Angry as one may be at what heedless men have done and still do to a noble habitat, one cannot be pessimistic about the West. This is the native home of hope.
—*Wallace Stegner*
The Sound of Mountain Water

The Native Home of Hope

For Flannery and the Northern Rockies: outposts of hope.

The Native Home of Hope

People and the Northern Rockies

edited by Thomas N. Bethell, Deborah E. Tuck, and Michael S. Clark

with an introduction by William Kittredge

and photographs by Mike McClure

Howe Brothers   1986

SALT LAKE CITY   CHICAGO

published by
Howe Brothers
Salt Lake City, Utah

Manufactured in the United States of America

Excerpt from *The Sound of Mountain Water* by Wallace Stegner.
Copyright © 1969 by Wallace Stegner.
Reprinted by permission of Doubleday & Company, Inc.

All photographs are by Mike McClure, with the following exceptions:
pages 10, 17, 29, 35, 43, 52, 57, 75, 89, 96, 130, 135, 159,
174, and 184 by Mike Clark;
pages 63, 83, 111, and 151 by T. N. Bethell;
page 142 by Kathy Kelly; page 105 by Mike Meloy;
page 121, courtesy of the Montana AFL-CIO archives;
and page 165, photographer unknown.

LIBRARY OF CONGRESS CATALOGING-IN-PUBLICATION DATA
Main entry under title:

The Native home of hope

   1. Rocky Mountains Region.   2. Rocky Mountains
Region—Social conditions.   3. Rocky Mountains Region—
Politics and government.   4. Interviews—Rocky
Mountains Region.   I. Bethell, Thomas N.   II. Tuck,
Deborah E.   III. Clark, Michael S.
F721.N37   1986   978   85–21858
ISBN 0–935704–26–4 (pbk.)

Contents

Preface

A PHYSICIAN FRIEND IN MONTANA TELLS A STORY about absenteeism at a Mission Valley health clinic. One morning an employee called in to say he would be late for work.

"There's a bear out there sitting on my truck and he won't get off."

"So? Go out on the porch and shoo him off."

"I can't. There's another bear sitting on my porch."

Living in the Rockies is different. Not everyone has been kept away from work by bears, but there are plenty of other good stories to be told. This book is one effort to do just that—to let citizens of the Northern Rockies tell their own stories about themselves and their homeland. *The Native Home of Hope* (which takes its title from Wallace Stegner's characterization of the region) grew out of the work of the Northern Lights Institute, a regional research center created in 1981 by a group of citizens concerned about the future of the Northern Rocky Mountain states of Montana, Idaho and Wyoming.

I was hired by Northern Lights Institute's board of directors to become its first executive director. My wife, Deborah Tuck, and I moved to Helena from the hills of East Tennessee and opened an office. During our first year we traveled extensively throughout the three states, meeting people and learning about regional issues, resources, and problems. As we traveled, our preconceived notions of the region were, one after the other, revealed to be inaccurate. At roadside bars, in the homes of new-found friends, or in the offices of government officials, we found new insights and information. We were struck by the images of the region which began to emerge.

Few regions of the country have a more engaging hold upon the nation's imagination than the Northern Rockies has. It is the home of Plains Indian culture, the territory of fur traders, the wild land of Lewis and Clark, the funnel for immigrants on the Oregon Trail. Here the golden age of the cowboy saw its beginning and end. Custer died here, Buffalo Bill began his career here, and Teddy Roosevelt shot everything in sight here. Hollywood put it on celluloid for us. Television gave us a nearly universal obsession with western history. All of these powerful images have little relevance to today's problems, but myths persist, reinforced by first impressions and by the seemingly self-sufficient sweep of the western sky.

Northern Lights Institute was created to poke at the myths and pursue ways of dealing with the underlying realities. Our travels exposed us to a wide range of people with contradictory perspectives about the future of the region. Few of these people fit the traditional stereotypes of western leaders. We began to think about a publication through which these people could express themselves and which would make their insights available to interested readers both within and beyond the region. Taped interviews, transcribed and edited, offered a way for people to speak for themselves. This book came out of those discussions.

Deborah Tuck was the project coordinator and conducted most of the interviews. Tom Bethell, a long-time friend and writer, did some of the interviews and edited the transcripts. Carol Abrams, our Northern Lights office manager, took on the job of managing most of the paper flow and transcribed most of the interviews. Mike McClure, long recognized as a superb photographer of Rocky Mountain life, is also an old friend of Deborah's. We met him one night in a Lander restaurant, and he offered the use of his pictures. We were overwhelmed a few weeks later when a package of exceptional photographs arrived in the mail. Duane Ward began collecting state and regional data which was later used by Dan Whipple in his factual guide.

Slowly the book began to take shape. With help from Northern Lights Institute's board of directors and friends throughout the region, we began making lists of people to interview. We wanted people who had been active leaders in their communities. We tried to find people who strongly believed in what they did and who were willing to talk about their beliefs for publication. We did not attempt to represent all points of view—an impossible task in any case—rather we sought people who could articulate different perspectives on what they and their communities had experienced during the past few decades. The interviewees are bound together, more than anything else, by a sense of place. Our hope was that these interviews would illustrate the diversity of experience and the range of opinion within this region and could begin to dispel some of the prevalent stereotypes about life in the Northern Rockies.

Our short list of candidates grew into a long one. We approached many people to ask if they would allow us to tape record conversations with them. Not a single person turned us down—a fact that speaks directly to the open, trusting attitude of people in the West.

Few were reluctant to talk. Most could not be stopped after getting over their initial surprise: "You want to listen to me? Well, I've been waiting for you."

We asked each of them to tell us about themselves, and we asked:

"Why are you here and not some place else?"

"When you think about the future of this region, what do you see? What are your hopes and fears?"

Rocky Mountain voices. High country hopes and fears. People who are, on the whole, strong, inquisitive, observant, proud, generally optimistic about the future, devoted to their communities. None of them would be so presumptuous as to say that they speak *for* the region. They speak for themselves and their families; they inspect the past and tentatively probe (as we all do) into the future.

Defining a vision for the Northern Rockies is not easy. It is especially difficult in a region so strongly identified with the nostalgia of a golden past. The history of the West, cast in a heroic glow, is still seductive, still alluring. Its images are deceptive. Life in the Rockies, for most people, has been a struggle defined by scarcity: of water, of good land, of justice. It is hard to speak of justice when the entire basis of Western life—ownership of land—is built upon the bloody conquest of native people whom we now allow to (barely) exist among us. Similar questions of justice now plague the region's unemployed workers— farmers, miners, timber workers, and smelter workers—who are on the move by the thousands seeking new jobs and new opportunities throughout the West.

The western landscape, for good and bad, has molded much of our image as a people. Perhaps it is our destiny as a nation to be drawn into western spaces. But the nostalgic images of the mythic past do not serve us well in adjusting to the realities of the present nor in planning a plausible future. As our population grows and our technology continues to outstrip our ability to fully anticipate its consequences, we must recognize the need to look further and further into the future.

We need to be constantly searching for new ways to measure our expectations, our limitations and our resources. Our questions may be expressed in economic or technological terms but the answers will almost certainly be political. This book is one effort to measure the rapidly changing political landscape of the Northern Rockies. Whether this region can effectively learn from the experiences of the past has yet to be determined. The shining western mountains still call us. Our challenge is to see whether we have the vision to guard for future generations the possibility that this region can remain what it has been for a fortunate few, the native home of hope.

This was a difficult, but a joyful, book to assemble. Long hours on the roads of the Northern Rockies invariably landed us beside the desks or on the fields or in the kitchens of most gracious and hospitable people. They told us their stories, shared with us their hopes and fears, made us newcomers feel welcome on the soil of this vast and lovely region. We thank them all— the ones we interviewed, the ones who helped, the ones who offered direction to the project and encouraged us to continue.

In particular, the editors wish to thank those who joined us in performing the interviews: Med Bennett, Richard Chapman, Penny Lucas, Mary Lou Reed, and Wilbur Rehmann.

As the manuscript grew and came together, we used the skills of some very able typists, who had the thankless task of transcribing miles of cassette tape into manuscripts fit for editing. They were Renie Hanson, Esther Leiter, Sherry Mergenthaler, Carol Stebbins, and Jean Stephenson.

The board of directors of the Northern Lights Research & Education Institute offered special insights and guidance along the way. The board members who shared in the conception and development of this project were Med Bennett, Colleen Cabot, Jack Pugh, Ken Pursley, Lou Reed, Ann Roberts, Jon Roush, Arnie Silverman, and Pete Simpson.

Thanks also to Bill Kittredge for being able and wanting to, Tara Townsend for reading and responding with a voice always honest, Dwayne Ward for the clearheaded and thorough data, Dan Whipple for his experienced and thoughtful advice, and Don Snow for seeing the book through to publication.

We also thank the William and Flora Hewlett Foundation, the Northwest Area Foundation, the Public Welfare Foundation, and the Charles Stewart Mott Foundation for their support.

Finally, our most special thanks to Carol Abrams, administrative assistant at Northern Lights Research & Education Institute, for her diligence in tightening the loose ends, keeping things organized, and preparing the final drafts for submission. Without Carol, this book might have never made it.

MICHAEL S. CLARK

Introduction

All of Our Friends

Jack Ray was one of the heroes of my boyhood in the far outback of southeastern Oregon. A slope-shouldered, balding little man, Jack dominated the late roughhouse craziness at our mid-July country dances. The Harvest Moon Ball.

"He can hit you like a mule kicking," my father used to say after those dances, winking at me and grinning at my mother's back while she served up a very late Sunday breakfast, steak and fried mush and biscuits and thick sausage gravy.

At that time I was maybe five or six years old, and I would have been asleep in the back seat of our car for a couple of hours when the shouting and fighting started around midnight. So I recall those scenes with a newly-awakened child's kind of strobe-light clarity, a flash here and there, all illuminated in the headlights of 1930's automobiles. Those ranch women would be crowded outside onto the porch where they could see—some wife weeping, their men out closer to the battle in the parking lot, passing bottles.

But what I see mainly is Jack Ray getting up off the ground, wiping a little trickle of blood from the corner of his mouth, glancing down at the smear on his hand, his eyes gone hard while some sweating farm boy moves at him again, torn shirts, the little puffs of dust their feet kicked there in the headlights. At that point my memory goes fragile. There is some quick slippery violence, and the farm boy is on his knees. Jack Ray is standing over him, waiting, wheezing as he breathes.

It's over, everybody knows it, and soon it is. Two more grunting punches and the farm boy is down again, and Jack Ray steps back, his eyes gone soft and almost bewildered in the light as a little shudder moves through the crowd, and someone shouts, and the bottles pass again. I see Jack Ray, there in those headlights, smiling like a child now that it's finished, the farm boy up on his knees, shaking his head.

No harm done; the air clear. I see it over and over, summer dance after summer dance. I see the kind of heroism my boyhood educated me to understand and respect.

And I hate the part that comes next. I grew up and ran the haying and combine crews on the ranch, and there eventually came a time when I hired Jack Ray to work for me. He had worked a lot of seasons for my father, and such men always had a job with us. Jack was maybe fifty by that time and crippled by his life—the magic gone—a peaceable man who seemed to have turned a little simple. He did what he could, chores around the cook house, and once in a while he drank. After a bout in town which earned him a week in the county jail, he showed up grinning in the bunkhouse. "Well, hell, Jack," I said, "it's a new day."

"Boy," he said, "it's a new world every morning."

Looking backward is one of our main hobbies here in the West, as we age. And we are aging, which could mean growing up and maturing. Or not. It's a difficult process for a culture which has always been so insistently boyish. Jack Ray has been dead a long time now. As my father said, he drank his liver right into the ground. "But, by God," my father said, "he was something once."

Right after the end of official American involvement in Vietnam, I heard Benjamin DeMott, a noted Amherst humanist, talk before a university audience in Missoula. The times, he said, they were changing. We have a new kind of freedom, he said. He seemed to be talking about a revolution in transportation and communications. About mobility. The air in America, he said, was ringing with possibility.

It seemed kind of true. Lots of people from Missoula fly to New York or Washington, D.C., occasionally, and call coast-to-coast any time they want. A friend in the film business, not wealthy or excessively successful, has apartments in Los Angeles and New York. His work demands, as they say in that game, that he be "bi-coastal." And besides, DeMott wasn't really talking about Montana. We've always had that kind of freedom. So we nodded along. Yeah, we thought, freedom, possibility, sure that's us. It's one of our most fundamental traditions.

A strange thing happened. An unshaven man stood up in the audience and interrupted. He looked to be a little drunk, and he was—more with outrage than booze. It was the poet James Wright, in town for a visit with his old graduate school buddy, Dick Hugo. "Sure," Wright shouted, "tell 'em that crap up on 123rd Street." He was talking about the black ghetto in New York City.

Well, we thought, isn't that rude and unfortunate. But then we smiled. It was, we knew, after all, only an east coast argument.

Possibility. It's the old American story. Head west for freedom and the chance of inventing a brand new life for yourself. Our heroes are always leaping the traces when their territory gets too small and cramped. They go out.

It's what you hear people say when things get too tight around the house. I've said it myself, "Think I'm going to go out for a beer . . . or maybe just ride around." And leave that woman home with her kids.

Back in the late fifties, living with my wife and our small children in our little cattle-ranch house, on a rainy Sunday afternoon in November, I always had the excuse of work. "I got to go out," I would say, and I would duck away to the peacefulness of driving the muddy fields and levee banks in my old Ford pickup. Or, if the roads were too bad, I would go down to the blacksmith shop and bang on some damned thing. It's an old American recourse. If you have work which is out of the house.

Moby Dick: "Whenever I find myself growing grim about the mouth; whenever it is damp, drizzly November in my soul; whenever I find myself involuntarily pausing before coffin warehouses, and bringing up the rear of every funeral I meet. . . ." Then he runs away to sea.

"Lighting out for territory," says Huckleberry Finn, with his broken-hearted optimism, right at the end of his get away down the Mississippi. Remember Boone Caudill, in our own best book of beginnings here in the Northern Rockies, *The Big Sky*. He was just doing what a true man was bound to do.

And it wasn't just the runaway boys in books. John Colter left Ohio at the age of thirty to head up the Missouri with Lewis and Clark in 1804. He stayed west another five years, earning his keep as a fur trapper in pursuit of the beaver. One fearsome Montana winter he took a legendary walk from Fort Lisa on the Missouri, traveling through what is now Yellowstone Park, to circumnavigate the Tetons—somewhere around a thousand miles on snowshoes through country where no white man had ever been before. Something wondrous and powerful drove him. Maybe it was a need so simple as being out, away.

Imagine those shining snowy mountains burning against the sheltering endless bowl of clean sky, and Colter alone there in Jackson Hole. Just imagine. We will not see such things again, not any of us, ever. Not even, really, in British Columbia or Alaska. It's gone. We know it is. Only one man ever got to be Colter. Not even Bridger, or Joe Meek or Jedediah Smith had a world so absolutely to himself. Except for some natives, who maybe never thought they were alone.

But our people kept coming. In 1836 Narcissa and Marcus Whitman came west with Eliza and Henry Spalding. The first white women had crossed the Rockies. Along the way they witnessed the last fur-trapper rendezvous, on the Green River in Wyoming. Think of those Presbyterian women amid the inhabitants of wilderness. Only seven years later Marcus Whitman was leading one of the first wagon trains west from St. Louis to the Oregon country. The thin filtering of migrant souls was turning into a great tide.

The New York newspaper editor, Horace Greeley, worried about them, wondering what they could be seeking, leaving behind the best of climates and agricultural lands, schools and churches and markets: "For what, then, do they brave the desert, the wilderness, the savage, the snowy precipices of the Rocky Mountains, the early summer march, the storm-drenched bivouac, and the gnawings of famine? Only to fulfill their destiny! There is probably not one among them whose outward circumstances will be improved by this perilous pilgrimage."

Only to fulfill their destiny!

Anybody sensible, Greeley suggested, would stop ". . . this side of the jumping off place." The only practice stupider than such migration, he said, was suicide.

It's easy to understand his puzzlement. The wagon trains were predominantly a middle-class, family venture. Poor folks couldn't afford a wagon, much less provisions. The basic outfitting cost up toward a thousand dollars. And in those long-gone days that was some real money. But seemingly sensible people persisted in selling their good farms and heading west.

Imagine half the population of Bozeman picking up sticks, selling out, and heading for one of our latter-day mythological frontiers—Alaska or Australia. Greeley was right, it was crazy, it was a mania, which seems to have mostly affected men.

What the hell was driving them?

Well, lots of things. Fear of mortal corruption and death. Cholera. By the spring of 1849 an epidemic had reached St. Louis. Ten percent of the population died of the disease. The road west from Independence was likened to traveling through a graveyard.

But mostly, we have to believe, they were lured by promises. Promises of paradise for the taking. Free land, crystalline water, great herds of game roaming the natural meadowlands, good fishing, gold, all in unfettered abundance.

What compelled men to believe promises of paradise on earth with such simple-minded devotion? Well, for openers, a gut yearning for freedom, escape, to hope and dreams and another life, the chance of becoming someone else. Freedom from want and the terrible weight of responsibilities; freedom too often equalling free, without cost. And who could blame them?

America, we will find ourselves in Thee. Who would you want to be? Teacher, preacher, bartender, merchant, farmer, governor? Sounds like a schoolyard game. Sounds like never-never land. All this we promise you . . .

White men wrote the books, so it's easy to understand why themes of territory and conquest were central in our legends and histories for so long. Some of it is the stuff of great story-telling, it's easy to write, and it's real enough, not a doubt about it, but it's a long way from all the story. It's not even the most important part.

My grandfather on my mother's side ran away from a Germanic farmstead home in Wisconsin the year he was fourteen, around 1900, and made his way to Butte. "I was lucky," he would say. "I was too young to go down in the mines, so they put me to sharpening steel."

Seemed to me such a boy must have been lucky to find work at all, wandering the teeming difficult streets of the most urban city in the American West. "Well, no," he said. "They put you to work. It wasn't like that. They were good to me in Butte. They taught me a trade. That's all I did was work. But it didn't hurt me any."

After most of ten years on the hill—broke and on strike, still a very young man—he rode the rails south to the silver mines in what he called "Old Mexico," and then worked his way back north through the mining country in Nevada in time for the glory days in Goldfield and Rhyolite and Tonopah. At least those are the stories he would tell. "This Las Vegas," he would say. "When I was there you could have bought it all for a hundred and fifty dollars. Cost you ten cents for a drink of water."

To my everlasting sadness, I never really quizzed him on the facts. Nowadays I look at old photographs of those mining camps, and wonder. It's difficult for me to imagine the good, gentle man I knew walking those tough dusty streets. He belonged, at least in those Butte days, to the International Brotherhood of Blacksmiths and Helpers. I still have his first dues card. He was initiated July 11, 1904, and most of the months of 1904 and 1905 are stamped, Dues Paid. It's a connection I hold to with some pride and tenacity.

However tenuously, it ties me to the commonplace communality within which we find the weave of our society here in the Northern Rockies. Or anywhere. Despite that portfolio of runaway schoolyard bravado and contrivance called The Western, our history like any other is predominantly an intricate tale of cooperation and compromise, of paying such dues and making do.

You go to any tavern and show any sign of weakness, and some poor beleaguered bastard will start telling you the story of his life. You always feel like you ought to listen, at least for a little while. Because some way or another, we all do it.

We find stories in the unpatterned endlessness of our lives, and we tell them and retell them, if only to ourselves, living them out and sharpening and reinventing them, defining and redefining ourselves, discovering significance. It's the most universal of human activities—inventing ourselves.

My grandfather died in an old-folks home in Eugene, Oregon. During the days of his last summer, when he knew the jig was up, a fact he seemed to regard with infallible good humor, we would sit in his room and listen to the aged, bemused woman across the hall chant her litany of childhood, telling herself that she was somebody and still real.

It was always the same story, word by particular word. I wondered then how much of it was actual, lifting from some deep archive in her memory, and now I wonder how much of it was pure sweet invention, occasioned by the act of storytelling and by the generative, associative power of language which is so vital a part of creativity. I couldn't help but think of ancient fires, light flickering on the faces of children and storytellers detailing the history of their place in the scheme of earth.

The story itself started with a screen door slamming and her mother yelling at her when she was a child coming out from the back porch of a white house, and rotting apples on the ground under the trees in the orchard, and a dog which snapped at the flies. The telling took about three minutes, and she told it like a story for grandchildren. Then she would lapse into quiet, rewinding herself, seeing an old time when the world contained solace enough to seem complete, and she would start over again, going on until she had lulled herself back into sleep. I would wonder if she was dreaming about that dog amid the fallen apples, snapping at flies and yellowjackets.

At the end she would call the name of that dog over and over in a quavering, beseeching voice—wish I could remember that name—and my grandfather would look to me from his bed and his eyes would be gleaming with laughter, such an old man laughing painfully and wheezing, his shoulders shaking.

"Son of a bitch," he would whisper, when she was done calling the dog again, and he would wipe the tears from his face with the sleeve of his hospital gown. Son of a bitch! He would look to me again, and I wouldn't know what the hell to do beyond aimlessly grinning acknowledgment that some mysterious thing was truly funny, and then he would look away to the open window, beyond which a far-off lawn mower droned, as if this time he were the one who was embarrassed. Not many moons after that he was dead, and so was the old woman across the hall.

"Son of a bitch," I thought, when we were burying him one bright afternoon in Eugene, and I found myself suppressing laughter. Maybe it was just a way of ditching the grief I felt, for myself, who had not known him well enough to understand. Now I wonder if such knowing is possible. But I have his picture on my wall, and I can still look to his image and find relief from the serious weight of my own foolishness. It's like a gift.

These voices from the Northern Rockies, in *The Native Home of Hope,* are also a gift. "Wyoming is as much a state of mind as a place where you walk on ground." That's the voice of Jack Pugh, a man from Green River, a miner and member of the Wyoming legislature.

"Government," Pugh says, "won't succeed unless its something people will believe in and defend."

Over and over, these voices remind us that pure political consensus-seeking and problem-solving will be an ultimately defeating process—unless we stay continually aware that we are manipulating the materials of dreams and hope.

Sandra Viall is a young divorced woman with three children, the youngest with cerebral palsy, who lives in Missoula. With the help of a Head Start job and supplemental social security grant money, welfare money (until her eligibility ran out), and food stamps, she has been trying to work her way to a degree from the University of Montana as a physical therapist. It is a tough go. Sometimes she thinks of other lives: ". . . there are lots of little towns in Montana where your children have the freedom to grow and gain responsibility because you don't have to be checking on them all the time. . . . And there are lots of people who are willing to reach out and help their neighbor. You've got the helping hand. In fact I could probably go back to my parent's farm and live there and raise my kids, but it would just be an existence. I'm getting a little bit old to have my parents support me, though they do try to help me much as they can with food supplies. But I go down and help them out during the summer too. In that way, I try to pay them back. But going to live there—I still wouldn't be educated."

"People give up in different ways," Sandy Viall says. "They stop looking for higher education; they stop bettering themselves; they just kind of 'sink back' and go along in this world . . . ."

It is such giving up, on a massive scale, that is the most real danger our national culture faces as it grows more and more complex and distant from the individual. It's a malaise many of us came to the Northern Rockies to escape. Here we can still work in direct connection with the power structure of our society. We can make ourselves heard, and, if we are persuasive enough, we can effect positive changes.

Jack Pugh knows what is possible: "You have to understand that I went from being just another guy who worked in the mines and came home and drank beer and watched TV and talked about football and went hunting and fishing—from that, in a three-year period, to the state legislature . . .

"Because that country is so big out there, we don't feel enclosed. We feel we can still go out and do things. . . . Throughout history, there never was a rugged individual in the West. Nobody survived here without major cooperative efforts. Stegner says we have to go back and learn from that and use that sense of community to build institutions as magnificent as our scenery, so that we can indeed survive as a region."

Pugh is not alone in feeling a community responsibility. In a scattered way, we've had a run of exceptional luck in our draw of socially responsible political figures here in the Northern Rockies—I'm thinking of my favorites from Montana, such as Mike Mansfield and Pat Williams, genuinely good people who have given their lives and energies to the public.

Such luck is not unaccountable. It comes to use because we live in a place where it is still possible for a good and relatively uncompromised person to succeed in public life. Al Larson of Wyoming is another of my favorites, a truly conservative old-style country statesman. Larson grew up on a farm in Nebraska, and like Mike Mansfield, became a history professor. Unlike Mansfield, he stayed out of politics until his retirement from teaching. But then he got himself elected to the Wyoming legislature and served his first term in 1977. While Al Larson is a man actively grappling with the problem of Wyoming's future, he also finds some virtue in things as they are. "We ought to level off our population at a little over 500,000 and try to make Wyoming more of a tourist place and keep our wildlife going and our loneliness. We need that in this country. We'll need it more fifty or a hundred years from now. I think that less than ten percent of Wyoming has ever been plowed, and I don't think it ever should be plowed. I think the rest of it ought to be left the way it is, as much as possible." How lovely to hear a politician extolling the virtues of loneliness.

In reading these interviews we begin to find threads of purpose which run through them all. These are people talking and retalking the significance of their lives and their striving in their society, deep in the old process of reinventing themselves and their notions of the good life over and over, as we all do in our continual hunt for meaning in our days. It is the most basic and continual of human activities, and that is the reason why storytelling such as this has always been of primal worth. It is in such narrative, both personal and historical, that we discover ourselves—who we have been and who we could possibly be— both individually and politically. In these voices we find those resonances of human fallibility and strength which remind us to proceed always humanistically, with compassion, as we search for a way toward truly imaginative and fair public solutions to our mutual problems.

Our landscape is ultimately a country of the mind, inhabited by people who came here seeking freedoms—and their children and grandchildren. They still come.

Our history is one of native Americans and Mexican Americans and Swedes and Finns and Britishers, sheepmen and wilderness freaks, miners and worn-out working stiffs in bunkhouses, merchants and working mothers—name your category —all coming to live in our city-state enclaves, watersheds and counties and reservations, towns and fledgling cities, and all at least in their secret hearts working to achieve some positive effect in the world.

But the freedoms they come seeking—the liberties we as westerners have grown up cherishing—are more and more constrained, and we hate it. Simple as that. And we have to live with it. Another simple fact. There is no more running away to territory. This is it, for most of us. We have no choice but to live in community. In this we are like those pioneers in their wagon trains. We must come to understand that true freedom, from now on anyway, can only be created by our own laboring, amid freely assumed responsibilities, and cannot be found somewhere over the next hill.

Reality is always invaded by dreams. At their best, these interviews act as doorways. They open and admit us into private complexities of connection and yearning. Once again we come to understand that all our deepest secrets are the same. And once again we learn the kind of empathy which should always inform our drive toward the making of coherent and humane public policy.

WILLIAM KITTREDGE
MISSOULA, MONTANA

Jack Pugh

I GREW UP IN THE BIG CITY OF DALLAS, AND had all the big city I could take. When I got to be thirty years old, I decided that the universe was no longer expanding, and that if there was anything I wanted to do, or any place I wanted to be, it was time to go do it and be there.

I'd always had the same idealized romantic notion of the Rockies that many people who don't know anything about the region have—although I'd been up here, backpacking and vacationing, several times. And so I decided I wanted to live somewhere in the Rocky Mountains. A company here in Sweetwater County, the one that makes Arm & Hammer baking soda, came to Texas recruiting people to work. I applied but they didn't hire me.

About a year later, my wife and I were up in Colorado, doing some mountain climbing, and on the way home, I just said, "This is it. The hell with it." My wife said, "Fine, I'd like to go, too," which made it somewhat easier. So I got home, called the company, and as fate would have it, they had an opening. They flew me up here and offered me the job and I took it.

So here I was. And it took me about two years to become a citizen of Sweetwater County and Green River. I have a friend who calls it "the suitcase syndrome." So many people moving in, and they're never sure they want to stay. They came up here for a job, which is absolutely the worst reason to come to Wyoming, in my opinion. But there are dollar opportunities here for a working-class person that just don't exist elsewhere—if you can get a job in a mine. People come out of Utah where they may have been working in a refinery in Salt Lake City making $6 or $7 an hour and they get popped into a mining job as an ordinary laborer at $2 or $3 an hour more than they were making in a more responsible job.

It took me two years to decide I was a citizen here in Green River, as opposed to being a citizen generally of the state of Wyoming. I spent that first two years flitting about the countryside, all the mountain ranges, everywhere else too. Then I just realized my suitcase was completely unpacked.

Now the town has gained some real prominence for me. Green River is a comfortable little place to live, but people need to understand—and they seldom do, from outside the region—that this is hard country. These towns can be damned hard to live in. But once you cope with it, that makes them rewarding places. For me now, it's almost impossible to separate the city of Green River from the countryside at large. The people who live here come and stay, *want* to be here.

On the surface we have this flimsy boomtown look, and of course we all know about the lack of cohesiveness and the breakdown of community networks and social networks, and I use that rhetoric a lot in the public arena. But there is a core here that we all understand. We seldom articulate it. It's like a fraternity sometimes. We don't have a secret handshake, but you can see people looking at each other and saying, "He

Jack Pugh lives in Green River, Wyoming, and represents Sweetwater County in the state Senate. He is a miner, a member of the legislature since 1978, and a director of Northern Lights Institute and the Wyoming Outdoor Council.

couldn't cut it—he left—but *we* can cut it, can't we?" That sort of thing builds.

Maybe that's endemic to small towns in the West. I don't know how to break it down as to which is most home—the city of Green River or Sweetwater County or Wyoming. At one point I could have made some distinctions, but now it's all part and parcel. Wyoming, in spite of the fact that the borders of the state are artificially defined political boundaries, is as much a state of mind as it is a place where you walk on ground. And so are the towns, often. I think this is one.

Who do I spend my time with? Well, over the past couple of years I've spent it with politicians. When I was in the mines I spent it with just regular old working people, eight hours a day. But they were also the people I sought out, to go hunting and fishing with. I don't spend a lot of time with anybody. I'm not reclusive, obviously; I wouldn't be a politician if I was. But when I have time that is not obligated to some group, or to some cause, I spend it by myself for the most part, especially since I got divorced.

You have to understand that I went from being just another guy who worked in the mines and came home and drank beer and watched TV and talked about football and went hunting and fishing—from that, in a three-year period, to the state legislature.

I hadn't thought much about running for office, but I had decided to get active in the environmental movement in the state, because it was the only public interest sort of activity going on. Environmentalists were the only people who were raising issues before the legislature, taking on the big federal agencies that managed the land in the state, saying things that had to be said. I got involved in that, and I gained some prominence locally, because we took on the trona companies on a couple of big air-quality issues.

But it's not quite enough to go down to the legislature and talk to the legislators. I thought it might be better to be one of the people who gets to cast the votes and to argue from that side.

Well, in 1978 the great reform movement got underway in the Democratic party in Sweetwater County, and a man whom I did not know, but who since has become one of my very best friends, took on one of the old dragons and blew his feathers off. I got to know the people who ran that campaign. In particular, I got to know a great political street fighter, a United Church of Christ minister who was a real prophet—in the sense religionists use the term to describe people who raise issues of social conscience. He just had a frank talk with me one day and told me to run for office. I thought it was flattering that he thought I had that kind of moxie. I vacillated about it, but then in the last week before the filing deadline, I thought, what the hell, and I did it.

I had absolutely no constituency, since I'd only been here a little less than five years. I did have the hunters and the fishermen, because I had always been right out front on issues that concerned them.

We put together a damn dedicated little crew. I had to take on the unions, which didn't want me to get through the primary for the probable reason that I was working in a non-union mine, even though I said everything they'd expect a working man to say, and meant it.

I made it through the primary despite their opposition, and in the general election I upset, by a surprisingly large vote, the only Republican who had been elected to the House of Representatives from this county in forty-seven years. It was a surprise, because his family had pioneered in this area, and he was a well-loved man, active in school-board issues and very successful. But I beat him. And here I am now, in politics.

There was a time when I used to kid myself about politicians and the political process, and how it was all soiled and tainted, and we intellectuals ought to stay away from that crap and read poems and go to plays. That was what was wrong with me in Texas, I'm convinced now.

I like to read poems and books and hear great music and see the ballet, but it's not enough. I found out when I got into the environmental movement with the Wyoming Outdoor Council that I had some real skills in just those areas that I had always been suspicious of politicians for. I can scheme and connive with the best. I am very manipulative and not above screwing around with people to get them to go in the direction I think they need to go. And obviously I am making God-like judgments when I do that, but we all have to make those judgments. Maybe the great failure of liberals is that we analyze— we worry too much. Either we're right or we're not—time will tell—but we've got to *move*.

I didn't like finding out that I could be political. It made my white horse stumble. But I decided that the political process, as inefficient and as cumbersome and unresponsive as it is, is the only thing we have to deal, in a pedestrian way, with those grand questions that we all care about—social justice and equality.

I haven't gotten cynical at all about such things. Actually, two things have happened to me since I got into politics. One, I've become somewhat radicalized about the way things ought to be—radicalized notions similar to the outrage I felt in the late sixties and early seventies but never acted on. But, at the same time, I have become surprisingly optimistic about the chances of getting some things done. We're never going to get where we ought to be, but there is a chance to make progress in small incremental ways. As soon as we all learn to be patient about that and understand that that's the best that can be done and that even though they're small gains they require hellacious struggle—then I think we can be satisfied, to some extent, with the political process.

I have my own notions, like everyone else, of how the world ought to be—how to make the right mighty and ascendent. In particular, I think back on the progress made in civil rights, since I grew up in an area where race was a big issue. I participated in civil rights demonstrations in Dallas, and my old grandma, who had been a worker in the Ku Klux Klan auxiliary after World War I, disinherited me and my brother for that kind of activism. It was a small amount of money but it was a big trauma for the family to have that kind of clash, and the experience meant a lot to me. So when I run up against barriers, institutional barriers, constantly I try to argue with people that you've got to open the system to everybody, and yet you can't convince them. That kind of thing heightens my anger. That's what I think I mean by radicalization.

To channel that, you become the best and worst of politicians. You become shrewd, cunning, and manipulative, and you understand that the other guys are shrewd, cunning, and manipulative. And you understand what you're both doing with each other, and you don't express your anger, not really. You simply use the system as best you can to push the issue, whatever it is, to the forefront and try to get some movement.

We've had some notable successes in Wyoming the past year or two, particularly on women's issues. I've never felt as good about any political activity as I have about helping to bring about the advent of programs to deal with family violence and to provide shelters for battered women.

In retrospect, it was probably easier to pull fiscal conservatives along on that than I thought at the time, because we seem to have developed some real sensitivity to these problems. Because of the boom towns, those are highly visible problems in Wyoming. Spouse abuse and child abuse are endemic.

But the point is that we were able to take steps to address specific problems that fit within grander notions of justice. We did it by getting women all over the state to raise hell with their legislators, and then, while they were raising hell and twisting arms, we could sit down there in the legislature, with the liberals and bleeding hearts, and play hardball politics. The rhetoric was emotional, but we had to make horestrading decisions in order to go anywhere.

We wanted a full-scale, statewide shelter program. We got the issue raised prior to the session through publicity and press conferences, and we went from one locally funded shelter in Cheyenne to a statewide program that has four operating now with two more being planned and two more somewhere on the back burner. We did that in the space of a year.

We came back this year knowing we needed more money for the program and we knew we were going to have a fight. But an interesting thing happened. In the House we got the funding *doubled* from what Governor Herschler had recommended, even though the Senate kicked it back down. Eventually we ended up with half again what had been recommended and approved by the appropriations committee. So that was a considerable coup, and it was brought off by people who are typically considered bleeding heart liberals, who were playing some real hardball politics. We got it done.

The state legislature in Wyoming is unlike most state legislatures, we're still a small state where we all call each other by our first names. There's no "Governor Herschler" in the state of Wyoming, despite what I just said. It's "Ed" or "Gov. Ed." There is no Senator Wallop or Senator Simpson; it's "Malcolm" and "Al." That's just the way the state is—still is—and that's good.

When I talk about hardball politics, I don't mean it in the way it might be construed in New York or California, where people are really getting rapped around and probably some things happen that none of us really wants to know about. What I mean is just that we simply box people around and have a little fun with their politics and their rhetoric sometimes. It requires a pretty close ear. With some of the more conservative members of the House, whom I get along with very well, I just looked for weak spots and played on them. Maybe an emotion, maybe an off-hand comment they tossed off somewhere, something that can be turned against them to your advantage. Sometimes it can be done casually because we're so informal with each other, but for the same reason, it can be very serious.

We have the Right-to-Lifers, very sincere people who genuinely believe in what they're doing, and we have to go through an emotional, traumatic exercise in the Wyoming legislature every year around the issue of state funds being used to pay for abortions for low-income women. In 1981 I helped to kill a bill that would have outlawed abortions completely unless the mother's life was in danger. But 1982 was a budget session, and we had a footnote to the budget precluding the use of state funds for abortions unless pregnancy occured as the result of

sexual assault or incest, or unless the mother's life was endangered. I was asked to introduce an amendment that would allow state funds to be used for abortions based on amniocentesis, a test to determine whether a fetus has genetic deficiencies involving brain development.

I introduced the amendment with the understanding that one of my colleagues, a legislator who is conservative and also a doctor, would explain it. Then another colleague who is a Mormon and a rancher got to the microphone. He got to the microphone and allowed as how he had just had lunch with his nine-year-old daughter, and he said she had asked him:

"Daddy, is it really true there's a man in the Wyoming legislature who would kill little babies, just because they're retarded or handicapped?"

And he said he told her:

"I'm sorry to say so, but apparently it is true."

It got quiet in there.

I got the microphone back. Usually in the House people are doing things during the debate. They're reading something or shuffling files or writing notes. But they stopped what they were doing; they knew the personalities, and they were watching and listening very carefully.

All I said was that I hoped my colleague had also explained to his little daughter that there were also men in the Wyoming legislature who insisted that these babies be born regardless of the circumstance but who then consistently refused to support proper funding for the programs needed to care for them.

I had been introducing amendments to increase developmental disability funding during the whole time I'd been in the legislature, and my colleague had consistently voted against them. It was probably the best comeback that I could have made, because most people reacted negatively to what he had said. Normally we try not to attack each other personally, and when I responded that way even the gallery got quiet. He flushed red. My knuckles were white. What I wanted to do was jerk him out of his seat and knock the stuffing out of him, but my speech was effective. The result of that exchange was that the vote on the amendment was very close. We lost it, but otherwise we would have lost it by a big margin.

The Wyoming legislature, unlike so many legislatures elsewhere, still has the capacity to be touched by average people. The shelters for battered women are good examples. That was a grassroots movement from the very beginning, and we took it all the way through, and people who had been feeling really washed out about government came to us and said, "This really restores our faith." It was a good issue, but without hardball politics, it would have gone nowhere.

Where did I learn to think on my feet? I don't know. I've always been glib. I can't pinpoint a place or time. I grew up in what I guess was a typical low-income situation. My father was a Depression child—his family lived in a tent on the Trinity River near Dallas for four years. We were always poor and I lived in hand-me-down clothes. I hardly ever saw my parents. They were both at work *all* the time.

I don't know how kids who come from that sort of environment make it, but I could always more than hold my own in a classroom. However, I would have left high school before I graduated if I hadn't been an athlete. I went to college at North Texas State, Sam Houston State, and the University of Houston. I'm about twenty-five hours shy of a degree. The educational system was not something I ever functioned all that well in, but one teacher who really stands out in my mind was my junior English teacher, a graduate of Columbia who organized modern jazz dance recitals and made us read good litera-

ture. She's the one who kicked me along and got me to at least graduate.

I've always been a reader. When I was in grade school, I bought one of those old canvas army packs from a surplus store, and on Saturdays I'd ride the bus downtown to the library and browse around there for an hour or two and load that thing up with books. My routine was to go to the library, get my books, and then go to one of the big theaters and see the movie and the serials. Yes, I always was a reader. I got that from my father. He read science fiction and loved it. The few hours that poor man had to himself, he would be on the couch with a book. I'm sure that was my example.

Without some sense of community, we'll be bickering endlessly over issues that divide us, especially the water issue. People will still fight each other over water out here. When you're talking about agriculture in the West, you're really talking about ranchers, because ranchers have always wanted to develop water. There's a lot of lip service paid to questions of technology, of engineering, of where you're going to put it and how you're going to do it and how you're going to control access to it; but it's really a social question.

Wyoming is always under pressure to develop water resources, but it's bogus pressure in my opinion. You can justify the expenditures for these projects—and they cost a lot of money, even the small ones—only if you have a use for the water. Agriculture in Wyoming has a very uncertain future; it's always been marginal. I think ranchers have the idea somewhere in the backs of their minds that if we just go ahead and build reservoirs we're somehow going to save agriculture. And that's not the case.

As the demographics of the state change, the significance of these projects is that they're going to siphon money off what probably ought to be spent in our social service networks, the so-called infrastructure projects, and so on. We have some community-based programs that function extremely well because we are a state of small communities. They could suffer from funds being siphoned away.

That family-violence shelter program I spoke of earlier—it operates out of Cheyenne with a bureaucracy of two people, the director and a part-time secretary. The funds go to people in the counties and towns and cities who are putting programs together that work in their communities, putting the programs together and staffing them and running them. That's why the program works. It's a truly community-based program. The funds go where they should go, and there should be more funds.

But the shadow of the water issue looms over this program and others like it. The water issue can generate a lot of expensive rhetoric by politicians. You know: "By God, we're gonna build you a reservoir and you can entice industry with it and save agriculture with it and ride boats on it."

I think a nagging doubt may be growing in the developers' minds about whether reservoirs will save anything. They'll never say that. They'll go down, they'll sink in their reservoirs still trying to build more, convinced that that's what will enhance the future of Wyoming—build a reservoir everywhere you can stick a dam. It's an issue that has its own powerful momentum because of so many, many years in the forefront of political consciousness.

In spite of all the rhetoric about water development, the biggest issue at the moment is how we handle public school financing. We're going to have to commit a lot of funding to that. The Supreme Court overturned our system of public education, as it has done in so many states, ruling it unconstitutional because we have these pockets of prosperity where minerals are developed and that creates a concentration of wealth in those areas that other counties can't share. So we're going to share the wealth, and how it gets shared is going to be a difficult issue to resolve.

You talk about your social questions and the legislature! As you know, in rural communities, the school system is the focal point of the whole community. We have only two real cities, Casper and Cheyenne, and you don't see it as much there, but in every smaller town, by God, they know about their schools. They keep an eye on them. They watch. They pay attention. Water is an emotional issue. This one's maybe more so. There are at least two issues you can get killed over in Wyoming and this is one of them.

Looking ahead, I'm convinced that the growth game here has changed dramatically, partly because the Rocky Mountain states are so dependent on the state of the national economy. The minerals industries can't boom unless there's a nationwide demand for those minerals. I think we have built-in limitations on growth, such as climatological and water limits.

Politicians in Wyoming are starting to talk about the bust they know is going to come. Most of them are convinced it won't come for another 150 years. But they're not sure. They're starting to wonder about what "economic diversity" really means and how you go about insulating against a large-scale decline, if indeed we can do that.

Recently I spent a Saturday with the Sweetwater County Association of Governments as a panel member in a seminar on stimulating small business. They wanted me to talk about what state government can do. So we got into talking about short-term capital and long-term debt, which is where the shortfall is: How do you get enough money to sustain your business until you actually make some money with it? And we talked about small-business investment corporations and such.

One of the things that will probably come to the front will be the issue of using severance tax money—not increasing it, but redirecting it from the minerals trust fund to develop a small business structure. I think that's an issue that will be relevant all through this decade, and I think we'll see in the next few years a lot of activity in the Wyoming legislature in response to the "New Federalism." Since this is a conservative state with a tremendous general anti-welfare bias, I'm not all that optimistic about funding in the social welfare areas.

To get those issues articulated properly we really need to have a group of legislators who don't care if they get reelected or not. It will probably cost most of them their jobs to say what they ought to say, and they'll need allies.

Wallace Stegner describes the Rockies as the native home of hope. In that context, he meant that people don't realize how deeply imbedded in our community psyche our landscape and our affinity with it is. People who would flatten your nose if you called them environmentalists can go teary-eyed over the countryside out here—just hard-nosed old suckers.

Stegner also pointed out that the vast spaces breed a sense of solitude, and therefore introspection, and that when that comes together, somehow the mix produces optimism. Because that country is so big out there, we don't feel encolsed. We feel we can still go out and do things.

But he said that the rest of the nation wants an awful lot from us, and if we are going to survive as an entity and not be overwhelmed by the demands being made on us, we're simply going to have to take a look at what has brought us to this point: the traditional sense of community.

Throughout history, there never was a rugged individual in the West. Nobody survived here without major cooperative efforts. Stegner says we have to go back and learn from that and use that sense of community to build institutions as magnificent as our scenery, so that we can indeed survive as a region. I think he's exactly right.

Belle Winestine

I WAS BORN IN HELENA IN 1891, WHICH IS QUITE A WHILE AGO. My mother died when I was born, and my father married again when I was three. My older sister and I were brought up by a very strict stepmother, so we were very well behaved.

I remember her arrival—it was the same week that Helena won the election to become the capital of Montana. The competition was between Anaconda and Helena, and it was quite a fight. We were all staying at my aunt's house on Lawrence Street, and down the street past the front of the house came this long parade of fancy-decorated carriages carrying important politicians bringing the announcement that Helena was now the capital of the new state. I had no idea what the significance of all this was, but I was very impressed with the torchlights and the carriages and the bands playing. It was quite something.

It was fun growing up in Helena, where I had a brief career on the stage when I was about five. Warren Dahler, whose father was one of the bankers here in town, was in high school at the time and wanted very much to be a great actor. The Dahlers lived up here on 7th Avenue and had a woodshed behind their house, just as everybody in Helena did in those

Belle Winestine's long life spanned the development of Montana as a modern state. A native of Helena, she was active in her youth as a leader in gaining women the right to vote. Later she became an administrative aide to Montana's Jeannette Rankin, the first woman to ever serve in the U.S. Congress. As an author, playwright, and political activist, she was a major force in state literary circles until her death at age 94, in March, 1985.

days. And Warren decided to put on a performance of *Hamlet*. They revamped the woodshed into a theatre with a stage and curtain and box seats at each side—very boxy-looking box seats—and a few benches across the front.

Warren asked Mamie Cruse to be Ophelia. She was the daughter of Tommy Cruse. Maybe you've heard of him? An Irish prospector who struck gold in 1876 and built the great Drumlummon Mine—he named it for his home town in Ireland

—and built the town of Marysville to house his miners. He named the town for Mary Ralston, the first woman to live there. He became a millionaire several times over. He gave a large contribution to build the cathedral here. Mamie was the only millionaire girl in Helena and she had a woman who stayed with her twenty-four hours a day, because old Tommy Cruse was one of the only two or three millionaires in Helena and Mamie was the only kidnappable child. The Sweeney children, neighbors of ours and friends of the Cruses, were going to be in this play too, and they wanted my sister Frieda and me in it, and we thought that would be very nice. But Warren Dahler didn't want us in his play. Old Tommy Cruse said, "If the Fligelman girls aren't in it, then Mamie won't be in it either." That settled it, and we became great actresses on the spot.

We practiced evening after evening in the Cruse dining room in their big mansion just back of where the capitol is now. Warren Dahler had the feeling that Helena could not appreciate *Hamlet* as Shakespeare wrote it, so he went through it and improved on it a good deal. I'm sure Shakespeare would have been thrilled to see what he could have done if only he'd tried a little harder. And Warren acquired a long black union suit and looked very Hamlet-like.

Finally we had a dress rehearsal in the woodshed theatre that the boys had built, and then we put on the show, charging fifteen cents a ticket. I played the part of a page and had one line to say. When the queen toppled from the throne and fell to the floor, I was supposed to come in and exclaim, "Look to the Queen!" But just as I was to come in, a piece of scenery fell on me and I couldn't get on stage. I got there about two minutes late. Everybody was already looking at the queen. And I had practiced my one line in front of the mirror for weeks and was planning to say it with such elegance, and here they were,

all staring at the queen. Well, I said my line anyway, and it occurred to me, early in life, that we say a lot of things that aren't strictly necessary.

In the audience sat old Tommy Cruse in one box with a niece who ran the household, and in the other box sat United States Senator Clark and his family. And the parents of all the actors sat on the benches—a very distinguished audience. Only Tommy Cruse was so thrilled to see Mamie playing Ophelia that he took the entire cast and their mothers up to Marysville to put on a performance for the miners.

Marysville is twenty miles from Helena, up in the mountains, and there was a great trestle that the train had to cross, and I remember the queen's mother down on her knees in the aisle of the train all during the trip praying that the trestle would hold up. And when we got there and Warren and his mother were unloading the scenery at the Miners' Hall, Mr. Cruse said, "You know, you can't charge admission here tonight. You have to put it on free. It's a present for the miners."

Well, Warren said we couldn't possibly put it on free or we'd lose our professional standing. They argued back and forth. Finally Mr. Cruse said, "Well, if you want to charge admission, you'll have to find yourself another place to put it on. You can't do it in the Miners' Hall." They then decided to put it on free, and it was a great success up there. That was the final performance of the Warren Dahler Shakespeare Company, but it gave us quite a taste of what could be done artistically in Helena.

There were lots of things to do. In the winter we could slide on our sleds right down to the Gulch—it was called Main Street then, very citified—which took us across the streetcar tracks on Park Avenue. There was a streetcar that ran out to the Broadwater every half hour, and why no children ever got killed, sliding down and bumping into it, I never knew.

The Broadwater, of course, was the great swimming pool, or natatorium, about three miles out from the center of Helena. It was the largest covered natural hot mineral water natatorium in the world. If you left out any of those other adjectives it wouldn't be the largest, but with all of them included, it was. We had a wonderful time out there in summer. They had the big Broadwater Hotel, which Colonel Broadwater built in 1889, where people came for vacations, and people from Helena would come to for picnics, arriving by horseback or bicycle or the streetcar.

The streetcars were really very handy. In the summer we had open streetcars and they were lots of fun. They charged ten cents a ride, as I remember. Nobody ever used pennies out here. You rarely paid less than ten cents for anything. It was ten cents for a bunch of grapes, ten cents for admission to the Broadwater, ten cents to rent a swimming suit there. It was five cents for a loaf of bread, but you always bought two loaves. They weren't quite as big as they are today, but a loaf would feed a family of four for dinner.

Nobody in Helena saw pennies very much. My sister came home from her first year at college carrying a little purse full of pennies because they were so new to her. She thought it would be impressive to give the streetcar conductor ten pennies for a ride, and he said, "What are these?"

"This is ten cents," she said. "These are pennies."

And he said, "Maybe you have a dime? I'd better have a dime."

I think anything east of Billings we would have called "back East," but we never thought of it as being superior. Helena was quite an advanced community in its way. We had an opera house where opera companies would come out to from New York, and we had very good plays.

It was quite an elegant opera house. The manager was a man named Miner, who was also the manager of the railroad ticket office here, and he and his wife always sat in the same box. I remember one night when everyone as usual came with opera glasses and before the performance began they looked at the boxes to see who was there. Mrs. Miner was wearing a very low-neck dress and a very fancy diamond brooch that was apparently pinned right to her chest. It looked that way, and the entire audience became terribly worried about it. All the opera glasses were trained on her chest, and the next morning all the telephones in Helena were busy.

"Did you see Mrs. Miner last night?"

"Did *you*! And how did she have that brooch attached to her?"

Well, it was finally explained that she had used a piece of what we called court-plaster in those days, something like a Band-Aid but with no bandage part on it, to glue the brooch to her chest so that it created this staggering impression.

Mrs. Miner was sort of the social arbiter of the city. People felt that she knew what should and shouldn't be done. I remember when someone was invited to a dinner party and wasn't quite sure what to wear, she would phone Mrs. Miner and Mrs. Miner would say, "After six, black lace." And the whole town knew it the next day. I don't know how it got around so fast, but we were up on social etiquette.

I became involved with getting women the right to vote when I was a student at the University of Wisconsin. I hadn't known much about it before. My sister and I were very good childhood friends with Genevieve Walsh, whose father was the famous Senator Thomas J. Walsh, the man who exposed the Teapot Dome oil-leasing scandal, and her mother was an ardent woman suffragist. When I was in about the fourth grade, we learned from Genevieve that there was such a thing as a fight for equal suffrage going on. Many women in Montana were fighting for it, but they weren't organized. They would go to the legislature to get the constitutional amendment put on the ballot, but the effort would always lose out in the legislature.

Well, one day in 1913 when I was a senior at Wisconsin, the telephone rang at the student daily paper where I was the editor of the women's page. "This is the state headquarters of the Wisconsin Women's Suffrage Campaign," a woman said to me, "and we're going to have a hearing at the legislature tonight, and because you're the president of the women students at Wisconsin, we think you ought to be down here and talk ten minutes on why the women students at the university want suffrage."

Well, I was quite giddy at the idea. I knew suffrage was right, but I didn't know you had to have *reasons* for being right, and I didn't know any reasons for suffrage; I just knew that theoretically women ought to be able to vote.

"I'm sorry," I said, "I just can't do that tonight."

"And you will talk ten minutes," she said.

I said, "I'm sorry, but you'll have to excuse me, I can't do that."

"And wear your most feminine-looking dress," she said.

"I'm sorry, but I won't be there . . ."

"Be sure to be there at eight o'clock," she said, and hung up the phone.

I was terrified! My assistant editor was there, and I told her what was going on, and she said, "Well, don't worry, you'll think of something to say. Just tell them that the legislature is spending thousands of dollars educating both women and men stu-

dents to be good citizens but when they let only the men students vote they are only cutting half the coupons on their investment."

She was a lot smarter than I was. "That's marvelous," I said. "I'll say that. But that won't take ten minutes. I have to talk for ten minutes. That won't take more than two minutes to say."

"Well, I'll be there," she said, "and I'll stand at the back of the room, and when it looks as though you can't think of something to say, I'll start clapping, and when one person claps, the whole audience will clap, and you'll have time to think of something."

Well, I went to the meeting. I couldn't see over the lectern—they didn't know I'd be this short—and they had to find a box for me to stand on. I stood on it, and all I can remember is ten minutes of clapping and clapping and clapping. And I never knew whether they clapped for something I said or for what I didn't say.

They didn't get suffrage in Wisconsin then, but I became a suffragist. And a few months later, when I came back to Helena, I got a job as a reporter on the Helena *Independent*, and began paying attention to Jeannette Rankin's campaigns for suffrage.

Jeannette Rankin was at that time about thirty. She was born in Missoula in 1880, and had graduated from Montana State University in 1902 and gone to New York to study welfare work and become a social worker. Then she went out to do social work in Seattle in 1909. I think she was doing some work with the students at the University of Washington when she noticed some leaflets somewhere and realized that this vote-for-women business was going on. She called up the state headquarters and volunteered to help, and they gave her some literature, and she went out and put posters up in all the barber shops in Seattle, figuring that since only men could vote she'd put posters where she knew the voters would see them.

They won the campaign in Seattle that summer for women to vote in the state of Washington. It was the first successful referendum since Idaho in 1896. She went on to work in women's suffrage campaigns the next year in Washington, D.C., and in California the year after that. The referendum passed in California, and she thought: Why shouldn't Montana women vote?

By that time Montana was the most backward state in the region—women had won the right to vote in Wyoming back in 1869, when it was still a territory. So she came back to Montana in 1911 and went to the legislature, talked to some of the members and got them to hold a joint session where she could talk to both houses and get them to put the suffrage question on the ballot.

The men in the legislature thought it was quite an amusing thing. They agreed to have a joint session, and they gave her bunches of flowers and made it all very pleasant for her, but everybody was just making jokes about it.

Well, Jeannette Rankin had this wonderful idea, which she must have gotten partly from the campaign in Washington State. Maybe she'd given the idea to the organizers there, I don't know, but she felt that there had to be a campaign, not just at the legislature, but throughout the whole state. Organize the state. And that was what she did, from 1912 to 1914. She became field secretary of the National American Woman Suffrage Association in 1913, with national responsibilities, but she was also the chairwoman of the Montana State Suffrage Committee, and Montana was her first organizing priority.

She was a genius at organizing, and she made speeches all over. She went to every county in the state and talked in ranch kitchens—women from neighboring ranches would ride over to these meetings, and she would talk with them about why women ought to vote and how to get their husbands to support the referendum. And she went to at least one schoolhouse in every county and told the children to be sure to tell their fathers to vote for suffrage so that their mothers could be good citizens.

She made speeches in every town and city and organized other women to make speeches too—street speeches—and as far as I know, it was the first time women ever made street speeches in this state, except for the Salvation Army, and that was quite different. To go out and make a public speech for something political was for a lady something unheard of.

I remember my own first street speech. I was twenty-two, a reporter for the Helena *Independent*, and terrified. I prepared my speech very carefully and stood on 6th Avenue across from the post office one day at about 12:45. Men were going home for lunch, and I figured I'd talk as they were walking back to work because they would have had their lunches and would be in good moods to hear my arguments. Well, I stood there and there wasn't a soul on the street. Not a soul. I didn't know what to do. Finally I decided I would just talk. To the world. I began shouting. And as soon as I did, people came running from all directions, and I had a good audience in no time at all.

That night my stepmother said to me that she believed in equal suffrage but she didn't believe a lady should speak out on a street corner. It just wasn't done. "If you speak on the streets of Helena again," she said, "you can't come home."

So I thought that over. And the next time I spoke on the street, I stayed at the Placer Hotel and charged it to my father.

After that, they let me come home, and I did a lot of street speaking after that.

As a reporter I got an awful lot of women's suffrage news into the newspaper. I was their first woman general reporter—they had a woman society editor, but they'd never had a woman general reporter before. I thought the editor was probably amused that I wanted to be a reporter because the other reporters were so much taller and I looked kind of ridiculous. They got me a little bit of a desk. In later years I realized that probably one of the reasons he was willing to hire me was that my father owned a department store that was one of the biggest advertisers in the *Independent*.

The paper theoretically was opposed to women's suffrage. It was owned by the Anaconda Copper Company—as was every other paper in the state except the Great Falls *Tribune*—and the mining company didn't want women voting. The wives of their miners were worried about conditions in the mines, so naturally the company didn't want women to have anything to do with voting.

Well, there was this very wonderful doctor in Helena, Maria M. Dean, who was also a very earnest suffragist. She and I used to get together in the afternoons two or three times a week. I would go down to her office and we would talk about women's suffrage; then I could go back to the paper and report that there had been a suffrage meeting that day and write a column about what we wanted.

The editor came over to my desk one day and said, "The Federated Women's Clubs are going to have a convention in Lewistown next Saturday. I'm sending you to cover it." I was pleased, but awfully worried. Lewistown was seven hours away by train, and I knew I would have to send the news by telegraph, and the only telegrams I had ever even seen were the personal kind—ten words with the last word as "love"—and you couldn't use *that* to write up a convention.

Well, he told me to go to the editor of the Lewistown paper if I needed help, and then as he went out the door, he looked back over his shoulder and said, "Jeannette Rankin is going to be at that meeting. One of the speakers." That got me really excited.

Jeannette was the first speaker on the program, and she looked perfectly elegant. She came out on the stage in a gold-colored velvet suit with a great plumed hat to match. She had a marvelous personality. As soon as she came out the air was electric.

"You shouldn't have to tell men why you want to vote," she said. "As soon as you tell them you want to vote, they always ask why. 'What do you want to vote for?'"

Now the women's clubs hadn't gone on record in favor of women's suffrage, and there were a lot of anti-suffragists in the audience, but they listened.

"Men don't tell why *they* want to vote," she said. "They vote because it's right to vote. People have to get things done that need to get done and that's the only way you can do it. Women's needs are sometimes quite different from men's needs."

This was back in 1914 and women's interests were indeed different. She pointed out that women were, for instance, interested in pure food for their families. They wanted food inspections and they were interested in safe streets for their children; they wanted controls on traffic; they wanted to limit the number of hours of work in jobs occupied by women. She went on and on and she was very, very convincing.

I met her that afternoon after the meeting was over. We both gave speeches in the park on suffrage.

I remember when I went to write the story that night, I went to the editor of the Lewistown paper to send the story from there, and he said: "Didn't she look like a young panther—ready to spring!" She was so full of life. It was just wonderful.

That was really the only time I actually saw Jeannette Rankin during the Montana suffrage campaign. I put on a lot of meetings in Helena; her headquarters were in Missoula, with a big office in Butte, too.

At the end of the campaign we put on a big parade in Helena followed by a mass meeting at the auditorium. It was the week before election day. The parade marched down Main Street with three bands playing and people wearing vivid yellow "Vote for Women" sashes. The national head of the women's suffrage organization came out from New York to address the meeting.

The arguments against suffrage were really exactly the same arguments that are made today against the Equal Rights Amendment. I remember how well she addressed them:

"People say that men are the sturdy oaks and women are the clinging vines," she said. "They say women shouldn't try to do things—they should cling and let the oaks be sturdy. Yet I've often noticed, when I walk through the forest, that all of the sturdy oaks that have clinging vines around them are a little withered at the top."

A week later we won the referendum. We got the vote for women in Montana.

Some months later, Jeannette was in Helena and called me on the telephone.

"I'm thinking about running for Congress," she said "What do you think?" Of course no woman had ever been elected to Congress.

"Good!" I said. "Where are you?"

"I'm down at my brother Wellington's law office," she said.

And I said, "I'll be right down!" And we started a campaign headquarters on the spot. Later I learned that she had previously convened a committee of women from around the state who said they were afraid of frightening the men—that if she ran for Congress, the men would all feel they had done the wrong thing, giving women the vote. So they said they couldn't be responsible for her running, but when she called me, I said, "We'll start right away."

So she ran, beginning that day in 1916. She had campaigned all over the state just two years before, and she campaigned again in all the same places, where people greeted her as an old friend.

Two weeks before the election we sent a penny postcard— you could send a postcard for a penny then— to every new woman voter in the state. We had the voter registration list from every county. The other candidates would send out printed postcards: "Vote for John Doe for Sheriff. He is Honest and Courteous." Every candidate was honest and courteous. Well, we wrote our cards out by hand. We addressed them personally—not "Dear Mrs. Smith" or "Dear Miss So-and-so" but "Dear Mary" or "Dear Agnes," using the first names from the voter lists, and then we wrote out: "We are in Helena now and wish you were here. We're going to vote for Jeannette Rankin and hope you are too," and signed it with just the initials of the person who wrote it.

Well, the people who got these cards worried from the day they got them until election day. "Who in the world could have written that card to me?" It kept Jeannette in their minds until election day. I think it helped a good deal. In any case, she was elected by a good majority and went to Washington the following spring to take her seat in the House of Representatives, and I went with her as her administrative assistant and secretary.

It was the special session of Congress that President Wilson had called to get the United States in World War I. Jeannette had run on a peace platform—a pledge to keep us out of the war if she could. Of course, in that same election, Woodrow Wilson's reelection slogan was "He kept us out of war." But soon after the election, the Germans began indiscriminate sinking of neutral merchant ships, including American ships, believing that possibly they were carrying arms to Germany's enemies. Once they began sinking American ships it seemed that almost everybody in America wanted us to go to war.

Wilson read his War Message to the Congress on April 2. I can remember him saying, "This is going to be a war to end war." The Senate voted it up the next day with only four opposing votes. But the House had voted to have an unlimited discussion first, before voting, and the debate took several days. It wasn't until April 7 that they took the vote, and that was at 3:00 in the morning after speeches had gone on day and night.

In the meantime, the congressmen who had offices up and down the hall from ours would come in and tell Jeannette that she must vote the way her constituents wanted her to. They knew she had campaigned against the war, but they said if she wanted to be reelected, she'd have to vote for it.

"And after all," they said, "you *do* want to be reelected."

It just floored me no end! It had never once dawned on me that people went to Congress to be reelected. I would tell these men that you go to Congress because there are things you want to do for your country! And Jeannette said she couldn't pay for her reelection to the next Congress with the lives of her friends' sons. She wouldn't do that.

All week Jeannette's office was filled with visitors. Many, many pacifists came in, hoping she would stand by the pacifist position she had campaigned on, but most of the visitors were for war. Many suffragists came in and said that if she voted against war, the public would think women were just sentimental and shouldn't be taking part in congressional decisions. They said she would set the cause of equal suffrage back twenty years if she voted against war. (Remember, Congress didn't pass the 19th Amendment giving women the universal right to vote until 1919, and it wasn't ratified by the necessary thirty-six states until late in 1920.)

She was terribly distressed. Nothing, she felt, could make her vote for our going to war, yet she felt she couldn't betray the suffrage movement. If the suffragists felt their cause needed a vote for war, maybe she ought to.

I remember the night the war vote was finally called. Wellington, her brother, was quite anxious to get me out of the office, because I felt just the way Jeannette did—*nothing* would make me vote for war. He wanted me out of there while people were trying to persuade her to vote for it, so he sent me over to the Capitol to find out what was going on and when the vote would be called.

I remember walking over in the darkness. The dome was all lighted up, and pigeons were flying around it. It looked as though they must be the white doves of peace, but it didn't work out that way.

When the vote was finally taken, there were fifty-six votes in the House against war. "I want to stand by my country," Jeannette said, "but I cannot vote for war. I vote No." Then she sat down and cried.

Jeannette was not reelected in 1918. She became a Washington lobbyist for the National Council for the Prevention of War. She was elected to Congress again in 1940, again on a peace platform, and she was the only member of Congress to vote against war after Pearl Harbor. Again she was defeated for reelection. She opposed the Korean War and led a march on Washington against the Vietnam War in 1968, at the age of eighty-eight, five years before she died.

Jeannette did a lot of good things for the good of government and for the good of the people while she was in Congress. She supported the Butte miners in 1917, for example, when they went out on strike during the war and were accused of being anarchists and German sympathizers and the owners said they would flood the mine rather than recognize the union. Jeannette said that if the owners couldn't run their mines, the government would.

But I think that, without question, the greatest thing she did for the women of the world was to make the first vote of the first woman of the world to sit in a national parliament, a vote against war. I think it was terribly important; I think she set an example.

I left at the end of the first year. Hattie, Jeannette's sister, took over in the office. I must say, after a few months in Washington I had much more respect for the Montana legislature than I did for Congress, because what they try to do in the legislature is so much nearer the people than the political trades they were making in Washington. I was quite haughty about it.

I met my husband, Norman, in Washington. He was working for Herbert Hoover's Food Administration during the war. He had been examined for the draft, but had flat feet and wore glasses. In those days, if you had any such terrible thing as flat feet or glasses, you couldn't be a soldier. Today, if you're lukewarm, they'll take you.

After we married, we lived in New York. I was all ready to tell *The New York Times* how to run a newspaper, but they weren't the least bit interested. It was the year that women first began to cut their hair and wear it short. It was very new, and the effect was somewhat startling. As short as I was, and with my hair cut, they thought I was a child. They said they didn't have a children's department in their paper. The other papers said the same sort of thing.

Around 1919, before my first baby was born, I designed six maternity dresses and sent an explanation to the *Ladies' Home Journal*, which in those days was *the* big women's magazine. At that time, maternity clothes were unheard of. You just wore your ordinary clothes until you got very conspicuous and then you didn't go out in public for about four months, except perhaps at night when nobody would see you.

I submitted my designs and waited to hear from them. When I was nine years old, I had written a poem about love and sent it to the *Journal* and got back the most impressive rejection slip. It was printed! I had never received a printed note, and it called me "Dear Madame." I thought it was something to be called "Dear Madame" at the age of nine. Well, this time I got another printed slip, but it was accompanied by a personal note from the editor, Mr. Bok, whose grandson is now the president of Harvard.

"The *Ladies' Home Journal*," he wrote, "does not mention babies before they are born."

Norman had better luck as a writer. He got a job on *The Nation*, but after about a year, we decided that we'd better get over to Paris and become foreign correspondents. It was a very unprofitable trip. We came back to New York after several months abroad with two small babies and no jobs. And then my father wired us that the last of his business partners had retired, and if Norman wanted to come to Helena and be part of the firm, he was welcome. We thought it might be a good thing for people with a family to eat once in a while, so we came back, and although we've done a lot of traveling, we've lived here ever since.

The second time Jeannette Rankin voted against war—the *only one* to vote against World War II in Congress—I was in Helena, and all the people I passed on the street downtown were just furious about it. They all said she should have voted for war. But I have this very strong feeling, and I had it before, that murdering people doesn't get you anywhere! The people who get killed in war are not the people responsible. The people responsible are not in the war; they're the big bosses.

And I must say, when I hear people arguing against abortion today, I keep thinking, "How can people be so excited about killing a fetus when they don't get excited about killing adults whose parents have spent eighteen or twenty years feeding and clothing and educating and inspiring them with the idea of doing something for the world?" It's murder when they kill people in a war, especially when the people who are being killed are not responsible for what they're fighting for. Half of the soldiers, I think, don't know what they're fighting for, and that applies not only to our soldiers but to the enemy soldiers.

I think that if I had been in Jeannette's place in 1941 I would have voted the same way. I would have prayed and prayed for some brilliant idea of how to talk directly with the head of Japan instead of having to kill millions of people first and then talk. Why they couldn't sit down around a table the way they do after the killing, I don't know—except, of course, that the one who gets to boss the discussion is the one that can kill the most people who have nothing to do with it.

Today, if we have one of the nuclear wars, we won't have to worry any more about who's going to be the boss. There won't be any bosses. Civilization will be wiped off the face of the earth. With these MX missiles they're putting around here, our defense will kill us as well as our offense. I went to a lecture recently showing the development of our nuclear system since the first bomb. They get new things every year. Heaven help us if we wipe out civilization with an old-fashioned bomb! It has to be brand-new to do what we expect to do.

I don't see what war is going to bring to anyone, except ruin. We used to say, just a few years ago, "The day is coming when we'll have to do something." But the day is here, now. It's not coming, any more. I wish I knew what we should do. We should try to make direct contact, I think, with the people of other countries. If we could send a million people, or even a thousand, to Russia, for instance, to visit, if each person could befriend someone in a foreign country, really become close and warm friends, I think that's probably the only way we'll ever save people from being blown up by other people. A lot of people are terribly bigoted to start with. You can't make friends with them. But if you can pick out enough of the friendly ones, I have a feeling that's the only way it's ever going to get done.

Pete Simpson

Pete Simpson is a scion of one of Wyoming's most illustrious pioneer families. His father Millward served as governor, his brother Alan is now a U.S. senator. Pete, a cultural anthropologist, served two terms in the Wyoming House of Representatives. He is known throughout the state as an accomplished stage actor. The former dean of instruction at Sheridan Community College, Pete is now the executive director of the University of Wyoming Foundation.

YOU ASK IF THERE'S A POSSIBILITY OF DEVELOPING A REGIONAL SOLUTION to our water problems. The answer is yes— there's a *possibility*. Take the Little Horn as a classic case; the Little Horn doesn't get put to much use in the state of Wyoming. It runs out relatively rapidly. Somebody discovered there might be a profit in boosting the water out of the canyon before it gets to the Montana border. Well, we got into wrestling matches over that, in the legislature and everywhere else. It was highly controversial. The biggest problems didn't have to do with what might or might not be done with that water here, but what would happen to the usages claimed downstream. It went through the Indian reservation, for one thing, and that created a huge legal barrier to the use of that water.

I will bet that the settlement of that case will be as expensive as the Big Horn-Wind River case has been up to this time. The legislature has fed three million dollars into *that* case, and will probably spend another two million dollars to finally settle it.

You have Governor Schwinden in Montana complaining that "the governor of South Dakota is selling our water." A lot of legislators here in Wyoming talk the same way. The mighty paradox of this whole damn game is that the potential exists for all kinds of interstate rivalries, now that the "New Federalism" has brought us a whole refocusing of governmental responsibility from Washington on down. That could aggravate something that's already a parochial nightmare in the water situation. We have an interstate compact which is essentially a non-pact. Wait until we find some good uses for that water up here, then we'll see how strong that compact is.

Questions about future use begin with upstream storage. I think the biggest portion, particularly, is attached right now to instream flow. There are two schools of thought on this point. Many contend the best storage is damming it up, while others, including many ranchers, contend that irrigation and upstream use is the only way to keep streams recharged and that it is better storage in the long run.

But those arguments are losing some of their weight. With the population increase of the past ten years, the influence of farmers and ranchers—which is still considerable in this state—has been relatively depleted. There's still a heavyweight number of ranchers down there in Cheyenne, but not as many as there used to be; and there's crossbreeding in agriculture—white-faced cattle and oil. Ranching is not what it was ten to fifteen years ago. A whole lot of mineral influence is inside the ranching influence.

I keep thinking Wyoming has a chance to cut out some new directions and make some things happen that might not be happening in other states. I am hopeful that this state is not going to be another Colorado, for instance. Many indications suggest it never will be, not the least of which are its general topography and its relative balance of resources.

The history of this part of Wyoming has been shaped by an extraordinary collection of settlers—old safari leaders and counts and countesses and dukes and all manner of British noblemen who became great cattle barons. We have our own third-generation nobleman serving in the United States Senate today: Malcolm L. Wallop. That's quite true. His lineage is peerage, and he has the potential, once he retires from the U.S.

Senate, to take a seat in the British House of Lords. His uncle has the seat now, because his father refused to take it, which means that after his uncle gives it up, it comes back to him.

The Wallop who came to Wyoming must have been a fourth son. Although I am not personally familiar with Malcolm's family history, the pattern elsewhere is familiar. The oldest son would have had the title, the next one would go into the military, the third into the clergy, and the fourth would be shipped off to the colonies and end up in Wyoming. Some made fortunes. About three months before the outbreak of the Boer War in 1899, from what I have been told, the Wallops got the contract to supply the English army with cavalry mounts and draft horses for the quartermasters corps. Well, the Boers shot every horse they saw, so the Wallops made a sizeable fortune from the Boer war.

There's much of that kind of history around here. Jack Ellbogen comes to mind. His ranch happens to be the IXL Ranch; the brand is, in fact, derived from the Ninth Lancers—the roman numeral for "nine" and the initial letter "L." Some people refer to this whole group as the "Mink and Manure Set," but it's very influential in this valley, and always has been.

Regarding my own family history, we've never paid much attention to my mother's side, but someday I want to write about it. It has some eminently writable things involved in it, starting with a Dutch immigrant who lived in Chicago and was farmed out as a young boy to work for an uncle. He started at eleven years old as a "ticket boy," a coal-scuttle-hauling boy, and became the owner of the damn ticket brokerage in later life. There were plenty of these combination travel and rate-setting agencies. And then he sold the whole thing to take up mining in Wyoming, and built a mine out here called the Kooi Mine.

He got himself a whole townful of miners. A group of Polish miners came over and became the miners in that town. The old railroad promoters would make all the arrangements for immigrants to go to a specific place—they would pass clean through thousands of miles of the United States without ever seeing any of it, on the way to a home in southeast Oregon to herd sheep or, in this case, to Kooi, Wyoming, to mine coal.

And Polish families still populate the town today. Look in the telephone book. All the Legurskis, the Zowadas, the Awuloks started in the mines out by Tongue River and Ranchester, all through that area. There's something very interesting about that whole process—the coincidence of this area opening up at the same time that some coal-producing areas in Poland were playing out. Entire villages there were losing their traditional means of support; they were moving whole villages out here, just before the First World War, around 1910–12.

Dad's side of the family is really a good deal more colorful, because it's four generations of Wyoming. I'm the fourth generation, and my children are fifth-generation Wyomingites, which means little or nothing except that Fin Burnett, my great-grandfather, fled the west wing of Pierce's army—the Union frontier brigades—in the Civil War and got to Fort Casper with a sutler's train. (The sutler was the equivalent of the army P.X. [post exchange] and was the provisioner of tobacco, some food stuffs, camp luxuries, leather goods, and the like.) He went out of Omaha, and ran that sutler's train on the Bozeman Trail during the two years it was open. He hauled the dead bodies of the Fetterman Massacre in his wagons back to Fort Phil Kearney, outside of present-day Story, on the Bozeman Trail during that terrible winter in 1872.

He was there in the days of Portugee Philip's Long Ride. He fought in the Hay Field Fight at Fort C. F. Smith; then he became what they called "boss farmer" on the Shoshone Reservation over at Lander. This was a post the federal government created on some reservations to help acculturate reservation Indians and teach them farming. His daughter and my grandmother, Margaret—"Maggie Finn"—went into the convent at St. Stephens and worked at the mission on the reservation. She helped translate both the Shoshone and Arapaho languages. She also taught Latin. After she met my grandfather, Billy Simpson, who was a cowhand, she taught him enough Latin so he could start reading the law. You could "read the law" in those days and pass the bar. She tutored him, and he read the law and passed the state bar, and she married him. And he stopped the cowhand business and became a criminal lawyer in this state—a very remarkable, famous and successful one—although he sometimes would drink his way through a fee in a week.

Ol' Bill Simpson was the only man who ever sent Butch Cassidy to jail. And then they let Butch out for a little while, on his own recognizance; but he came back because he'd given his word to Bill.

My dad went to Harvard Law School. He never did graduate, but he went all the years that were necessary, and then came back here and passed the bar. And the very first case he ever sat in on was his own father's murder trial, of all things.

My grandfather had gotten into an embroglio with a chap, and ended up shooting the guy. He was acquitted, but before the trial began, my dad was asked to come back. He'd been planning to go to work for Manley Hudson, a diplomat and lawyer assigned to the American Embassy in England; so he was on his way to the Court of St. James, in London, but instead he took a train ticket the other way, to Wyoming.

And then he courted my mother over the damned mountains for three years. He always claimed he wouldn't have had to court her so long if he hadn't proposed to her on top of the mountain. When she answered "yes," *sotto voce*, his ears were plugged from the height—he says he never heard her. If he had, he claims, I would have been at least a year and a half older. Anyway, they were married right here in the church downtown, and the reception pictures were taken here in this house. I was born in this town and spent my first few weeks in this old house.

Every summer of my life I remember this place, but I never fancied I'd be back in the state to stay; I never really did. I pursued a scholarly career, which I deeply loved and still cherish, but I came back here to find, to my pleasure, that my ties are indeed very deep. And I relish being home.

When I look ahead and think about changes, it makes me feel that all of us with ideas about what Wyoming might become ought to be up saying and doing what we can as often and as effectively as we can, to make sure that we aren't swept along and inundated by some tides that we might have had some control over, had we had the wit. Because there are just a hell of a lot of things that are already beyond our control, in terms of what we can do as a state to adjust to the years ahead.

I have a feeling: Wouldn't it be lovely to have the same political environment in this state ten years from now that we have here today? This state has a very intimate association between politicians and their constituency—a very direct and therefore, I think, a very democratic way of dealing with our political problems. We can hope to maintain it, but I have the haunting feeling that it's related to sheer numbers, and that we may just lose it by dint of circumstances as time goes on.

Change is here. So we have to step somewhere in the middle of that stream and either divert it or channel it or find some other way to direct it. And we can. Your voice, my voice, the voice of anyone in the state of Wyoming, can make a difference, if we choose to use it. That's important, still.

I really think the only time you can alter a current is when you drop into an eddy. When the current starts to circle, then you have some control over how it will come out of that eddy. I think Wyoming is in an eddy right now. What appeared to be a really big flow began with the coal and uranium booms of the 1970s, reinforced by the fear that followed the Arab oil embargo of 1973. But the disarray within OPEC has really caused a slowing of that current, and things are beginning to swirl within this state now. The surveys taken for this last election showed that the positions that were *major* bones of contention six or seven years ago—things that were almost fighting words on environmental issues—have become accepted as the baseline from which we work now. The head-long rush has not swept over the state. I think that, as a result, we're in a period where decisions can be affected. That's a very apt metaphor, especially when you look at the political results of this last gubernatorial race, and maybe at the political results of the past gubernatorial race, and maybe at the political results of the past four to eight years. Perhaps because we're in that eddy, we have a caretaker—Governor Ed Herschler—in the State House. He neither forcibly plans nor does he detract from planning; he simply acts on popular wishes when and if they become visible and strong. He reads these things quite well and he takes care of the folks. He's governor in a time when we're left more or less alone to indulge ourselves in our own particular swirl of circumstances. That's of interest, you see, in terms of the regional focus here. We may not be the only state in an eddy; I don't know, but I'd sure like to find out.

The debate about placement of the MX missile has some similarities to the energy-development flow-and-eddy pattern,

but there are some profound differences, too. The pressure to base a "dense-pack" missile complex down in Cheyenne will arouse the same kinds of arguments that are aroused up here in Sheridan when you talk about any large-scale technological device that uses Wyoming water.

The overlay of the implications of the MX missile, which have to do with the nuclear freeze and nuclear war and other large national issues, is different from the notion of using Wyoming, or setting Wyoming aside, to produce energy for the rest of the United States. There's a similarity, however. Can you secede, or can't you secede? There'll be a lot of arguments about Wyoming's "responsibility to the nation's defense" or to "the nation's government." Those arguments are familiar from the energy debate: we're responsible for the nation's energy self-sufficiency; we're the fuel for the national furnace. On balance, there may be more similarities than differences.

When we come up against these kinds of arguments and expectations, it's all the more important to keep struggling with this idea of defining a region and its true interests.

You know, my one comment at one of the first meetings of the Northern Lights Institute was that there's a "river-line" region here that's very important to understand. We're defined by our rivers. That's why I've always maintained, and will continue irascibly to maintain, that one of the priorities of the Northern Lights Institute should be to conceptualize the regional ramifications of the drainage of these major river systems —the Columbia, the Yellowstone, the Colorado.

Here in the state of Wyoming you have many separate city/state regions, all of them contending politically and culturally, and all in fact buried in their economic bases. The politics of the state divides itself up into conversational topics that relate to the Casper oil nexus, the northeast Wyoming cattle nexus, and so on. "City/states" is not a bad way to conceive of it. Western settlement can be perceived as urban settlement as well as, or perhaps better than, it can be conceived of in terms of agricultural or rural settlements.

I read a very provocative treatise by Gene Gressley, on regional differences and similarities in attitudes—the things that stand in the way of cooperation as well as facilitate it. He points up the difficulties and the potential of regional political action. At the heart is finding some means of making states aware of their common needs. They're already aware of the list of faults and arguments they can find with the easterners and the feds and the big corporate entities. This again is where an institute like Northern Lights comes into play. If Montana, Wyoming and Idaho come to be aware of the means they can use to combine their actions on better ways of managing their water, we're talking about the basis of regional political action.

When and where do we become mini-Bureaus of Reclamation? When and where do we encourage private enterprise? What state is best able to encourage what project? What interstate funding prospects are there?

Information is needed out of which we can design a regional approach to shared, regional resources, and water is the key.

Charles Banderob

Charles Banderob is the president and a founding member of the Montana Senior Citizens Association. At 83, Charles continues a Banderob family tradition as a farmer, organizer and advocate for the common man. Born into a Montana homesteading family, he has lived and farmed in the Yellowstone River Valley since 1907.

MY FATHER HOMESTEADED. I was born in Bowler, Montana in 1905, and in 1907 we moved to Huntley, on the Yellowstone River about fifteen miles east of Billings. The Huntley Project was the first large-scale federal irrigation project in the nation. It was authorized by the Reclamation Act of 1902 and completed and opened for homesteading in 1907. My father filed for a homestead in June, and we moved down there in September. Grubbing a farm out of sagebrush and greasewood land was the major project for the next three years.

Many homesteaders came to that valley. It was laid out principally in forty-acre tracts, and each individual could homestead forty acres, provided he had the money to pay the filing fees, which quite a few people didn't have. The fees cost from $135 to $165 per forty acres, and many families just didn't have that kind of money in those days.

During the day we would grub the sagebrush and pile it up, and at night we burned the piles. It would be a contest to see who had the biggest fire. The whole Project—which covered about 24,000 acres—would be lit up with sagebrush fires.

35

First there was the homesteading, then the coming of the roads and the schools in 1908 and 1909, and then after awhile it became apparent that forty acres wasn't enough—not that there wasn't plenty of work on forty acres—but with the prices we were getting, you couldn't get enough production out of one tract. I think we got six dollars a ton for the first sugar beets we grew in 1909, and production was less than ten tons per acre.

I remember carrying a spike, similar to a knitting needle, to break the crust around the beets when we thinned them by hand. We'd block them with a hoe and then thin out the little cluster we left, down to one beet. Miles and miles, up and down the beet rows, we crawled, doing that work.

In 1917 we managed to acquire some additional land, but the only land we could afford was twenty-five miles from home. Driving a team and wagon, or going on horseback that many miles each way was hard work, but what an experience for us as youngsters to live in the days of free range when you turned your horses and cattle right out on the prairie grass and paid no fee for it, except when the rustlers took some of them. We witnessed the change from the era of free range and big cattle operators to the elimination of free range by homesteaders and farmers who took it up.

The land we bought when we expanded was dry, which means just the opposite of how it sounds, because it was land that would produce a crop without irrigation, or so we believed. We ventured into other crops. Feed crops brought a little more —oats and corn and hay, which then were the main sources of energy for agriculture operation. This was in the early stages of the introduction of dryland farming in Montana, and it worked really well at first—1917 was a good dryland crop year, and 1918 was pretty good. Then the weatherman changed the picture in 1919. It was a real drought—lasted for five years in some parts of the state. The wheat crop didn't get over eight inches high and was very thin. We couldn't get anyone to come in and thresh it after we'd headed it. We had to carry the wheat stacks over to the next year. We had a little better year in 1920, but not much better. From the two years' crop, we had sufficient wheat to make it worthwhile for a threshing outfit to come in and thresh it for us.

The year I met my wife and got married was 1927. It was so wet that fall during and after the beet harvest that we could only haul a half-load of beets with four horses, because the mud was so bad and the ruts on the road were so deep. In November, when my wife and I drove from Huntley over to Roundup to get to our wedding scene, it took us four hours to make the fifty miles. The ruts were about eight inches deep, just clear of the axles of a car, and the mud had frozen. When we met a car, why, we'd have to stop and hoist one car out of the ruts and then drive by, and then go back and push them back into the ruts. Today that's a main oiled highway through there— U.S. 87.

That winter, during the months of January and February, the wife and I had a total of $2.25 income on which to live. Work just wasn't available. We had vegetables that we had produced, so we could live, but as far as finding any employment, it just wasn't possible, beyond getting some contracts to cut ice for some folks. Fortunately that year turned out to be a pretty good crop production year, but then came 1929.

In 1929 it began to get dry again, but the crops had enough reserve moisture that they did pretty well. You couldn't get a good price for them, though. We could get $2.10 a bushel for our wheat the fall of 1929, but it cost us $2.50 a bushel to produce. So we put it in a granary, to hold for a price of $2.50 or better. Well, we wound up peddling that wheat out to hog farmers in the summer of 1931 for seventy-five cents a bushel.

Many of the farmers around here went broke then, starting in 1929 and then in the drought during the 1930s, and of course there were real serious problems for the small business concerns as well as the farmers, and not only in this part of Montana. Other parts of Montana had suffered earlier and longer. There were so many farms foreclosed on that the farmers revolted and organized against the foreclosure auctions and founded the Farmers' Holiday Association to try to cope with the fore-closures and the evictions. Family after family loaded up their belongings and joined the caravans of the Okies and the Arkies who were on the road, looking to find better possibilities else-where.

We managed to hang on. We still have the homestead that we homesteaded in 1907, and we acquired some additional land, but just adding more acreage is not the answer. Return for the products you produce is what's needed. It's got to have buying power equal to or a little above the cost of production, or otherwise you just can't stay in.

That was our problem in the 1930s, and it's the problem today that needs to be addressed much more seriously than it is. Whether you are a laboring person, or a farmer, or a small busi-ness person, if the return for the hours of labor you exert doesn't give you buying power comparable to a halfway decent stand-ard of living, then your family is going to be crowded out.

There are approximately seven transactions between you as a producer and you and the other laboring people as consumers, and it's cost-plus at every transaction, plus times plus times plus, and that creates surpluses of products on the market, depressing prices further. In my judgment, that is the major cause of economic depressions and the economic exploitation of the masses of people.

A certain percentage of the people—they can be of any extraction and any degree of education—are going to be crowded out and eliminated in the process of excess buying power being accumulated by a few and taken away from a percentage of the rest. It depends on many things—the health and age of the family and temporary changes in the economic situation. If you just happen to be fortunate, you'll possibly survive, but if you're not and the combination of circumstances isn't right, then you're eliminated.

A family came out from Iowa in 1911 and homesteaded the forty acres of land right across the road from my folks. They built a five-room house there and put running water in it. They worked the land, the same as we did, and borrowed $7,200 above and beyond the money they brought with them, but that property was sold in a foreclosure sale in 1929 for $67.50—house, barn, and forty acres of land. That family was elim-inated.

The party that bought that property lost it to Yellowstone County for the taxes. There was $1,600 owed in delinquent taxes and water fees and I bought it from Yellowstone County in the spring of 1932 for $1,250 with the taxes cleared up. Now that's buying land below zero.

We grubbed along on that piece of property for about fifteen years before we got on our feet a little better, but between 1944 and 1947 particularly, prices were much more favorable. Prior to that, though, it was necessary to establish the federal farm loan programs and the production credit programs. I couldn't have bought that property without a federal loan, and the pro-duction credit associations set up under the federal Farm Credit Administration in the 1930s required that you get credit against your future production, and the commercial banks and money-lenders didn't have a sympathetic attitude. I remember learning about that back in 1927, when I went to a moneylender to borrow $100 to go get married, and he said "Charlie, when a feller figures out how much money he can loan, he might just as well figure out how much money he can give away." And I said, "Thank you," and walked out.

Many of the merchants were financing farm families through the production season. One merchant might carry a family for awhile, and then he'd transfer them to another merchant, to carry them for a period of years. Many of those families were never able to get out from under that debt. They needed money for groceries or they needed money to farm with. Many of them hadn't sharpened up enough to know how to keep good records on their operations, and they would pay over and over again on the same machinery. One of the things that really got to me was the business interests taking advantage of poor people, some of them brought in here from foreign countries and not abreast of the English language that well.

We did considerable talking about it among the people, and finally we got some organized action. The Farmers' Union came through the area in 1928 proposing that farmers band together. There had been earlier attempts by the United Produce Association and the American Society of Equity. Then the Farmers' Union came along with an education program to develop a basic philosophy and a cooperative program to help you buy supplies and market your products on a cooperative basis.

The philosophy and the promotion of the Farmers' Union did quite a lot to change the attitudes of farmers throughout much of Montana. The wife and I joined the Farmers' Union in 1928 and are still considerably active members at the local and county level. I served on the State Board of the Montana Farmers' Union for some years, and that gave me an opportunity to really see that organized action is one of the major ingredients that people need to have, in any walk of life, whether they are farmers or laborers or small business people.

The real crux of the problem is how to arouse their awareness of the need for organized action on behalf of all people, not just some of the people, and to not seek special privileges for special groups. This today is a real hassle. It's becoming more and more necessary for people to discover that you don't have security for yourself unless you also seek that same degree of security for others.

I don't believe there is any individual who has a full and complete grasp of the intensity of the impact of the Reagan administration's policies—on society as a whole and on senior citizens in particular. We think we understand what the cuts have meant, but the actual severity is not known at this point.

Wherever you go, the uppermost problem in the minds of the majority of the senior citizens is: What is going to happen to our social security? How are we going to live if they take more and more of this social security away from us?

By "social security," I mean more than the basic Social Security pension system that the bipartisan commission wrestled with. I mean the whole collection of programs. It's worrying the senior citizens to sickness.

One woman at a meeting the other day put it this way: "How in the world do they expect senior citizens to live on $325 a month and pay doctor bills that run into the thousands, every stay in the hospital?" She had just finished three months in a hospital and a month in a nursing home. One particular pill that was prescribed cost a dollar apiece, and she had to take

one every day, and then she had her rent, and her food, and her heat to take care of. It just doesn't fit together. And then they talk about cutting more.

Coupled with the mass unemployment that we have now across the nation, these kinds of conditions are driving people to insanity. The young families, right when they need a job and a steady income, are cast aside. And the little insurance and retirement they had accumulated, that's washed away from them.

The thinking of rank-and-file people has got to be brought to bear. We've got to find ways where the various groups that are concerned can work closer and closer together on these issues. The problem, after all, is corporate monopolism, which is international in scope and more powerful in many cases than the government of any nation. It manipulates nations to the detriment of their societies.

The masses of the people are disturbed by this administration's military expansion. They have difficulty uniting themselves against it, but day by day this unity is developing. We have developed war machinery that is beyond the comprehension of the individual, and people recognize that it doesn't solve the problem and that it can't solve the problem and that it is becoming an unnecessary burden.

People are willing to look for other information—for a better way out—and are taking some action. The military acts like a cornered beast, and a cornered beast or a cornered man is in no position to reason. Many of our parents, or our parents' parents, left Europe because of the military oppression, only to discover that we're all wrapped up in the military here and now. And with the intensity of the military machine of this day, it just isn't going to be possible to cope with it and maintain a society of humanity unless the rank-and-file people do the reasoning.

The most encouraging thing is that there are lots and lots of people, and people have a way of being able to think, and there are avenues by which to appeal to them. But unless we, the rank-and-file people, organize our thinking and our actions to the point where we are a countervailing power sufficient to keep a semblance of balance for a logical society for mankind, we are going to be placed under complete military domination. If we allow that to happen, the suffering will be intense, and the thinking ability of people will be ground down very severely, and the shaking off of the shackles of military control will be a long drawn-out struggle and very bitter, serious battle.

Organizations will come and go, but there will have to be organizations that plant the seeds of the needs of the people, and there will be ways to bring those seeds to fruition. We have to go out and keep working at it, and we've got to recognize that time has a way of doing great things.

The Farmers' Union experience gave us insight, as a family, to grasp the opportunity that arises when other groups develop concerns and the opportunity to help them focus those concerns. I worked on the Green Thumb Program, which was founded by the Farmers' Union and the AFL-CIO and some other liberal groups to develop a work program for senior citizens. The idea behind it was that many farmers were moving off the farm and into town, because of their age, and when they got to town they were still able to do quite a few things if there was something there for them to do. They still needed some income, so Green Thumb was put together to develop work programs on community projects for senior citizens.

Well, in 1973 there was a Governor's Conference on Aging held in Billings, which had been held there for a period of years.

The senior citizens who attended were having problems with both federal and state programs affecting them and they wanted to request some changes. Well, they kept being told, "No, you can't do that at the Governor's Conference on Aging, because it's not that kind of an organization." So finally they said, "Well, we'll form an organization of our own, so that we can take that action."

They walked out of the conference and went across the street to the Liberty Theater to discuss forming their own organization, and they elected a committee of four and instructed it to proceed and formulate the Montana Senior Citizens Association. Well, I had attended the meeting and expressed myself, and I was elected to that committee. The four of us then developed the skeleton proposal for the Montana Senior Citizens Association. We decided to base it on the twelve subdistricts of the State of Montana, with a Board member from each, because Montana is a pretty big state when you get to traveling around and visiting people.

In addition to that, there was a theory that we should also have a regional organization of senior citizens. Federal funds were made available through the Community Services Administration to help develop both the state and the regional associations. Anyway, we were able to establish organizations that were really hard-hitting on behalf of senior citizens and the elderly poor. There have been many variations in the philosophy of what these organizations should do, but, all in all, we've survived thus far. And the state legislators have been forced to recognize our importance, and, with other organizations, I guess we get some recognition nationwide. The point is, anyone with the desire to help bring about improvement can find a niche where he can do whatever little part he can, and sometimes the little part is the most important.

For old people in rural areas today, the economic pressure has intensified. In the past, families were larger and there were more children and grandchildren to take care of parents and grandparents. Now we have smaller families and parents and grandparents who live longer. There are more old people and fewer younger people to take care of them, and with the increased cost of medical care and the higher cost of living—well, taking care of the older folks just isn't economically possible. So we have government programs to help. But while we have developed a Social Security system, and some employment programs from time to time, there is a constant struggle with those who cannot understand anything but dollar-and-cents values. They lack the ability to apply any humane values to society or to see to it that people have a reasonably equitable opportunity to achieve a common, decent standard of living.

Instead they will exploit the masses until they force them into the grave. The constant worry of not being able to meet the cost of the things you need finally just breaks down your health, bringing on sickness or suicide. Exploitation is the same, whether you are a young person or a senior a week or two from the grave. It matters not. We have considerable to do in this field.

This is an opportune time. The masses of the people are more disturbed and concerned than they have been for many years. We need more people who will dedicate themselves to the mission of going out among the people and helping them to become active in whatever activity they prefer to help bring about change. Again, this is not for the benefit of some of the rank-and-file people, but for all of us.

It's an interesting proposition to ask yourself, "Why does the human mind do as it does?" Think back to the cowboys and the sheepmen, fighting each other over the range. The cowboys were really death on the sheepmen, and yet every cowboy wore woolen shirts and sheepskin coats.

This always focused very plainly the lack of an overall concept of humanity among people. We had the opposite concept historically: The West was dominated by Indians, and we had to eliminate the Indians to bring about the necessary improvements. It is a sad commentary, in my opinion. The Indian is another human, and if there is a Christianity, he was created by the same Creator as the rest of us. And if there's any basis for division, it must be for some reason other than the Christian way of life. It must have to do with the exploiting of people for monetary reasons.

Our education system has taught us more about how to efficiently exploit other people than it has taught us how to develop a total society of mankind. So I say our education system has failed us, and I want to continue to work on that.

"Live and let live" was basic to the attitude of my family. They worked hard and had to do without many times. They never wanted extravagant living conditions, but their analysis of the situation was that all people should have the opportunity to have a reasonable, decent standard of living. Poverty, in a nation with the ability that this one has to produce in abundance, is a disgrace and a blight on a thinking people.

Little by little, I've been able to whittle out a concept of "why" and "how" and "what are we going to do about it." The opportunity is here. The people are out there. I hope that in the years I have left, I can stir a few other people into action, because to have mass unemployment and to have granaries full of wheat and nowhere to go with it are blights on our society, and to have the deprivation and the suffering we have is a disgrace to our intelligence today. And no one is going to do anything about it, except you and me.

Humberto Fuentes

LET ME TELL YOU ABOUT OUR PLANS for the *Mercado*. The word means "market" in English, and that's part of what it will be, as well as a construction project and hopefully a source of income for the Idaho Migrant Council. But it will also be a showcase, or a way of expressing our abilities.

How did we get started on this project? Well, for the past several years the Idaho Migrant Council has been very conscious that things were getting more difficult economically and that we needed to develop strategies to become self-sufficient. That's one reason we changed into a membership-type organization, as opposed to just a provider of services.

It's important, we felt, to have people belong and pay in, even if they pay a minimum amount of money, because that way they feel they own the Council. They participate. Their attitudes change and people see membership in the Council as a form of community involvement.

To generate funds and help aim us toward self-sufficiency, we started buying properties around the state. We purchased an office in Blackfoot about six years ago that used to be a health center, and we have another one in Burley as well as

Humberto Fuentes is a founder and currently the executive director of the Idaho Migrant Council. For over 20 years, he has been an advocate for the rights of farmworkers in Idaho and other Western states. The Council is headquartered in Caldwell, Idaho, where he lives.

some other property. We've tried to acquire sufficient assets to assure that the organization will continue, whether or not we have federal, state, or private funding.

Based on that premise, we put together a plan to look into economic development ventures. We set up a subsidiary of the Council, and we were able to leverage money from the banks and from the federal Small Business Administration. So at first we helped quite a number of Hispanic businessmen who were struggling or needed technical assistance and other folks who wanted to open up their own businesses. We saw that there was a tremendous potential among the Hispanic population to participate in the business world, and that's how we got started. Then we were able to persuade the federal Economic Development Administration to commission a multi-county study of economic needs. That was the beginning of planning the *Mercado*. We knew there was a tremendous potential for the Hispanic market because more and more, the radio stations and businesses were beginning to cater to Hispanics because of their numbers, especially here in Canyon County.

So then we got a small grant from the governor's office to do a more specific site-selection study—a study of traffic flow, the economy of different areas, and so forth. We came up with about ten sites and narrowed those down to three, and then to one, which was in Caldwell, about thirty miles west of Boise. And just at that time, the Reagan administration decided to kill the Economic Development Administration.

"Oh, here we go," we said. "It's just our luck. When we're ready to submit a proposal, the agency gets killed."

Well, somehow EDA revived. The administration didn't succeed in killing it outright—although its operating funds were cut back—so we decided to take a chance and prepare a proposal anyway. With the help of the EDA representative here in Boise, who's been a good friend of the Idaho Migrant Council for a lot of years, we put together a package and submitted it.

Under the law, EDA can only fund part of a project; the rest has to come from private sources. So we went to the city council of Caldwell with a presentation, trying to get it to apply for Community Development Block Grant funds, so that the council would be the one to loan us the money to build. We almost did it, but there was a lot of opposition. Anyway, we still submitted the application, and the EDA approved it! It gave us a letter of authority, which means the project was authorized for funding when we met all the other requirements, such as

coming up with private financing. We then put together an overall package. The Mercado is financed with a $960,000 grant from EDA, a $200,000 loan from the National Rural Development Corporation in Washington, D.C. and a $432,000 loan from the Provident Federal Savings and Loan Association in Boise.

The Council will have its offices on the upper floor, and we'll have other offices for lease to professional people. (We've already had quite a few inquiries.) In the lower part, we plan to have a good lounge and a Mexican restaurant—we're talking to the Arriba people here who want to branch out to the Caldwell area—and some other types of cultural business: maybe a curio shop, or an import/export shop. The building has a small open plaza, with a Spanish motif.

So we're very excited about it, because it puts us right in the middle of the area where we work. It's quite a step for us to get into this big of a project and to get into the economic development area, which sometimes is very difficult to understand.

So the *Mercado* is more than a structure; it's also an image-builder and a source of encouragement to our community that we can put things together. It's also going to be helpful to us to show the *Mercado* to the Anglo community, which sometimes views us narrowly and sometimes sees us as troublemakers. "They get drunk every weekend and they fight," that type of thing. "They're not smart enough to do anything but field work."

I was born in Tamaulipas, one of the northern states of Mexico. Earlier, my father and his brother had come to the United States to work—his brother worked in the mines in Pennsylvania—and when my father married, he brought his wife to the United States where two of my older brothers were born. Then, during World War II, the family went back to Mexico.

In the late forties or early fifties my father decided to come back. It helped that my two older brothers had been born here, and I think that I was about nine years old when we crossed over at Brownsville, Texas. Just like so many of the immigrants that come over, the first thing we did was get hooked up to some contractors with a truck. They put six or eight families on the back of the truck, and we followed the crops up to the Northwest to a labor camp at Caldwell, which was the first labor camp I ever saw in my life. We lived in it for a summer during the working season, and then we went to the apple orchards, and then up to Weiser, which is about sixty miles from here.

We just kind of followed the routine and went from there to Blackfoot. We picked spuds, or potatoes, and from there went to west Texas to pick cotton, and from west Texas in late October we would hit the Rio Grande Valley and be there for two or three months. And then we'd start the cycle again.

It's sort of fun to look back, because in those days a crew was like an extended family. It was a little community, and we would go everywhere together and we knew everybody. But it was hard, there's no question about it, and not all that much has changed. In fact, the cabin we lived in back in those days is still being used by farmworkers in Weiser, and the camp—well, there's a couple more toilets. It's still pretty bad, and even though some camps have improved, in some of the older, smaller communities, the labor camps are still the same.

Eventually I was drafted and spent a couple of years in the service. I thought about coming back to try to do something for farmworkers because I had first-hand experience. Then, when I got out, I got married and settled down and worked in the fields. After that, I went to a community college in Oregon using my veteran's benefits, and I started to help organize farmworkers. This was in the early sixties.

While I was still a student, the college hired me as a counselor to help other Chicanos get scholarships, since we had a fairly large Hispanic student population there. Well, we ran into some difficulties with the school administration, and I was fired, along with two other men. We went to federal court, during the old Office of Economic Opportunity days, and claimed that the college's migrant programs should have a policy board composed of farmworkers themselves, not just the college trustees, because the trustees were making all the decisions and the farmworkers had no say whatsoever in determining the programs that the money was being used for.

That's how we began. We had a pretty strong group of people supporting us, and we finally got a planning grant from OEO to set up the Idaho Migrant Council. By that time, we had gotten thrown out of work in eastern Oregon, so we came over to Weiser and started organizing in all the labor camps and getting councils set up and people excited about participating and getting help. The state was doing *nothing* for farmworkers at that time, so we formed councils throughout the state and had organizations in every labor camp in the state. There was a lot of excitement because we're talking about the sixties.

We got the planning grant in 1969 I believe, and spent almost all of 1970 organizing and getting our legal structure in place—our boards, our policy manuals, the whole bureaucratic system that was new to us at that time.

We incorporated in 1971, and then we got a small OEO grant to provide support services to farmworkers, and we began dealing with housing, early childhood education and bilingual education.

Sometimes people elsewhere are surprised to find there's a Hispanic population in the Northern Rockies. I've been in meetings back East where first they think you're talking about Iowa—they have trouble back there remembering the difference—and then when you get them straightened out on Idaho/Iowa, they say, "Chicanos in Idaho? I never heard of that. What do they do there?"

All of them have heard of Idaho potatoes, but they never seem to have associated Idaho potatoes with work. Well, we pick the potatoes they eat in the East.

Actually, Hispanic people have lived in Idaho since the earliest mining days, a century ago. They were being brought in to do mining before 1890, when Idaho became a state. And there was at least one Hispanic businessman here in Boise who had a hardware store.

During World War II, when there was a manpower shortage, there was a lot of pressure from the growers in Texas and California to recruit Mexicans, and a lot of Hispanics were brought in. I would venture to say that in the years of the *bracero* program, almost all the immigrants were farmworkers. And, in the course of following the cycle, they came to this region.

Now things have sort of changed, partly because agriculture is more mechanized and partly because people acquire education and are more economically mobile. Hispanics traditionally view education with great respect. Even an uneducated farmworker will talk about education as a way out for his kids, so more and more people like me have begun to settle down. Now we see Idaho as our home.

A lot of us still go back to Texas from time to time, and we try to maintain the culture. And I'm beginning to see the effects of some of the battles we fought with the universities to get more

Chicanos admitted, and with the schools to offer bilingual education. Now there are a few teachers, a few lawyers, a few Chicano doctors who can serve as models. They encourage other Chicanos. I guess what I'm saying is that we're diversifying more. We have a few Chicano businesses popping up around the state, and I think that's an indication we're making some progress.

It's only recently that the Census Bureau began keeping track of the Hispanic population in the United States. In Idaho, according to the Census, there are about 39,500 Chicanos. We estimate that it's more like 55,000 or 60,000—about six percent of the state's total population, which was about 940,000 in 1980. There are many areas that the Census Bureau misses, and, obviously, they don't count the undocumented population, which is high not only in Idaho but throughout the Northwest.

The majority lives in Treasure Valley, which encompasses about five or six of the southwestern counties. The second largest population is in the south-central part of the state: Twin Falls, Burley, Rupert, and other towns there. And then the third, lesser population, is in the eastern part of the state: Idaho Falls, Blackfoot, Rigby. The Treasure Valley, the Magic Valley, the Snake River Valley—the agricultural part of the state—that's where most of the Hispanics are. They are still mostly employed in agricultural businesses such as Simplot and Ore-Ida. More recently the electronics industry has come in. Hewlett-Packard employs a number of Hispanics, but most Hispanics in Idaho are still employed in agriculture—picking, packing, canning, shipping.

Traditionally the state has been very narrow-minded about farmworkers. The attitude, especially in the early years, was,

"We need these people. They're a necessary thing we have to put up with. But we don't have to feel responsible for them." So the communities didn't feel responsible for farmworkers at all. They were just something to put up with, three or four months out of the year. There was no need to discuss their problems or set up any type of assistance programs. In the winter, they should move on. And they were *encouraged* to move on. If a Chicano ran afoul of the law, the authorities would agree not to prosecute if the Chicano agreed to leave the state. That was how Idaho took care of the Chicano problem.

When we formed the Idaho Migrant Council and began addressing these issues there was a lot of resentment toward us for even speaking out. But now, I think, we're making some headway. Attitudes in some of the communities have changed, as I've said.

But still the state refuses to act. To give you an example, it was just last year that we were able to get the legislature to enact a law requiring farmers to provide a toilet for the farmworkers out in the field, and we had a lot of opposition to this very minimum law.

And now, with the federal budget problems and the recession, the priority for farmworkers is even lower. That's the reality. We've always had to fight harder to get federal social service programs that will reach the Hispanic farmworker. Well, now the economy is so bad that middle-class people are hurting, which means that the cry of the Hispanics is not being heard.

The energy problem, for example, has hit farmworkers particularly hard because they depend on their vehicles. And there's never been enough money for farmworker housing, and now there's even less.

There's been a debate on housing for years. Should the farmer provide it or should somebody else do it? Well, the farmers threw the ball to the federal government. The federal government has never exactly gone out of its way to provide decent, sanitary housing for farmworkers, but now the Reagan administration just throws the ball back. And the state has been a bystander. Didn't get involved. Didn't think it was a state problem.

Well, now we have the "New Federalism," and the Community Services Block Grant, which gives the states more responsibility for anti-poverty programs but less money to fund those programs and more latitude to spend the money on other things. We're getting hit hard. The state Office of Health and Welfare is prepared to spend $10,500 to cover 55,000 Hispanics. That's the way the state approaches its responsibility to farmworkers. It comes down to twenty-six cents for each Hispanic in the state, and you can't even buy a cup of coffee for twenty-six cents, but that's the commitment we see right now from the state to the farmworkers.

It was that attitude that forced groups like ours to go to the federal government in the first place. We could not get the states to accept responsibility. At the national level we could at least get programs enacted and some monies appropriated specifiically earmarked for the benefit of migrant workers. Now, at the state level, we're going to be competing against many other groups. In theory, a poor person is a poor person whether brown or white or red, but when it comes time to equitably divide the few dollars that exist, we run into problems.

We're in the process of developing strategies to deal with this problem. It used to be that the state—whenever a brown face appeared at their door—would refer them to us, so maybe we'll have to do the same. When a family comes to us for help we'll just turn the problem over to the state. I don't know what they would do. They have a very limited bilingual staff.

We do know a thing or two about putting pressure on the state, and we will have to do it, especially in the area of education. The state is really cutting back, and we already rank forty-seventh, I believe, in per capita expenditures for education. If that's how much emphasis they put on education as a whole, you can imagine their enthusiasm for bilingual education and special programs for Hispanics.

About six years ago we conducted a study with the Civil Rights Commission to determine the drop-out rate among Hispanics from first grade through high school. We had to do it that way because the educators themselves weren't even keeping records. The drop-out rate among Hispanics was eighty-six percent. It's a very serious problem.

When I came to this country, I had gone to school in Mexico, so I knew how to read and write and do arithmetic. But when you cross over, you enter a different world and when you don't understand what's going on, you're penalized. We keep trying to point that out.

It became so bad, we had to sue the state four or five years ago. We pointed out that there was a state law requiring the state to guarantee students an equal opportunity to learn, regardless of race and native language. The state had been saying, "That's the school district's problem," and the school district would say, "No, it's the state's problem." Meanwhile, the state was getting Title I migrant education grants and other kinds of federal assistance for low-income students. Our suit was thrown out, but we're very persistent, and we appealed. It took a couple of years, but finally the case was heard at the Ninth Circuit Court of Appeals in San Francisco and we won. It was the first time in history that a federal judge here in Boise got overruled. You can imagine the reaction here.

The case went back to the local courts with the Mexican-American Legal Defense Fund helping us. Finally, in February, 1983, the state agreed to settle out of court. They promised to implement a state-wide monitoring system to ensure that each school district comply in setting up programs for students with limited English speaking proficiency. We try to keep up with their efforts and we periodically remind them of their promises. Obviously, what we could have gotten three or four years ago would have been a hell of a lot more than what we could bargain for now, because of the budget cutbacks and because of changes in the national attitude toward bilingual education.

It's a struggle. We operate migrant Head Start programs throughout the state and we try to implement a bilingual curriculum to help prepare kids to do better when they enter the school system, but the wages for teachers here are so low, you can't get a bright Chicano to come to teach. There are no advancements and such low pay that they get discouraged and go to California or Arizona, where they can do better. So there are very few competent bilingual teachers in Idaho and very few role models.

It seems to me that, until recently, Idaho has been predominantly agricultural, with the idea that education is secondary to sweat. Educators here have not been aggressive in advocating more funding or better approaches to teaching. They've had a dormant, "don't rock the boat" kind of attitude, and a lot of the teachers were farmers' wives, and it was just a second income.

Now you can see how bad the situation has become. The universities can't meet the minimum standards for accreditation. If higher education is in that kind of situation, just imagine what the elementary and secondary schools are facing. Now we're in an age of high technology, and kids are not being prepared for it. You can take the handicap of an average Idaho student and multiply that by two with our children, because they enter the schools with a language barrier.

We're also working on voter registration, and I think we're going to see some very positive results and tremendous change. Before, the few established Hispanics opposed our way of doing things, but they're coming around, and there seems to be broader agreement on what needs to be done, especially in the area of voter registration. Ten years ago there were many divisions among our own people, as in the black movement. Now I think there are potentials for stronger coalitions and stronger approaches to making an impact on the political scene. As yet we don't have an elected Hispanic official in the state, aside from a few school boards. There's nobody at the city, county, or state level. We're hopeful that will change soon.

Our approach is to focus more on local than on statewide offices. We have to get people excited, and we haven't had enough good Hispanic candidates to do that, so a lot of our folks are just negative about politics. "Democrats or Republicans, it's all the same." Come election time, politicians get interested in our problems. They eat tacos at a fiesta but after they get elected we don't see them until the next election.

Our folks are beginning to see that, and we're saying we need a change. We've played it kind of safe. First we wanted to get a lot of people more knowledgeable about the political process, and now, with more Hispanics in the state being more aware, there are more people willing to volunteer time for voter-registration drives. That's a positive change.

On the whole, I'm very optimistic about the Hispanic community here and about what we can do. Of course, if the economy doesn't recuperate, the employment picture for our people is going to be very bad. We're already seeing more competition in the fields from people who wouldn't be willing to work there in good times, and we're seeing more mechanization. But we have faced roadblocks before and gotten around them. The economic hard times that a lot of middle-class people are now experiencing have been to the Hispanic a way of life. We have experienced it and we endure.

Still we must do away with the discrimination and the barriers. In the early days, we faced very, very hostile opposition. I think that has changed to an extent. Discrimination and prejudice are still around—more subtle, more camouflaged—but I think now we have more people who understand our arguments. They understand we can talk intelligently just like anybody else, and they realize we have views that we will express. Our views might not necessarily be the same as theirs, but, after all, that's what this land's supposed to be about.

Reed Hansen

WHAT HAVE I LEARNED ABOUT WATER AFTER EIGHT YEARS ON THE WATER BOARD? Well, I'm not through learning. Nobody has all the answers. Some think they do and come up with short, snappy solutions. I guess I've learned how much I don't know. Don't believe anyone who says: "This is where we're going to be in twenty years." We're all guessing. Some opinions are based on fairly decent information, but it isn't set.

What have I learned? I've learned a little bit about fish, a little bit about power. All I knew before was just putting water on my ground; just bringing it out of the canal and raising crops and selling them. Now I see other perspectives. They didn't occur to me before because I was busy making a living. There was a particular period of time when people we called "environmentalists" were so upset. Well, they had a right to be! As I look back, they had to take a club to get our attention, like you do with an old mule. You hit him on the head right hard to get his attention; then you can get to work.

Power needs and fish needs and agriculture needs compete with each other. And how do you arrive at some sort of balance? I don't know. The balance is what the public says it wants.

That's why it's so important that we start listening to each other, so we can make some reasonable decisions. Reasonable decisions won't totally satisfy the fish people, or the power people, or the farmers, but you can't really put all those people into separate little categories, because they're all mixed up in each other's interests.

It's a matter of getting information and then presenting it. I don't want to use the words "educate the people," because I don't think that's quite right. I hear that all the time. Presenting as much information to people as possible and soliciting understanding and responses are maybe ways of "educating," but to me "educating" implies that I know it and I'm going to communicate with people and tell them what I know. I don't like that at all.

I don't want to call the shots for people. That seems arrogant. Environmentalists can be arrogant, and farmers can be arrogant, and poor people can be arrogant, when they set out to "educate" you. Inform the public and hope you'll get some good responses and good dialogue. They'll educate themselves.

I'm very proud and impressed with the way the Department of Water Resources and the Water Resource Board have gone about it. This style started before my time. It's essentially to come to the people with questions: "What should we be concerned about? What are the problems? What do we deal with?" Then you take that through a series of public meetings all over the state, again and again, and go back and read the transcripts and study and analyze them. Then start getting data and information and come up with some drafts with lists of alternatives. Then go back: "Did we listen? Did we hear you right? Is this what you told us? Is this what you meant? These are some tentative conclusions on where to go: What do you think?"

When you have the responses, you go back and determine if

such-and-such an issue was addressed. Then you come back with a firm, written policy. Then once again you go out and make a judgment; have all the hearings you can possibly have.

The most joyful part of my job is the public hearings. I just love them, because if they're conducted with the right attitude, you can just *see* the interaction. If you can keep emotions down, it's just tremendous. You hear a lot of crazy and conflicting things, but once in a while there's a little magic that gets in the air. Everybody's listening to everybody else, and suddenly you can just hear minds turning. They're not quite so mad and suspicious; they're thinking.

It's a pretty good way to operate. The only problem is getting the people to come out. Sometimes they don't. And you have to have the time to go through the process; and it takes money. The lay Board has to be willing to put in a lot of time, but the staff does a lot of the time-consuming work.

We've had a good staff. But, with the funding cuts that the state is experiencing, capability is being harmed. If ever there was any fat in the Department of Water Resources, it's gone, and the ability to do the job it should do is being impaired now. Response time is slow. Long-range planning is difficult.

Some positions have been eliminated and some people have just quit. Some of our most talented people have said, "I don't need this. No future for me here. I'm going somewhere else."

You've heard all the standard stuff about bureaucrats: fat, lazy, not working hard—lumping them all together that way. I think politicians like to use that as a justification for not maintaining or increasing taxes. Ultimately you create a self-fulfilling prophecy. The most capable people leave and the less capable stay.

State government is no different from any other entity. Sure there are some people who are being carried and who hide and

Reed Hansen raises potatoes on his family farm in the Snake River Valley near Idaho Falls, Idaho. He is currently a member of the Idaho State Legislature and also served for eight years on the State Water Board, the public agency which regulates water use in Idaho.

do nothing, but I've seen that in private business. I had a little of that preconceived image of bureaucrats myself at one time—until I started working with them. Why, I've seen them sweat, and I've seen them work really hard—nights and holidays. They take their responsibilities very seriously. We get better than we deserve, in my opinion.

After eight years on the Board, people can't fit me in a camp, and I think sometimes they don't trust me, because I can't be fitted in a special camp. If I wanted to take a selfish view, I could side with a lot of power companies and fish people, and there would be no more development. Do you realize what that would do to the value of my water rights? Holy smoke! If no more water permits were being issued in Idaho and I'm sitting there with my water rights, it would be valuable. But I want to be able to develop more water, and more farmground, if the need is there, and develop the capability to grow. I take the position that we should try to provide for more growth, against the day when we need that capability.

I want it all, really. I want fish protected, even though I don't fish anymore. All I do now is climb mountains a little bit in the off season, when I can afford it. That's my only recreation: I love to trek. A few years back, in 1977, I went to Nepal and spent a month there. Three of my brothers and I just got the idea and we went and trekked. We got to the base camp of Mount Everest, and it was wonderful! I'd go back tomorrow.

I've been on a farm since I was five years old. My dad was a potato dealer, and he bought a farm when his family was really young and moved out to the farm. I've been farm-oriented ever since. I now operate the family farm as part-owner. It's been incorporated—a very small corporation. I've stayed here all the time, except when I was in school and in the service. It's my chosen field.

My oldest son was graduated in the spring of 1982, and he chose to come back to the farm. This is his first year. My other two boys have expressed no desire to be part of the farm at this time. One's in college now, and the other was graduated a year ago and doesn't know what he wants to do, other than be a mechanic.

The opportunities for young people to get into farming are pretty tough now, unless they have a dad or someone who will let them move into an established farm and ease into ownership with low payments or with an inheritance. Otherwise, I just don't know how a young fellow can do it. Some bankruptcies are going to occur among young farmers in the next few years. They don't have the assets. Society chooses not to finance people like that, and that in turn accelerates the move toward larger farms. I don't know how you get young people into farming.

Am I glad I did it? Well, a newspaper reporter interviewed me last year, and I'll tell you what I told him. I was at the University of Idaho but did not graduate. I quit in my junior year and came home to do what I was studying to do, and that was farming. If I'd known when I came home what I was getting into, I wouldn't have had the courage to do it. That's the truth. I couldn't have done it. But then I suppose everyone could say the same thing.

Well, my life on the farm has been a rollercoaster. I'm healthy, I'm happy, I'm not broke, but it's my choice, and I guess I'm glad. It's been a great life, but I don't feel I've been rewarded to the extent I ought to have been, or to the extent that some others have been.

I'm not asking society to say, "Well, because you worked hard we're going to give you a subsidy to increase your income by some kind of factor so that based on your investment you can have an income comparable to a licensed engineer or an attorney." It's a free enterprise system. I made my choice.

I have trouble not discouraging my son, though, from doing it. He had a degree in business management from Brigham Young University, and I'm sure he knows what he's getting into, but when he decided to come back it made me a little nervous.

It made me feel like saying: "You better not do this. Hey, you're wasting your time. For hell's sake, get into something else. Don't commit your life to *this*." But, there again, I can't predict the future. He's smarter than I am and has worked as hard as I did. Maybe he'll be quite successful and happy; I don't know.

People have a perception that a farm is a great place to bring up a family. It isn't quite today what people think it is. In my youth, when I was growing up, it was great—although maybe I wasn't sensitive to the problems my folks had. But it's so high-pressure now, so specialized, so intensive, that I found I wasn't even talking with my kids as much as I should, even though they were right there. Because of the economic pressure to specialize and succeed, you run in and have lunch and get back to work. You aren't communicating like you should.

Farming has evolved to where it's like other occupations. We've lost something. That's my observation. I'm not crying, just pointing out that the perception that people have—that this is the last bastion of the "Great American Way"—isn't quite right. The old farm, where everybody worked together and milked the cows together is gone. It used to be that everybody had pigs, chickens, cows, horses, eggs, cream, and everything.

I don't know the future of the potato market. I'm scared. I pick up bits and pieces of information that other parts of the United States are doing all the research they can to develop a potato as good as ours, to be grown in Missouri or Kansas or back East, that the public would like as well. And they're so much closer to the markets—it's scary! And if we can't preserve our share of the market, preserve our potato—it's a super eating potato, just an outstanding potato—if another area can match it, then we're dead.

What makes the Idaho potato so great? I think it's a combination of soil, climate, temperature, and growing season. The soil is volcanic ash; mine is, anyway. It's good soil—really deep and light—and we don't have really high temperatures here, and the spuds don't grow really fast. They have a mealyness, a distinct eastern Idaho taste. There are people in western Idaho who come over for eastern Idaho potatoes.

We're totally mechanized. It just evolved that way over the years—you had to, to compete. And we're not through yet, I suppose. The pencil tells you—or at least the way I try to use the pencil—that it's time to move up to this piece of machinery, and I do it. And harvesting is better with mechanization, but we've lost something. In the 1940s, during the war, kids came out to pick. Classes were dismissed for that. The farmers here would never have gotten their harvest in if it hadn't been for the high school and junior high kids and teachers coming out and harvesting. There was tremendous commitment in those days.

I remember those days—I was in junior high and high school myself. I remember an ex-governor of the state of Idaho, Brazila Clark, who was quite elderly, who came out to pick potatoes and to do his bit. There was no fanfare or publicity. Food was needed. It was a beautiful time, in terms of spirit and the commitment of youth. The public was united, and it was for the country, not just for "me." They just poured out. Beautiful! If only there hadn't been a war.

I see bigness everywhere— bigness, bigness, bigness, with farms and business both. I like the concept of something more personal where you are the boss of your little enterprise. Bigness really troubles me with the giant chains and all the mergers going on. Eventually the individual loses any influence.

When you feel you can't influence either government or economics—that you don't amount to anything—it's a bad situation. I usually deal and sell with General Mills, as a producer of grain. I really have no influence with them at all. I don't count. The local management is very nice, but they don't set the prices. They're so big. If I said, "Well, I'm not sure I like the way you're doing things—I'm going to Pillsbury," they wouldn't care. It's all the same to them. It gives me a helpless kind of feeling.

With farm produce, it's a buyer's market nine times out of ten. I'm not suggesting there's a conspiracy: it's been a buyer's market historically, and there are many more farmers than there are grocery chains on the other side. That, of course, gives them an advantage.

It's a weird occupation, farming. You can't pass your costs on. When I make a deal with a potato buyer, he makes an offer and generally that's about it. Not much dealing goes on. I can say, "I don't choose to sell today." But when I do sell, I can't say, "Okay, I'll sell at $2.75—*plus* my freight and my taxes." I don't say that, because I can't.

Let me go back to a conversation I had with my banker last fall. Grain was bad, spuds were going down, and I was pumping him about what might happen to prices in the months ahead, presuming that he had better information that I did. "What do you hear?" I asked him.

"Well, you know," he says, "one consolation is that there'll be a shake-out. There'll be some folks who will have to quit farming. There'll be some people who just won't get financed, and they'll have to get out, and that will make it better for the rest."

I've been in the game thirty years, and I said, "Let me tell you something. In thirty years I've seen a lot of farmers forced

out, but I've never seen one acre of ground idle because of it. Someone always moves in and buys or rents that piece of ground. It doesn't go idle. So a shake-out is no consolation to me. Some one has been hurt."

These pieces of ground go back into production, but control seems to be moving to the vertically integrated types of institutions—the processor, the dealer, the conglomerate, the bank, or someone back East who needs a tax advantage.

With farming, supply and demand doesn't work the way it does elsewhere. If the demand for steel diminishes to the point where Republic Steel goes bankrupt, U.S. Steel doesn't necessarily come in and buy up Republic's productive capacity and crank it up again. In farming that's what happens.

It's not necessarily a matter of weeding out the inefficient, either. That took place at one time, but anybody who has survived until now has proven himself to be pretty darned efficient. Today it's your economic resources that determine your survival, not your efficiency; it doesn't matter how efficient you are. A young farmer can work eighteen hours a day, and it won't solve his problem. When he runs out of equity, it's over.

With the trend to bigness, availability of capital is even more important, otherwise you can't play the game.

I hope we can preserve our quality of life here, preserve it close to where we are now, or improve it. That's my desire: keep what we've got. I like this community and this state. It has industry, it has agriculture, and it's a nice place to live, really, compared to what I hear about Chicago and California and those other places. People leave those places to come here. I want to preserve what they come for and still provide for growth and economic opportunities for my children, my neighbor's children, and their grandkids. Somehow, in the quaint little hunter's and fisherman's paradise nestled in the nice mountains, you have to live, too. I don't want to create a rich man's paradise here. We're entitled to make a good living and feel that we can get our teeth into something. You've got to provide for that and preserve it. It's the old trade-off: it's not all one or the other.

We might have to give some things up. I'd be willing—I guess—to give up some open spaces. I'm willing to accept that the city of Idaho Falls will be closer to where I farm, just so it doesn't leapfrog it and just so it isn't growth for growth's sake for some chamber of commerce or some real-estate developer. I don't want only the realtors making state policy; I don't want chambers of commerce to be the only planners.

I said that to a guy in a meeting a year ago. "You know," he said, "I'm on the Chamber of Commerce here."

"Oh," I said. "Well, I used to be on it, myself. But I think the rest of us need to speak up. Help make policy. I'm not sure everything I want is right, but I want to be heard."

And I want to preserve the opportunity for my kids and the next kids to make judgments. Let them decide whether the fish have to go because they've got to build some dams on the Salmon River, instead of my saying, in effect, "Well, kids, we decided the salmon were going. Sorry." Who do we think we are?

56

Rudy Autio

Rudy Autio is an internationally known artist and sculptor. A native of Butte, he was an early staff member of the Archie Bray Foundation in Helena. His primary medium is ceramics; he also paints and works in bronze. A member of the faculty of the University of Montana since 1957, he now teaches on a part-time basis. Rudy lives in Missoula, Montana.

BUTTE? IT'S A HELL OF A TOWN AND ALWAYS WAS. I can remember walking around the streets of Butte when it was exciting as hell, with great characters in the streets—Shoestring Annie, Whistling Sam, and Jerry Murphy, the chief of police. These are people I can still remember from when I was a ten-year-old boy, loose in the streets of Butte.

You might say it was a privilege to grow up there. It was very special and very international in feeling. There were a lot of different ethnic enclaves in the city—the Irish and the Finns and the Yugoslavs—and each of them had their own little microcosm of a social unit, with their own church and stores. You could almost exist within your own culture. I learned to speak Finnish at home, and it was reinforced in the neighborhood, in stores, and in the Finn Hall during all kinds of activities. As a consequence, I became very much immersed in the Finnish culture, although of course I wasn't conscious of it. But when I started school, I probably wasn't very fluent in English.

Both of my parents came over from Finland. Dad worked in a Montana mining camp at Southern Cross, where my parents met. They were married in Butte about 1917, and Dad worked in the mines practically all his life, while Mother worked in the boarding houses. They were active in the Finnish community all their lives. Dad was a musican and played the violin, and in the early days he played in all the Finn saloons. Later he got religion and became a very straight guy—a pillar of the church.

There was a great enthusiasm for culture in Butte—thirst for it. None of the miners wanted their kids to do what they were doing, so there was this pressure to get an education, but not necessarily a liberal arts education. The idea was not to end up in the mines *as a miner*. It was fine to go to the School of Mines, and become a mining engineer, because that was a cut above being a miner. They would see those engineers marching through the mines and think that that's what they wanted their sons to be.

I'm not sure there was pressure to be an artist or anything else in particular. Working in a grocery store was admirable enough, just so you didn't end up in the holes. And the only way to guarantee that was to get at least a high-school education. There was a lot of support for that.

I had some excellent teachers in Butte, particularly some great Irish teachers in grade school. They were fantastic. I like to think the Irish have a great affinity with the arts. They're very supportive in the areas of music, drama, plays, and poetry especially. My art teacher in grade school was a great Jewish lady by the name of Mildred Chamison. She was also very supportive.

In high school we had a teacher named Pop Weaver, who was an artist of the *beaux arts* school who painted posters like crazy—a legendary character around Butte. The old-timers remember Pop Weaver. We had to do a lot of portrait drawing. He could just sit everybody down with a piece of paper and a pencil and pose someone and we would do portraits all day long. Nobody thought it was feminine or sissy to be interested in art. Pop Weaver was a rough, tough old guy with a broken nose. You didn't mess with Pop Weaver.

I think, looking back, we had a very good public schools program in Butte, and when I was a youngster, the WPA program—the Works Progress Administration—was active. It would send artists into the schools, and they would have evening programs. I suppose those programs were largely intended to keep people occupied during the Depression, but I learned a lot from them. There were good people involved in those programs.

When I came out of high school we were in the middle of World War II, and I went into the navy; then, after I got out of the service, I enrolled in Montana State University—it was Montana State College then—and spent four years there. I started in the architecture program, but I didn't last. I spilled too much coffee on my drawings and things like that. And since there were better looking girls over in the art department, I was persuaded to go into art, where I got into ceramics. They had a good staff and we had a great group of art students. Everyone out of that class has done well in the art world including Peter Volcus and Harlan Goudy, who has been head of the art department at Knox College in Illinois for many years.

After we both finished graduate school, Peter and I went to Helena, working with the Archie Bray Foundation, which we kind of got started. It wasn't our idea, but we were the workers there, the drones who put the bricks together, and it was an ideal situation to work in. But calling it a foundation is a little bit misleading, because there's no endowment or any other financial support for the operation of the place. It's merely a collection of artists who work together.

Archie Bray left some land and some buildings—a place for artists to work. He was a very interesting, very generous guy—rough and tough and hard-nosed about running the Western Clay Manufacturing Company—but he had a vision of supporting the arts and he was intensely interested in seeing his vision develop. We made bricks by day and ceramic pots or sculpture in the evenings. During the early years, the brickyard supported us, before we raised our production of art goods to the point where we were paying for our own operation. Gradually we began to sell more pottery, and by the time I left, which was in 1956, it was pretty much on a break-even basis.

Archie wanted his foundation to be not only a center for ceramic art but a painting and wood-making center and a place for music. It was a crazy idea for a brickyard, but why not? People in Montana like crazy ideas.

I've been very lucky to have been able to do a lot of things that I've wanted to do. The Archie Bray Foundation was a great start and opportunity, even though we were poor as church mice for a hundred years, or so it seemed. It was a very intense involvement in art, and exciting—I really didn't know one thing about clay in those years.

From time to time I've been tempted to leave. I've been on teaching assignments in different areas, but my roots are here and I like it here. There's sort of an undefinable kind of life here that you become used to, particularly if you grow up here. I think I'm lucky in my work, because I have the opportunity to travel and see other parts of the world. I don't think I have any built-in prejudices one way or another. I love the Yuma desert, I love Brooklyn, and I think New York is great. Practically everywhere I've been, I've been positive about. The only thing I didn't like was the smog in Los Angeles, and we've got that here in Missoula now.

I had the opportunity to go to Finland to work in 1981. I'd been in touch with the director of the Arabia ceramics factory, and he wrote to me from Helsinki, encouraging me to come at just about the same time that I got a grant from the National Endowment for the Arts which was to be used in any way I felt was important to further my career. I'd always wanted to go to Finland, because it has a strong ceramics tradition.

When I arrived, Arabia provided me with a studio, a place to live, and a salary—the whole shooting match—which I hadn't expected. I worked there for two months, initially. It was wonderful getting to know the artists there, and I had a show in Helsinki—primarily work that was fired in the Arabia plant. I returned the following year, dragging Pete Volcus and Jim Leede with me, and we all gave demonstrations and lectures at the University of Helsinki, and to other potters' groups. I remembered my Finnish, even though I hadn't practiced it for years.

The climate in Finland is practically identical to Montana, especially around Missoula. It's a beautiful country. You have to remember, the population is small, about four million people—you could fit them all into the Bronx. As a consequence, the cultural centers are small. After a while you get to know all the artists who are as advanced and as accomplished as we are here. But they go by the rules a bit more; there's a little cleaner edge. I don't think they have the same sense of adventure as we have in our painting or sculpture or clay.

There are some things they do that I admire. For one thing, Finland supports artists by actually giving them annual stipends to live on. Once an artist becomes established, he's assured of surviving, because he doesn't have to search out sources of income for himself. Finland is a small country and recognizes that it doesn't have a support base for the arts. There's a short-

age of rich patrons. That's one reason for the stipend system. That doesn't mean they give it to everybody. You have to earn your laurels and credentials and recognition. They're discriminating about making grants. I think something like that would be the best way to help artists in our country. We're rich enough that we could afford to do something like that, if we spent our resources wisely.

Can artists find financial support in Montana? Yes and no. If I had stayed at the Bray Foundation and continued to work there, I probably would have continued to survive, but I don't know how broad my horizons would have been. I was doing architectural murals at the time—relief work on public buildings—and there were architects and clients who supported my work. Had I continued to do that, it's possible that I might be doing well; I don't know.

Having moved to the university, though, I've acquired the university as patron, and it has made possible a more independent kind of approach to work that is paying off now in different ways. I'm getting some national and international recognition for it; if things had gone differently, I might still be doing saints and walls in churches.

It's all art, and I like leaving my mark on buildings when the work turns out well. It's a little like having old friends scattered around. There's one in Helena; there's one in Polson; two in Great Falls; one in Cut Bank; Bozeman, Anaconda, Butte. There's a metal relief in what used to be the Metals Bank and Trust in Butte, and a brick relief in a church there. I just recently found out that it split the congregation when they installed it. But it's been up for a long time—twenty-five years or so. The congregation adjusted.

On the whole, I can't think of a better place than Montana. You don't have the pressure of some cities where artists are stealing from each other's work, they're so frantic in their race to get shows. You don't feel that here. And I can be good friends with the cowboy artist even though our work may be very different. I'm not sure I would respect everything he does, but we can be friends. He may not understand what *I* do, but with ceramics, there are a lot of things that people will more readily accept because it's clay.

But then there's the other side of that coin. If you're in ceramics you're never quite accepted into the first rank as an artist, because ceramics has always been a humble craft. But I think ceramic art is ultimately going to receive the recognition it deserves. I think some of the best artists in this country are working in clay.

Are there things I still want to do? Of course. In the fine arts you never do resolve all the questions. I think every piece I do is better than the one I did before, but there is always the potential for realizing something else—just finding out things.

Montana is still a good place for artists to live. I'd like to see more support for the arts, but I'm not sure just what form it should take. We have a lot of good writers in this state. And we have a hell of a lot of good artists who are, interestingly enough, not necessarily connected to any educational institution. Yet they're very hard workers in their communities. I don't know how best to reach these people and give them the kind of encouragement they need. A circuit-rider kind of approach, going around the small towns? It might work.

Years ago H. G. Merriam started the Montana Institute of Arts with the idea that it could develop into a statewide vehicle for recognizing and nurturing the arts. The only problem with the organization was that it lacked professionalism, so it has spawned a lot of little sewing circles that don't really get anywhere. They just tread water and sink half the time. You can't get the professionals interested in the MIA for that reason.

The Arts Council is a healthy thing. It has helped a lot of people through its support of the existing museums and its mounting of shows on a very professional level. My only criticism is that it starts to cost so much to run the bureaucracy that very little actually gets out the artists.

Beyond my art—looking at my hopes and my fears—I think about nuclear devastation. The mindless pursuit of these weapons troubles me. I'm not involved in politics, but I can see a snowballing of people actually beginning to believe that these things could be survived. I worry about an attitude developing that would erase any possibility of backing off. How to find people with the courage to back off, that's the biggest concern I have. I can't understand rational people sitting there and saying, "Yeah, it's survivable, and we have to build more of these weapons, more and more and more." It drains our economy; it drains our future. Our social institutions are folding, and all this activity is mindless.

In eastern Montana we're going through intensive coal development, and we're looking at possible future mining development in the western part of the state too. Well, fundamentally, I'm not opposed to that. I can't be. God knows I use stuff out of the earth—minerals and oxides and so on—in my own work and I think extraction can be reasonably dealt with; I think you can work out intelligent development along with preservation of the wilderness. It takes a cooperative attitude, of course. I don't believe in what Reagan is doing. That is a sell-out to me. But, on the other hand, I don't think you can lock up resources, either. People have to listen to each other.

There's nothing much left of Finn Town in Butte anymore. The neighborhoods I grew up in are wastelands. They're largely part of the pit—gobbled up. But there's a sturdy old building—the Helsinki Bar—that still stands, and I go in there and rap at the old guys once in a while. It still has a sauna that was built by an Irishman. The Finns had nothing to do with it except for bathing in it. The man who built it was a poet. He taught in Missoula for a while.

You know what I like to do in Butte, I like to go down to the M & M Bar and just sit there. Honest to God, it's like a circus world unfolding in front of you and I don't mean that in a derogatory way. It's a human level city. People are accepted on their own terms. I like that about Butte.

Colleen Cabot

Colleen Cabot has been in the forefront of virtually every important environmental battle in Wyoming since 1970. She was a lobbyist and the director of the statewide environmental group, the Wyoming Outdoor Council, when some of the state's most comprehensive environmental legislation was passed by the Wyoming Legislature. A Wyoming native, she is a former executive director of the Teton Science School in Jackson and a current board member of the Northern Lights Institute.

ENVIRONMENTAL POLITICS CAME TO WYOMING AT ABOUT THE SAME TIME THAT I WENT TO COLLEGE. I was drawn into the budding earth movement effort in 1969, working with some good people who were very concerned about this state and who were trying to focus general environmental concerns around specific things that were happening in Wyoming.

At that time, coal development was an issue and later, water development. A big dam was proposed for the Green River, and Project Plowshare—the "friendly bomb" project—was an issue. The idea behind that was to sink shafts deep into the earth and use megaton nuclear bombs to fracture big gas-bearing formations and then bring the natural gas out. They had done it in Colorado and proposed to do it in Wyoming, at Pinedale.

The big water project was to be a dam on the Green River, close to the headwaters. It would have involved inundating good agricultural land to create a very complex scheme of pipes and canals to move water from the Green River to the Sweet-water and then the Platte and up to Powder River, where it would be used in coal development. It was an incredible scheme, on the scale of something like moving the Columbia River.

The state supported it. The logic went like this: we can't let our water leave the state. We're a headwater state—we can't let our water go down the Colorado, where it's becoming more and more committed to the Central Arizona Project for the benefit of Los Angeles. This is a great chance to use it here.

Using water to support economic development was a powerful idea at that time. When I graduated from high school, in 1969, kids were leaving the state. There were very few job opportunities and the state was in a real slump. We were primarily an agriculture state, with quite a lot of oil and gas, but there weren't many jobs in those industries.

The state had undertaken an effort to get what it called "quality of life" industries to come here—electronics industries, and smokeless high-tech businesses. But there was also strong support for developing the state's vast coal resources, and relatively little fear of what the consequences might be, because we thought in terms of oil.

People look at oil as a fairly friendly neighbor in this state—even though it polluted the Platte to the point where essentially there was nothing living in it. But in the late sixties it was cleaned back up again.

Wyoming started to become environmentally conscious around 1967—passed some rudimentary reclamation laws and an air-quality act. The Wyoming Outdoor Council was active; it was started in 1967 by Tom Bell, the founder and publisher of *High Country News*. Governor Stan Hathaway actually got behind some of the early laws, and the early reclamation law was introduced by Wyoming senator, John Turner, who is from this county. And it was a good effort, but the philosophy at that time was mostly based on working with industry as a friend and saying, "We'll do whatever you guys think is right."

That worked when you had small industries and small-scale development. You could probably depend on people being responsible, in a corporate sense, but big resource-development projects created different kinds of problems.

And there were other proposals that we had to confront. They wanted to put a major highway down the Clark's Fork Gorge, for example. That is a tremendous canyon, with thousand-foot cliffs, and they wanted to pin a scenic highway to those cliffs.

That gorge was part of the route that Chief Joseph took north in 1877, to escape from the army—up this incredible canyon, with 300 warriors on horseback, and hundreds of women and children, in a place where people supposedly couldn't go. And now they wanted to put a highway there. It would be an amazing engineering feat.

People were staggered to see these huge projects coming to Wyoming: nuclear projects, big dams, big highway projects, the biggest mines—these things got people concerned and fired them up. Even conservative people for the most part, were concerned. Pinedale, for example, is a very conservative community. It is highly educated and has a very high ratio of college graduates to total population, but it is not particularly active environmentally. Cody, on the east gate of the Yellowstone near Clark's Fork Gorge, is *very* conservative—heavy Mormon influence; lots of Republicans.

These people didn't want to hear a lot of rhetoric from Stan Hathaway about preserving our quality of life. They were facing projects that they felt would destroy their communities. The nuclear thing was clearly a threat, after people found out what had happened with Project Ruleson in Colorado: the gas released was radioactive, and the area could become geologically unstable because of the size of the blast.

So people got active. Little ad hoc community groups were formed, and *High Country News*. And then the North Central Power Study came out in 1971 or 1972 and revealed that seventy-one power plants were going to be built in the Powder River Basin in a few years. It was mindboggling to think of the water, the people, the numbers of coal mines. We just felt that the whole state was going to go down the tubes in about two years' time.

A remarkable thing happened when Tom Bougsty and a couple of other people and I went to talk with Stan Hathaway.

The University of Wyoming was certainly not a very volatile place, but this was back when Kent State was blowing up, and college kids just generally made people nervous. And I've never seen anyone react the way Stan Hathaway did. We just asked him a few really timid questions about his quality-of-life policy and how it squared with these big projects, and he just blew up! *Anger.* Just complete, out-of-control anger. He was pounding on his desk, and we were just boggled, so we left. We didn't know how to deal with that. Obviously emotions were getting pretty high, but Hathaway thought kids like me should be grateful for whatever he proposed.

I finally got so involved with the Outdoor Council and environmental politics—going over to the legislature to fight the dam in 1971—that I became frustrated with college and quit. The University of Wyoming is not a very innovative place. If I had been in a more stimulating academic environment, I might have stayed, because I very much enjoyed education. But the university was frustrating enough, and juvenile enough, that I just decided to quit.

That was a very good experience for me, because for seven years I worked in environmental politics. During every legislative session, I was lobbying. By 1975 we had formed a group called the Wyoming Citizens Lobby, which was the first grassroots political movement in the state that was really effective. It was a network of 3,000 people statewide, and in this state, that's a lot of people. We sent them a weekly newsletter, and we had a WATS line; they could phone in for information. We launched a big effort called Export Coal. Our idea at the time was to get coal out of the state by train—we weren't thinking about coal slurry or any other technologies—so that we wouldn't have to have those big power plants here.

We had a really amazing campaign all worked out, with advertising and newsletters ready to roll. We were going to inundate the state. This was all engineered by John Jenkins. That's interesting—because this past year John Jenkins, the former environmentalist, was the gubernatorial campaign manager for Warren Morton, and Warren Morton was, at that time, the chairman of the House Minerals Committee in the state legislature who beat us on Export Coal. He found out about our campaign through an ad we had sent to the Casper *Star Tribune*, and he simply pulled all the bills that had been introduced on exporting coal—just locked them out of the legislative session.

There was no longer any focus for our campaign, but we went ahead with it anyway. We had planned a big petition drive. We changed the petition, and petitioned to protect our air-quality laws. The industry lobbyists were trying to get our sulfur dioxide emissions regulations amended and weakened considerably so that they could go ahead with these big power plants. In a week we got 7,000 names on a petition to protect the regulations.

In that session we actually strengthened our environmental protection. Wyoming had created a Department of Environmental Quality the year before, which covered air, land, and water quality. We actually had some of the best air quality regulations in the region—and the best reclamation requirements, for sure. In 1975 we passed the state land-use planning act, and we passed an industrial siting act which required industries to come to the state and tell what they were doing and offer mitigation to communities affected. We passed a water development act intended to ensure a broad base of citizen involvement in water development.

All of our major environmental laws were passed in those two years, 1974 and 1975. It was the peak, and over the next two to three years, we operated a holding action, trying to keep those acts in effect; trying to keep them strong; beating back attacks on them; adding a few good amendments here and there, and a few good laws.

The attacks came mostly from the big coal companies, and their parent companies. Both Exxon and ARCO had their guys down at the legislature in large numbers. Our logo for the Citizens Lobby was this wonderful graphic of a long line of industry lobbyists in an array of pinstriped suits with this little couple—a cowboy and a cowgirl—walking past them up the steps of the capitol. It depicted the Citizens Lobby against the horde.

The Citizens Lobby was a great grassroots effort. In essence, we staffed the legislature for the first time, and did it with about a dozen people. Each one of us was assigned to a committee and a bill, and we followed the bills through the whole process. The legislators and the lobbyists had never seen anyone do that before.

The legislature had no process and no provision for citizen involvement. It didn't publish agendas, and it didn't follow any timetable. The committee meetings weren't posted, and to find out about them in advance, you had to know a committee member. Sometimes we would watch legislators on the floor, and when we saw signs that they were kind of gathering and drifting away together, we would follow and attend the meeting. It was that intuitive. It was fun, and we learned the process really well.

I covered the committee handling land use questions, and helped Alan Simpson—now one of our senators in Washington, who was at that time a member of the House in Wyoming. I would go to all the committee meetings and record the votes. There was no record of voting in Wyoming, except for the third reading vote, and that's still the way it is, so there's no way to let people know what's happening and hold anybody accountable along the way. We kept track of all that. I'd tell Alan what the committee was doing, and he would use that information to go back to the committee with a counter-strategy, or to talk to his compatriots over in the State Senate.

Alan Simpson is a character. He was majority whip then, and he took the title pretty literally. He kept a big mule whip hanging on the pillar right behind his desk, and whenever things would get slow he'd roll that thing down the aisle and slap it at them. He had a wonderful sense of humor. I thoroughly enjoyed working with him because he knew how to use the information we gave him.

He's a very astute politician. He got a land-use bill through the Wyoming legislature at a time when the concept of land-use management was an absolute anathema; you didn't even talk about that kind of thing—exercising control over private land. Yet it was a fairly strong bill, requiring all the counties to submit a plan to the state within a certain period of time, and it was quite well-drawn-up in providing guidelines for them, with a commission to follow up, but requiring them to develop their own approach in response to local needs.

Malcolm Wallop, our other U.S. Senator now, was also part of the close little group of Republicans and Democrats that we depended on. But it's interesting to see how perspectives change. Alan Simpson is still the same person, but Malcolm Wallop is somebody that most of us won't have anything to do with now. We feel disappointed, betrayed. He's diametrically opposed to what he was doing out here.

Some people feel that when Malcom went to Washington he had to get involved in conservative Republican party politics, that he had to make a lot of promises to get anywhere, and now they're coming due. But I think that Malcolm doesn't have an established ethic. He loves Wyoming and believes, to an extent, in what we're doing, but he doesn't have a set of values that direct him in a political arena. In those days he was excited about being involved with this interesting group of young people who lived in basements. It was fun to meet with us and get some exciting new ideas going in the somewhat stodgy atmosphere of the Wyoming legislature. But I don't think he had any real gut level commitment, the way Alan, I think, does.

But you're asking about "*My Brilliant Career.*" Well, I hired on as executive director of the Wyoming Outdoor Council in 1976, and did that for two years, and felt pleased with the effort. I was very involved in water issues, and I got a grant and used it to expand our staff. We put on water workshops around the state, primarily aimed at helping people to look at their water resources as a community resource that they could do something about. It was a wonderful project for me, because it put me in touch with such a diverse array of people. At these workshops we had ranchers, housewives, lumber companies, coal companies, people interested in the historical uses of a river, recreationists, floaters, fishermen.

It was our best effort ever to involve a broad array of people —other than the Citizens Lobby, which was really incredible— and I think of it as a model that I'd like to see used as a framework for water planning in the whole region. It was a way of getting down to the community level, and getting people to see how they could use their resource and how it pinned into a larger framework.

But then I started to get tired of the other aspects of the job —the endless battles to protect legislation that was not radical, and the fight for budgets for agencies, year after year.

Finally, when I got really tired of politics, I went back to the university to finish my bachelor's degree. I felt better about being in school, probably because I was older. I discovered geography as a discipline, which suited me better than science. I studied all kinds of specific things—soil, geomorphology, paleoenvironment—which were fun to study but which also drew systems together. It was looking at the world as a whole.

In 1969, just before I went to college the first time, I'd come to Jackson to the Teton Science School to attend the six-week field research program. All through the years I've been talking about, I kept coming back, in the summers mostly, to teach or counsel or help administer the school. The winter I was completing my studies at the university, the director of the school called and said, "Colleen, I'm quitting, and I think you ought to apply for this job."

The Teton Science School was very serious about its staff; it had gone through a difficult transition. Ted Major, a Jackson high school biology teacher, had founded the school in 1967. He'd left, and Curt Rademacher had become executive director, and now Curt was moving on, and new staff members were being added and the school was growing and adding new programs in a new location. I couldn't have been luckier. The Board allowed me to go back to the university to finish up.

We've had a couple of rough years, but all of our programs are operating year-round now, and we're involved in a $1.2 million capital campaign to fix our buildings and start an endowment.

It's interesting that I'm back to basic field ecology; that's what we teach here. We take kids out in the field, and they measure the width of trees and look at their rings and figure out how things grow. They put out snow equipment and keep track on precipitation and weather and look at snow structures and measure what happens to snow as it compacts through the winter, and they catch little animals that live under the snow. It's all experiential education in the out-of-doors, and I think it should supplement every classroom experience.

Some science teachers have been bringing kids for years and integrate the Science School in their whole curriculum. The whole Jackson fifth grade comes out here—that's our youngest age group—and twenty-five to thirty kids come at a time, with their teacher. They stay for two and a half days, which doesn't sound like much, but it's usually their first time away from home, so you have that to deal with. The winter programs are five days long and add the challenge of being outside in a Wyoming winter. It's fun.

Recently there was an evaluation of all the Jackson school programs, and it was determined that unless the Science School was integrated into the school experience—if it was nothing more than an isolated experience for the kids—it wasn't cost-effective. The teachers grabbed at that. They all love the program, and they took the winter and developed a new curriculum, essentially making the Science School the core of the whole fifth-grade science curriculum, with pre-and post-Science School activities. Wonderful! We couldn't ask for more.

The kids come here again in the seventh grade. They have a different experience then, and learn to handle the winter environment, which is something they all need to know if they're going to live in the Northern Rockies, and then they come back in a select group and participate in an art and literature program. We use the outdoors as a creative element.

I love it—it's the best program we run—because it's a unique, cross-disciplinary approach to the environment. We use resource people, their teachers, and our staff. The program varies depending on the mix, but essentially we ask kids to respond to the out-of-doors in a new way. We want them to do more than just ski across it—we want them to observe it and learn what the tracks in the snow mean and where the animals are. We want them to respond to it: draw it, write it, express themselves about it, develop some feelings about it. It is a neat program, because our staff, which is essentially field geologists and outdoor educators, can share its undertsanding and knowlededge of a little piece of ground and then have an artist come in and show the kids how to draw those patterns that they're seeing because of the snow and wind and soil. Somebody talks to them about how to write about what we teach in a field journal or in a poem or a piece of prose.

We had a wonderful time here with Gary Snyder, the poet. He's involved in self-sufficiency: that's his political interest, beyond his creative talent. We got to talking: "Well, if you're really talking about your community, and how to live within the resources offered there—trying not to bring in a lot of outside energy or resources and trying to live on what's here—what would you do in Jackson Hole?"

It's a difficult question. Even the Indians couldn't winter over here, because it's too rugged an environment. This is a mecca for game (probably the largest concentration of big game left in the contiguous United States), but in the old days, the elk always left the valley completely in the winter. They could get out the south end. There are elk here now in the winter only because private land blocks the exit.

So it wasn't a place that the Indians lived. Actually, an archeology professor who works here in the summer says that mostly they came here to dig blue camas, a bulbous, edible rooted plant. They roasted it in large numbers, in big pits, and took it out of the valley. It was a food resource. They had rights to the meadows and they cultivated in a way that didn't over-utilize the resource.

It's interesting to think of that, when you think of all the big game here, but people couldn't survive here on game alone. Trappers took out the beaver, and there were a few homesteads, but they failed. People eventually turned to dude ranching. That's what sustained the economy from the 1920s through the 1950s, and it still does, with Grand Teton National Park. People come here to recreate, and to respond to this environment.

So we asked what was it that drew us all together. What is it that we all do? And we decided that we're all storytellers. The best guide in the world is the storyteller. He knows how to draw people into this landscape through wonderful stories of experiences on the land, and that's what we're here to do—to help people interpret this landscape and draw it into their own lives. That's why I like that program.

I don't have real skills as a storyteller, but I really want to learn them because I think storytelling is a complex way of communicating, with symbolism, with metaphor, with all kinds of techniques.

I wasn't happy as a scientist, and I wasn't really satisfied as a systems ecologist. I wasn't satisfied being a politician, either. I think my way of relating to the world is through the landscape, in an expressive way—helping people be a little more integrated in their lives. We all need to know why the leaves fall off the trees when they do, but we need to be able to respond to that little landscape in other ways.

In the West, our best landscapes are our wild ones, because we intuitively know that these wild lands are whole, healthy. When you appreciate that, you respond to the integrity in those landscapes; you understand the idea of integrity, and it influences your relationships with people—the process of just looking, subconsciously reacting, internalizing.

We forget, sometimes, that people in Wyoming love this country. Many of them make sacrifices to stay here. They can't get jobs; they have to face losing their children to outside interests; they have to make a lot of hard choices connected with loving this country. Many times, they'll make the wrong choices, because they don't understand cause and effect. They don't make this link: "If I make a choice to support a big power plant because I want some job opportunities for my kids so they won't leave the state, I'll be screwing up some intrinsic value—air, water, wildlife, horizons. I will be interrupting the integrity of this landscape."

Making those choices hurts people here. When you talk to people, one on one and not in confrontation, and when you get to know them, you know it hurts them to make those choices. And you know it's because they've lived in this kind of landscape and intuitively they know what it means to establish and respond to integrity—but our culture doesn't encourage that.

When I consider my hopes and fears for the future of this region, I think about something Arnie Silverman said: "What most people do, when they're thinking about the future, is recall the past." I find that an interesting comment, because I think that all of us think that it's very important to maintain our heritage. People who have lived an honest. self-sufficient life on this land want to be able to carry that forward.

Many people here do have a sense of the whole. Ranchers who have worked the same ranch their families started more than a hundred years ago obviously are doing some things right. They learned to manage heavy-duty intensive use of the land, and they've had to learn how to rotate ranges. Of course, a lot

of them did it at the expense of the public lands, by over-grazing them and nurturing their own.

But they don't think of their heritage that way; they think about it selectively. That's why Arnie's point is so well-taken. We can't just draw on the past and continue on, even though that's what a lot of people around here want to do. So when we talk about setting aside land as wilderness areas, many people don't want to do that, because other people will have access to that land, while the management of it changes. They think it's been fine up to now, so who needs wilderness?

Of course, "wilderness" is a loaded word and brings to mind such phrases as "the hippie badlands," and the elitist idea, "last one in, close the door behind you." Some people have lived here for three generations and have done fine. What's the big problem? What's going to happen?

Because people in the small communities in this region have neighbors and a church they've gone to with their families for so long, they have an incredible network of people who will help out when they're building fences or haying, or are ill or dying. The cooperative life works, and they think it will continue to be that way.

The changes, when they come, are wrenching. I have a friend who states it so well: "We're used to taking our kids into town on a Saturday night," he says, "dropping them off at the movie, going back home, picking them up later, and leaving them alone when we go some place. But you can't do that any more. Your girl will get raped; your boy will get knocked down. You can't leave your rifle in the truck and the truck unlocked."

Or the threat may be more subtle. A new guy moves in on the block, takes over the chairmanship of the local party or the presidency of the church—a dynamic person with a lot of ideas that perhaps don't fit the community. Or maybe the community accepts the ideas, but, in either case, people who were the power in the community find themselves disenfranchised. Suddenly it's not their community.

My people came here in the early 1900s as dryland farmers in the North Platte River area, and after they tried that, they moved into stores. My granddad ran a store in Glendo, then at Glenrock, and later on, in a little town called Midwest, north of Casper. Then my dad came in the 1940s, met my mom and married her. He's an oil man, so my people have all been tied to small communities, and to resources: farming, operating small businesses, and oil. That's really the range of the state, so I have a feeling for all those people's legitimacy here.

But, at the same time, I don't feel that we have the right solutions. That's why I think this project's a good one, talking about people's hopes and fears, because we have to listen to each other. We really face a challenge. We feel the rest of the country has screwed up. They've gone an industrialized, urbanized way, and we still hold onto a largely rural setting, even though most of our people live in towns and cities, and we're still tied directly to the resources we use.

Of course we have extensive connections all over the world to bring in the cars we drive, the TV sets we watch, most of the food we eat, so we're just as dependent as the rest of the world. But I would like us to pay more attention, nevertheless, to the idea of increased self-sufficiency, which means thinking in regional terms, because you can only do it on a regional basis. The goal should be to make ourselves as self-sufficient as possible, then bring in the rest of what is needed, instead of this starcrossed vision of the easy life where you sit down and have no skills and everything's served to you.

How do I define this region? I'm a provincial kid. I grew up in Wyoming and I have not traveled very much out of it. I've traveled to the East Coast, the West Coast, and Southwest, but I haven't really experienced any of those places, and I have no world view—I've never been out of the country. I have some connection elsewhere: my great-uncle came from Calgary, where he started the Calgary Stampede. He was the rodeo master, a trick roper, and his wife was a trick rider. I'd love to go there. I do feel that the Northern Rockies—Idaho, Montana, and Wyoming—have much in common because they haven't foreclosed options. They are still rural enough and their populations are still scattered enough that they don't have large urban centers that force their politics in one direction.

I would be tempted to add Utah, but Salt Lake and the whole Wasatch front have done some bizarre things to Utah. They have concentrated people and forced some decisions that haven't been forced in the Northern Rockies.

Nevada certainly has some basin and range country, but it's extremely arid. Our lives here are dictated by arid land and lack of water, but Nevada is on another order of magnitude.

Certainly the region doesn't extend westward past Spokane —the Cascades, really. You can understand the way people think and operate, up to the east side of the Cascades, but once you get into the maritime, heavy-duty rain forest, with lots of rain, lots of plants, lots of oxygen, and lots of people, it's overwhelming. I love to go there because it's so different. People *think* differently.

How people think in this region is not necessarily determined by whether you're an environmentalist or an exploiter. People really relate to this region because it's so powerful. A friend of mine, Jim Garry, calls this the heart of a mythological landscape. This is the core of the West; this is where America really became America. We really faced our continent and tried to do something with it—made a legend.

But, having done that, I don't know where we can go. I do feel that the Northern Lights Institute can be a vehicle. It represents a point in my own evolution, which is to go from politics, which is day-to-day crises, to education, which is a long-term view, and integrate that with long-term policy-making. It gets us into futuristic thinking, which is simply trying to get from here to there in a thoughtful way.

Talking to Med Bennett,* I'm struck by what he feels the world is ready for right now. We have been riding the wave of the masculine creative drive; that is, we've been coming up with new ideas and forcing them into our world and trying to make our way in that fashion. He really feels that we need to stop, take stock, and use the feminine, which is to draw together what we know, re-analyze it, get some sense of an overview, be open to new ideas, rather than just forge ahead. I think he's right. Obviously we're not operating that way yet. I think that's why women have to be involved, more than we already are, in this movement. Women bring a whole new perspective and a new way of operating that is not as aggressive politically. But because of that, I think it's still very difficult for women to be involved—because they're not used to being in the political forefront or being articulate. That's changing, of course, but we still have a long way to go.

---

*Med (Meridan) Bennett is a rancher and management consultant from Wilson, Wyoming. He was a founder of the Peace Corps, of which he has written in *Agents of Change* (Little, Brown, & Co., 1968). He has been actively concerned with Northern Rockies issues, having served as director of several public interest groups, including the Northern Lights Institute.

Perry Swisher

I BEGAN PUBLISHING *The Intermountain* (initially called the *Alameda Enterprise*) in Pocatello during 1952, when I was twenty-eight. It was a sometimes controversial, weekly comment-and-opinion paper. The writers were of different persuasions and they fought with each other and the world in general every week. I try to remember how I kept the damn thing alive, it was hand-to-mouth much of the time; but I published it for fifteen years.

We had some business support, but our secret was our readership. We weren't a county seat weekly, and we weren't a captive of Main Street. We didn't have a lot of circulation, but what we did have was scattered from hell to breakfast. No, that paper had subscribers because the newspapers were still pretty gray at the time; they hadn't yet recovered their self-respect from the objectivity binge triggered by the wire services. People wanted more than just the wire-service reports; they wanted to know what was really going on in their lives.

The Intermountain wasn't important because of its circulation numbers, but because when we decided to take off with something, we had an effect. From the Eisenhower years on through the mid-sixties, there wasn't much else in the way of a paper of advocacy or dispute being published in this region. We weren't always involved with the national scene. We certainly weren't among the central press during the McCarthy hearing, but before any of the papers in the country took on Joe McCarthy, we identified his underpinnings. We attacked the people who were supporting him and we did it by the book and Bible. We quoted them; we held them up to the light; we ridiculed them. We really went to war with the sons-of-bitches. That really had an effect even though we weren't a national paper.

I think one of the last things *The Intermountain* did which had a major effect was printing the speech that Marriner Eccles gave in 1965 to the Commonwealth Club in San Francisco. Eccles was head of the First Security Corporation of Salt Lake City, and he was once head of the Federal Reserve Board. I'd paid a lot of attention to him over the years because he was a pretty bright man; I liked the way his head worked. Well, he just lit into the Johnson administration's policies on the war in Indochina and the war on poverty at home. (You have to understand that at the time, Senators Wayne Morse of Oregon and Frank Church of Idaho were not yet doves; the war was not yet politically unpopular.) But Eccles simply ran the numbers on Johnson . He pinpointed the administration's shabby premises and held them up to the light. He described the consequences of that kind of policy, almost to naming the cities in which the riots would occur.

That week we stripped everything out of the paper including some of the ads (Marriner Eccles, you understand, was not given to brevity) and ran out the whole speech. Well, we printed up extra copies of it and sent it to members of Congress and to all sorts of people, and it really got some reaction. Many people in our own region rewrote their own positions on the strength of that speech. I think we made Eccles the first member of the central establishment to make a major criticism of that very bad policy, the consequences of which we're still dealing with.

There were a few other interesting papers scattered through the Rocky Mountains, such as *The People's Voice* which Harry Billings edited in Helena, Montana, and Cervi's *Journal* edited by Mr. Cervi in Denver. His publication was basically a paper of record for realtors, bankers, and lawyers, but he had his own ideas and he would wail away and serve his journal. He was a fearless son-of-a-bitch.

That kind of a paper doesn't exist in this region now. As the Vietnam War became the issue that we said it would, as the civil rights movement crested, as the pig in the python or war baby bulge occurred with that generation of kids hitting the campuses, the press became investigatory, just out of self-interest. The press changed and started covering something besides bridge club meetings in the local news and something besides the sports wire and Pentagon policy in the national news. A whole generation of new and very self-righteous young journalists showed up. Most of them spent their time biting tires, but they did change the press. I sold the paper in 1967 to some Boise interests because we were no longer conspicuous and I didn't think we had much of an excuse for existence any more. I did continue to write for the publication until it folded in the early seventies.

A few good papers have sprung up along the northwest coast, such as *The Willamette Week*—although it's quickly turning into something very different from what it started out to be—and *The Journal American* out of Bellevue, Washington. *The Journal* did some fine stuff for six or seven years, but now

Perry Swisher currently serves as one of three members of the Idaho Public Utilities Commission, a position that gives him an excellent forum for his outspoken and often controversial views on state and national issues. He was elected to the Idaho House of Representatives for four terms and to the state Senate for two terms. For several years, he published The Intermountain *a weekly newspaper in Pocatello, Idaho. Later he was managing editor of* The Lewiston Tribune *in northern Idaho. He makes his home in Boise.*

it's becoming a self-interest paper. I've never seen a paper do that so fast. They got so bad that when they were backing some particular hero for one of the local offices and he lost, they ran out a banner headline the next morning saying that he was ahead. They were sure the people had made a mistake. They were sure that when the final vote was tallied the paper would be vindicated. It's become that kind of a paper—went from beautiful to ugly faster than any paper I ever saw. They became puffed up bullfrogs sitting on their little pad, croaking away.

I've lost touch with the Montana papers. Their dailies were never worth much, but there's often been color up there. There was a photographer—I don't know if he's long since sold the paper—who started *The Hungry Horse News* just as a place to run his half-tone photographs. Most papers in the region didn't do a very good job of photographic display, and this fellow was horrified when he saw what the desk would do. He bought a paper, and, by God, he displayed pictures. I've always thought that a good photographer could often tell people more than a good reporter. I suppose that's one of the reasons I didn't resist early television.

I went back to Idaho State University to finish my degree after I sold *The Intermountain*. I didn't get my degree until I was in my forties. I met the university president while I was there and ended up working for him for six or seven years, directing university services to the communities and enrollment of more minority and poverty students. When I was finished at ISU, I went back into journalism as a managing editor of *The Lewiston Tribune* in northern Idaho.

The Tribune has always had a very strong editorial page, so I really wasn't frustrated by the change from *The Intermountain*. It was very knee-jerk, always arriving at the liberal position. But it's a strong, fearless paper; it's thrown away a lot of display-advertising dollars and a lot of legal business and job printing just to say what it thought. No, I wasn't frustrated by the change.

You know, there is more investigative reporting today, but it doesn't necessarily produce any better results. Reporters have just learned to be comfortable in the business of public service. They chase around, read carbons out of wastebaskets, and catch people in compromising positions. Now we have rat finks who sell their souls for wine and lobster. That's not investigative reporting. It's about as important as reporting who caught a cold last week. The interest in a scandal speaks to the banality of the human race, and it will cycle out again. It's already changing.

I spent a half-dozen terms in the legislature while I was with *The Intermountain*. Four terms were in the House and two were in the Senate. When I was young and starting out in politics, the Republican party was the more urban party in the West, and the Republicans were more concerned with state-level commitments. Except for the labor movement, the Democrats tended to be more aristocratic, like the Democrats of the Old South. That changed over time, and I changed parties. I was a Republican until my last Senate term when I became an Independent. In 1966 I ran for governor as an Independent because both parties had nominated anti-sales-tax candidates. The sales tax was a referendum on the ballot that fall, so it was pretty obvious that the state needed another option.

I suppose I'm with the Public Utilities Commission now because I was involved with energy issues as a legislator. I studied the potential for political exertion by utilities on major building projects like the Columbia River hydro dams and

I questioned the construction quality of the northwest pipeline for natural gas. I was caught up in quite a few energy issues over the years. In 1979, Bob Lenaghen was denied confirmation to the PUC by the Senate. Governor Evans then sent my name up to the Senate in his place, asked me if I would serve, and that's how I came to the PUC.

I think of a consumer advocate as someone who is always in the hearing room or at the legislature insisting that the consumer be protected from his own unawareness or his own lack of organization. I don't fit that definition of an advocate. I despise that approach to consumer problems. Most consumers are witless when it comes to the things I deal with. They didn't have the foresight to see that the era of cheap, federal hydroelectric power was drawing to an end and that their houses were lined with baseboard heat. They were not aware that the impact of AT&T divestiture could end universal telephone service in states like Idaho, Wyoming, and Montana. I'm not a typical consumer advocate because I'm not sympathetic to ignorance.

There's a new kind of ignorance here that didn't exist in the days when most Westerners had only a grade school education. Political sensibilities were much more acute, much more educated than today. People have a world of information available to them now, but it's of no use to them. Most adults have graduated from high school, many have gone to college, but they don't understand the effect of national policy on their daily lives. They're not involved with the issues. It's that kind of ignorance, the ignorance of non-participation, that makes them vulnerable. Historically, the Right could not get away with the kind and degree of manipulation it does today because people were engaged in the controversies.

When I fiirst ran for office, the turnout of voters in Idaho for any election was never less than second in the nation. I'm not talking about our registration, but about people over twenty-one voting. About ninety percent of the adult population would always be registered in the general election for president, but that's changed because of preoccupation with pleasure. Oh, I don't mean in the Roman sense of pleasure; I mean that you can now devote your time to your own pursuits. It's easier today to indulge your own interests without having to contribute to the interests of society as a whole. I think television has an influence that's still underestimated. People have become spectators. They watch discussions and portrayals of events which are integral to their present and future, and their perception is the same as though they were watching Monday Night Football. They are not participants.

We're probably not behaving any differently than the region's natives did when they first got hold of the horse. They lost their cool and went roaring across the Great Plains fighting with anyone who would fight back and giving up their local sustenance to go after the buffalo. When a great change occurs, whatever new freedom people get, they take. I don't think this speaks badly of society or its future. However, the casualties in the way of social policy and economic policy will be large at such a time. The fact that people can give each other permission to go do their own thing without the level of social, political, or job accountability that curtailed our ancestors is a new freedom. It has to be dealt with as we go. Meanwhile, it's pretty hard to get anything together except as a fast-food outlet. Any change is frightening. You don't know whether people will react to it or accept it. If a political or administrative change brings order when people see disorder as bad, then it really is frightening; then we have our own version of fascism.

Actually, I think Americans are too damn greedy, too selfish, to ever make good subjects. We may all wear the same clothes, think the same thoughts, watch the same TV programs, but we each think of ourselves as individuals. I think that's ingrained, and I think it's good insurance. That built-in cussedness prevents our cookie-cutter education system from turning out identical end-products.

It's not just a western perspective, although westerners have that conceit. New York City is filled with fiercely independent people. I have a ball every time I go to New York because I have to contend with more bodies and I can see how they handle that constant proximity. No, I don't think that's a uniquely western attitude at all. In my experience, easterners are much more individualistic in the sense of protecting their own rights. Television, movies, even Broadway, have created and perpetuated a myth of western individualism, but it is a myth. It's a nice myth, and as long as westerners think it's true, it probably helps.

I think I operate at different levels than most people who would voice their concerns for the region's future. I don't concern myself with who's going to be the beneficiary of a change, because it's so unpredictable. Often the people who are expected to profit from something fall off the edge because they don't have the experience necessary to deal with it, or they don't have the discipline to handle a new opportunity. Ninety percent of the people who came to this area moved on. They didn't know how to take what they'd found and turn it into something useful.

I learned a long time ago that when you make a change some people will benefit and some are going to lose. You make a change because you're persuaded it will help the community, the society, the state, or whatever. You make a change and then you see how the principals come out. It's my spectator sport.

I find it very interesting and almost always surprising.

If I were to plot a current social change on a time-condensed, exponential graph for this region, you would see the disappearance of surface and air transportation, the disintegration of universal telephone service, and the deterioration of public education. Idaho, Wyoming, and Montana have none of the ingredients for a modern society, except raw materials. We are not in a major corridor for communication or transportation; none of the states has a metropolitan center. That graph would show an isolation that will have us speaking the American equivalent of Basque within two centuries. I can't say whether that's good or bad; I can only say that if we don't change we'll speciate and stop thinking of ourselves as Americans.

We are making changes in the area of telecommunications. The PUC recently took a look at the quality of the telephone grid and discovered that gradual upgrading of service by Mountain Bell has eliminated four-party line service. We met with the Bell management and asked them what it would cost to convert the remaining two-party lines to a statewide single-party grid. All that's needed is electronic switching in the central stations. We held the hearings—which were poorly attended because no one had their last month's bill doubled—and issued the order to implement what we're calling OPUS, or One Party Universal Service. Everybody in the most remote part of Bell's Idaho jurisdiction will be able to have all of the things in the way of communication service that you would have in the most sophisticated system in the country.

That's important for the West. A significant number of people would be willing to live where they could pretend that they were pioneering if they could still have all the amenities. A young fellow whose family sold their interest in *The Lewiston*

Tribune bought a couple of tiny papers in Montana and two little papers on the Oregon coast. He's running the whole operation from a ranch near Eagle, Idaho, with his computer terminal. He lives where he chooses and how he chooses, and he uses the telephone to do it. I think we'll see more of that.

Like everyone else in this post-industrial cycle, we'll see some more light industry. We won't see a lot more because the quality of our graduate engineering schools can't sustain what most chambers of commerce are dreaming about. Students want to graduate from Stanford into Silicon Valley. Well, we don't have a Stanford. The fractured nature of our states made it impossible early on to develop central institutions of higher education, and I don't think I'd change that. The loss of any access to even the most limited humanities discipline in any of the subregions could not be made up by what would be gained at the center.

We're going to see fewer corporate farms in the future because they aren't flexible. Corporate farming is a bugaboo in this area; it ought to be in the Imperial Valley in California. The nature of our terrain, the remoteness of this region, the unbreakable costs of transportation, all add up to an inability of corporate farming to make it. A small percentage is already beginning to file for bankruptcy. If the pattern continues through the eighties, I think the number of corporate farms that go belly-up will exceed the number of so-called family farms that go belly-up. Oh, there will continue to be corporate farms here, but the southern Idaho paranoia that plowing would begin at the Wyoming border and end at the Oregon border is not feasible.

I'm most interested in what's happening in the rest of the world right now because I think outside events will impinge very importantly on this region. From my perspective at the PUC, I'm watching as closely as I can the statistics on the rapid destabilization of energy prices in the nonrenewables and the Iranian-Saudi conflict. Iran is a major oil supplier to Japan. If our State Department does its traditional tit-for-tat, perhaps the ban on the export of Alaskan oil to Japan will end. The Japanese currency would be strengthened and the entire Pacific littoral would change, and we would change. The most inland seaport on the Pacific is in Idaho at Lewiston, where the Snake and Clearwater rivers converge. At this point, it's a funnel, down which grain goes to the ocean, but if the export/import scene changes, then lighter containerized importation can move into that river channel. Imports that do come in could conceivably start using that waterway, avoiding much of the freight cost and enhancing our ability to deal with the surface transportation of manufactured goods. Making better use of that commodity export channel would be a very positive change for Idaho.

We now face the Pacific and its markets. In spite of television's atomization of a national consensus, our attitudes toward finance, regulation, and therefore toward political issues and parties remain markedly different from national attitudes. You don't have to go very deep into Alaska before you find half the people wishing it were still a territory, simply because the economic aims of the central government are so antagonistic to their own. I think the West as a whole is changing in that direction. We need to improve national communication, but I don't see us being pulled back toward the center. Our energy problems are being focused westward rather than east to the Ohio Valley's coal. We're looking into hydro power as a marketable resource that can displace oil and gas in the California market. Economic interests and social experience have pulled our attention from national preoccupations to a westward focus.

It's almost irrelevant that the majority of the region's land and resources are owned by the federal government. Policy would be a bit more exploitative if control were regional, but the knowledge that some part of the environment has to survive beyond this generation is already pretty well ingrained in people younger than I. I think corporate despoilers have to be dealt with at the federal level through tax treatment, land-credit collateral, and environmental legislation. I'm not pessimistic about the region's ability to recognize the problems, but I do think the states can deal with the corporate establishment only in a limited fashion.

We have a monument to corporate interference in the West just beyond our borders. We owe some very big bucks in Idaho for what is called the Washington Public Power Supply System. It constitutes a big debt in this country, and the system was primarily financed with AAA bonds and it was built on the most irresponsible kind of exponential growth for this region. The growth graph indicated that by the end of the century, the Pacific Northwest would be using as much energy as the entire country was using in 1970. Now when bankers and bondsmen buy in on that kind of incredible forecasting, the bottom line is greed. They're anticipating control of the machinery by which securities are rated and utilities are judged.

It's been a hideous thing to watch. It's confirmed in me— and I'm almost sixty years old—the prejudices I heard from my father's generation. Nothing's altered. It's the same as when the first longhorn cattle were brought here in spite of the winters which they couldn't possibly survive. It's not that different from what followed on the gold rush, the boom-and-bust cycle in the mining camps. It's not that different from when irrigation became a developer's project rather than an individual sodbuster's project. The region's political leaders have been

no defense against that kind of rape and pillage, and in that respect, the region hasn't changed.

I suppose water is the local issue that I'm most concerned about. Whatever else happens to agriculture in our region, the value of water is changing right now. People who have thought of the water in their canals as being worth $30 an acre-foot are now beginning to understand that the decimal point is one slot too far to the left, more like $300 and on its way to $500 a foot. The movement from the old cheap hydro-electric power into the high-priced thermal electricity means a virtual end to the high-lift, deep-well pumps. There's high altitude wheat growing in country that will revert to dry land because it will be too expensive to irrigate when we get out of the pump in the next ten to thirty years.

The character of our region is such that we have this perpetual motion machine that nobody can turn off. We get our water in the winter as snow, we get to use it, and it goes back to the sea. If anything makes life in this region possible for our society, it's that cycle. The problem is that our water is of great value as a commodity. If what's in place is destined to grow— and that's how civilization works—then the southern states will have to have water. The movement of the water out of the basins and into the Southwest and into southern California would make us a social desert. We'd be back where we were when the Oregon Trail was born.

The possibility that water from the Hoback canyon of the Snake River will be moved to the Green River canyon of the Colorado is not remote. Under a different scenario, the Bureau of Reclamation could divert the water from the Milner Dam to the south, or even more water from north to south, clear down on the main stem of the Columbia River. It's entirely possible for an entire subregion, like one of the irrigation valleys in southern Idaho, to disappear because of losing that water. Exporting raw resources is different from exporting water. When you export water, you take away some part of the life of the region.

I suppose it's human nature to say, "Well, we've got politicians in place who can protect us." Scoop Jackson from Washington and Frank Church from Idaho both wore that hat, but that's a very transitory kind of protection. Political parties do not represent a working consensus, but a day-to-day coalition. It will take an assertion by the judiciary to say that there are limits beyond which you cannot go in disrupting the lives of people.

I think the states have to solve their drainage problems river basin by river basin. Each drainage system is unique; there is no generic solution. Montana has one foot in the Missouri drainage and another foot in the Columbia drainage. They're two very different sets of problems. All these states are like that.

We reached an agreement with Wyoming and Utah that's working. We all share in the Bear Lake drainage, which is a microcosmal system like the Missouri. We hammered away for God knows how many years and finally arrived at a compact on how the water was to be used. Our compact is functioning to the mild disadvantage of Idaho, a little to the disadvantage of Wyoming, and very much to the advantage of Utah. It isn't entirely equitable, but it's working.

I think the future is absolutely not predictable. You can do some planning, some educating, and some raising of awareness, but right now you can't create a public consensus about a problem. It takes time for people to become aware of an issue, and I don't think that's all bad. Think about the opposite; think about professional planning; think about the Washington Public Power Supply System I mentioned earlier. That was not a decision of the people. Engineers, attorneys, and financiers made that decision and they built that monster. I don't want to live in a planned society, because I know that whoever the programmer is, it's not going to be me. No, I like life on the edge of a cliff a lot better.

Tom Preuit

TALK ABOUT YOUR SUGAR BEETS, one of the things that has changed this community the most has been the loss of the beet industry. It's been a struggle. Back twenty years ago there were more than 4,000 acres of sugar beets raised here at Wheatland. That had quite an economic impact on this community, because until they built the big power plant here we were basically an agricultural community.

Look what happened. We had 4,000 acres of beets in 1969, and in 1980 we didn't even get a contract from the manufacturers. We didn't have any beets. Then, the past two years, we've had a contract, but it's only for 900 acres.

It's a tough situation. The sugar manufacturer's expenses have gone up, just like all of industry. You see on the TV news where companies like International Harvester are about ready to go broke, and Chrysler's been over the rough haul. Well, it's no different for the sugar manufacturers. The returns are low. Sugar coming in from foreign countries has depressed the market. That's tough for the manufacturers, so it's tough for the farmer, too.

Tom Preuit operates a 7,000 acre family farm just outside Wheatland, Wyoming. He has been active in efforts by Wyoming beet farmers to obtain long-term growing contracts from sugar manufacturers.

It seems that the manufacturers, instead of going to the marketplace to get their money, are going to the farmer. Through the negotiations, they're driving down the price they'll pay for contracts, and the farmer is down at the bottom of the barrel, with no place to turn.

We have had support programs get through Congress, and they have given a fair return to the farmer, but the farmer gets less after we go through these negotiations with the manufacturers. The prices farmers receive today would have been realistic ten or fifteen years ago, but after the inflationary spiral that the agricultural industry's been through, our prices are kind of unreal.

There are alternative crops, but the thing is, they're all poor as far as financial returns go. You can raise beans; in this area we raise a lot of irrigated beans. A few years ago those beans were 29¢ a pound. After three years, they were down to 11¢ a pound. Back when they were 29¢, you could get almost a $600-per-acre, return. At 11¢ you're only going to make maybe $190 per acre, because the seed for those beans costs $35 per acre. There's no way you're going to make money after you figure all your other costs—fuel, equipment, and everything.

The cost of equipment has just gone out the roof. Back in 1972, I purchased a new 100-horsepower tractor for $8,200. Today a new 100-horsepower tractor will cost you anywhere from $30,000 to about $36,000. Fuel and fertilizer have gone up four maybe five times from what they were ten years ago.

It puts us behind the eight ball. You've been hearing the stories about the tough times ahead for agriculture. A lot of farmers will go broke this year, and a lot went broke last year. They're trying to get the Farmers Home Administration to be lenient and not foreclose on these farmers where they have some chance of repayment down the road.

I've been in the business a long time. I leased quite a bit of land. The land I purchased was much more reasonable than it's been in the last ten years. In this country we've had some pretty conservative ranchers who bought ranches years ago when land was cheap; they're going to be around for quite a while. They haven't gone out and leveraged their land in order to expand, but the people who are in real trouble are the young farmers who came into the business in the past ten or twelve years, when the prices of land and of equipment were skyrocketing. They wanted a farm, so they paid high interest rates, and they leveraged the land to buy more. They have enormous debts. It doesn't matter what crop they're raising; they're in trouble.

I've farmed for myself since 1957. We raise cattle, and we've raised about all the crops that are suitable for this area—beans, corns, sugar beets.

I grew up on this farm. I was graduated from Wheatland High School and attended the university for two years—then started farming. My parents live down the road. Part of my operation is leased from my father, and then I bought land and added to it. It's still a family farm, really.

We have a little over 7,000 acres. We run cattle, and we have about 400 cows. It makes a good unit. But if you wanted to purchase the operation, I don't know what it would be worth now; however, a couple of years ago you might have been looking at $3 million. For that amount of money, there's no return—not from just operating the unit.

We still have some family farms around here, but there's a lot of land around here that maybe twenty years ago had really good operations. But then something happened—maybe the manager died off, or the owners—and that land's been sold, and it's been on the market off and on ever since. It's never got back into stable hands, someone who would manage it and work to make a profit from it.

The people who bought that kind of land, probably bought it too high. They wanted a return from their investment, and it's just never worked for them. I can show you some really good farms and ranches that have been on the market ever since the old landowners passed away and it went into estate. The economics just haven't been there.

In this area, a year-round cattle ranch would probably cost you $6,000 a cow unit. You start looking at the interest, somewhere from twelve to eighteen percent on purchasing the land and the cattle. The return off the whole ranch won't cover the cost of the interest, but still there are people investing, trying to make it work. It's just out of the question.

Some are investing in the life style; some are investing in a business; some are speculators. They believe the land will always appreciate in value. We went through a period of ten years when land appreciated maybe ten, twelve, fifteen percent every year, year in and year out. We have real estate people here who believe it's going to continue. Right now, though, it's really leveled off. I see reports from Nebraska where they talk about farmland dropping as much as twenty percent from a year or two ago, and I can't help but feel the same thing is going to happen right here.

Back in the 1970s we had lots of investors—movie stars and people like that—who wanted to park their money in land because it was appreciating. But now the land has stopped appreciating and there's not much demand for it. It's awfully hard to sell. People can put their money in a bank and do better on interest, so land is going back down. In the long run, I think it's for the benefit of everyone, because it was too high. You couldn't begin to pay for it by operating it.

When I was in school, my father farmed 160 acres. That's all he had. Through the years, we've bought and expanded to build the operation we have today. Everyone's done the same thing—everyone who could. That's the only way people have stayed in agriculture. A person farming 160 acres today probably wouldn't have much chance of making it, although farmers are probably the most self-sufficient people on the face of the earth. They can milk a cow and raise a few chickens and plant a garden and live pretty darn good. Expansion hasn't been all that great. It's provided financial benefits a smaller operator wouldn't have, but when you had farm families on every 160 acres, you had many more people going to town and buying goods, and they didn't drive so far to save a few bucks. They didn't go to Cheyenne or Casper the way they do now. The roads weren't that great and you did your business at home.

Now people don't think anything about going to Scotts Bluff, Nebraska, or Fort Collins, Colorado, to do a little shopping at the malls. It's tougher for Wheatland, but I can't see where our town has suffered all that much. We have just as good a town and community as we had twenty years ago.

I like it here, myself. A lot of people want to see industry come in here and expand. They thought, "Build a power plant, and industry will come to Wheatland." But it hasn't. And really I'm against it, because if I wanted to live with the multitudes, I'd go where they live.

I've always been proud of Wyoming because we didn't have people falling all over us. You can get out on the highway without fighting the traffic, and you can go to the mountains and be there by yourself. I can take you to Colorado and show you the best trout stream in the whole dang nation, and you won't catch a fish in it; you get up there on a nice day and you'll be elbow to elbow.

My dad went through the Great Depression, and he talks about selling cattle for $7 to $12 a head. Well, let's see, the cow would sell then for $12 a head, which sounds terrible, but you could buy land for 75 cents to a dollar an acre. So, back then, one cow would buy you 12 acres of land. Today, as cheap as fat cows are, they're down around 39 cents a pound, so you're getting maybe $370 for that cow. You go out here and this land is at least $120 an acre, maybe $200, so that cow's not going to buy you more than two to three acres.

It all depends on how you look at it. I think it's pretty tough today, and I can't see what's going to turn the economy around. I'm a firm believer that we're probably not going to get it turned around until we go through another depression. I think people have to get back to basics. Our life style may have to come down a bit from where it's been.

A lot of people say Reaganomics is the problem, but I'm a supporter of Reaganomics, to be honest with you. I think what President Reagan had to do initially was on the right track.

I realize there's high unemployment right now, and things aren't where everyone would like them to be. I think labor has priced itself out of jobs. Laborers' wages are keyed to the cost of living index, you know. If the cost of living goes up 12 percent a year, they feel their wages should increase 12 percent. I don't think that's the right way to establish the wages of laborers in this country. Labor and the cost of living are kind of like a dog chasing its tail, because when wages go up they tack that increase to the price of the product, and that increases the cost of living, so it's just a continuous thing.

I think people in this country ought to feel fortunate they have jobs, even if they're poor jobs. A poor job is still better than no job at all. I don't think we can all be wealthy in this country. We've got to be happy with what we have, otherwise

our nation won't support the industries that have provided well for it for a hundred years.

You can see that in auto manufacturing, and the sugar beet industry is another prime example. In the past three years, maybe fifteen sugar plants have closed down. Once a factory goes down, it's not very often that it opens back up.

Congress wants agriculture to compete on the world market. I don't have any problems with that; I think we should. But I don't think agriculture can compete until labor in this country is willing to compete, too. You can't have organized labor demanding $15 an hour for what it produces and then tell the agricultural segment. "You throw your commodity out there on the world market and take what you can get." It just won't work, because we have to consume too many of the products that organized labor manufactures. We're big consumers of steel; we use tremendous amounts of fertilizer and tremendous amounts of power. If you break agriculture in this country, who's going to consume all that? Where's the backbone of the nation?

I didn't work to stop the power plant coming in, and I'm a pretty broad-minded individual. But we have an industrial park site across the road and I fought that tooth and nail. And the commissioners zoned for a big housing development back in my pasture, and I fought tooth and nail. But when they run me out, I guess I'll leave.

I really feel people here don't know how fortunate they are. They're maybe not as well off financially as they would like to be, but when you measure it in terms of the standards by which we live, they're quite wealthy. We have good schools and we have a nice community. I don't think you can beat it, myself.

I don't know how tough this economy's going to get. It's hard to say if I can ride it out. I think I'll probably be around

for quite a while, but who knows? Heck, maybe in a year or two . . .

Personally, I'm in a self-employed type of business. I manage my business. I hire several men, and if I feel I can't afford to keep paying those people—if they're not producing enough—I'm going to let them go. It gets back to competition. There has to be some competition for jobs, too.

I don't like to see everyone come to the government for a job. They expect the government to provide jobs. Government shouldn't provide jobs for people; that shouldn't be the government's function. Its function should be to govern and its concern should be with the laws that control the way we live.

Somebody has to pay for it. Why pay those people $12 an hour when they're only providing maybe $5 or $6 worth of work?

I think there's a place for farmers. I'm a dyed-in-the-wool ag-man, you might say. It's what I believe in. If my boy wants to farm—why, that's the only reason I keep the farm.

Several years ago I could have sold out and put the money into interest-bearing investments and been way ahead of the game, but the way I feel about the land, the only way kids today are going to get a chance to go into agriculture is if they inherit the farm. If he wants the farm, it's here for him.

That's what he wants to do, and I'm proud of him. I'm glad he wants to be a farmer.

Sandra Viall

I WAS BORN IN EASTERN MONTANA TWENTY-EIGHT YEARS AGO. I grew up there and was married when I was 19 and had three children. Then after six years of marriage I was divorced—mainly because of physical abuse—and I was without education.

I had gone to nursing school for a while, but when my divorce came about I was basically without the skills to find a decent job. I came to Missoula for my education and because my youngest child, Brandon, had cerebral palsy and needed really good medical care. I began studying physical therapy at the university, and Brandon received probably the best care he could get in the state.

When I first came to Missoula, I got on welfare and received Aid to Families with Dependent Children. It paid me $331 a month. I had Food Stamps, too, and a Basic Education Opportunity Grant to complete all my programs.

I attended school full-time until the spring of 1982, when a bunch of Reagan's changes went into effect. Then I was told that I could stay on welfare if I wanted to stay home and take care of my children, but I'd lose my welfare payments if I kept

Sandra Viall is a hard-working mother of three young children. Forced onto the welfare rolls after a divorce, she enrolled at the University of Montana, studied to become a physical therapist and taught pre-school children in a Missoula Head Start program. She graduated from the University in 1983 and now lives in eastern Montana.

going to school. I had to either quit school and go to work, or try to work and go to school at the same time. It was a real dilemma.

The thought of trying to find any kind of job at all was terrifying, so for the summer I went back to my folks' place in eastern Montana and thought about it a lot and decided that the only thing I could do was continue to go to school and try to find some work. As a result, I lost my eligibility for welfare.

I don't know how much the federal government really should be responsible for supporting people. I don't like to be saying the government should support me because I am divorced now, but these social programs were instituted a long time ago, and now, all of a sudden, they seem to be saying: "Hey, we made a mistake way back when, and we're just going to withdraw and get out of this," and they're doing it so abruptly that they're leaving people hanging in really bad situations without any kind of back-up support.

I think the people who are making the laws have never lived under the conditions they're talking about. When Reagan says he's not hurting the truly needy, how does he know? Has he gone down and talked to the truly needy? Does he know what truly needy is? I think he has no realistic idea of what's going on. He keeps talking about a safety net. There is no safety net. People like me don't quite fit anywhere. When things work out it's pretty much by luck.

I found a job working with Head Start in the fall of 1982, so now I work full-time, from about 7:30 in the morning until 4:00, and I go to school. They give me educational leave, five hours a week, so this quarter I was able to take one five-credit class, and one three-credit class, for a total of eight hours. I only had to attend lectures two hours a week, and the rest was lab, and I was able to arrange to do the lab work in the evenings.

That's better than nothing, but it doesn't compare to what I would have been able to do on welfare. Then I could have gone to school full-time, which means a credit of thirteen to eighteen hours. I would have been able to complete school much faster; I would have a degree; I would be worth something in the job market. I would be a physical therapist. I would be immediately employable in any hospital, or vocational rehabilitation situation, or in a rural health clinic. Physical therapists are in demand.

With welfare's help it would probably have taken me five years to get my B.A. degree and become a registered physical therapist: two years pre-physical therapy, two years in the physical therapy program, and a one-year internship. Now that's no longer possible. It's going to take me at least an extra year, maybe more. I can't work and take care of three kids and carry eighteen credits all at the same time. I'm not capable of that.

Welfare also made a difference in costs. For example, with AFDC I received Social Services, which paid for day care for the three children. Now I have to pay about $160 a month for day care for the two youngest children—the oldest one, Keenen, is in the first grade. And with AFDC I was eligible for Medicaid, and that's not to be taken lightly either. Now Keenen and Aria have lost their coverage, which means two out of three children with no health insurance at all. Their father was supposed to pay for health insurance, but he hasn't. He was supposed to pay $300 a month for child support, too, but he doesn't. I've tried to get help enforcing that, but I haven't been able to. And of course we were eligible for Food Stamps, so we were receiving about $400 a month, plus the additional daycare benefit, which was worth about $160 a month, and of course the health coverage. Right now, in the Head Start job, I make about $530 a month and I get $284 in supplemental Social Security grant money. It looks like more money, but it isn't, when you figure in the value of the benefits lost and the extra time I will have to spend in school.

People don't *like* to be on welfare. I would actually be receiving less money than I am now, but I'd get my schooling done faster, and when I finally did finish, my wages would be higher and I'd be paying more taxes. I don't know why the people who are so down on welfare never stop to figure that out.

If I really wanted to, I could sit back and sit on welfare

until my children were raised. I could say, "Hey, I'm not going to school and I can't find a job and I don't have any training and I've got three little children and one of them is handicapped. You're going to have to do something with me!" And they could be stuck supporting us for the next eighteen years. Instead I asked for support for four or five years so that I could go to school and get my education, and when I finished I would be paying back into the system. And they say, "No, we don't want to pay for you to go to school." What an attitude!

I don't know if there are any words that can describe what the stress is like, working full-time and going to school and trying to take care of children. I've talked to a lot of different support people—parents of handicapped children, and the Comprehensive Developmental Center here in Missoula which helps train the parents of handicapped children—so I've received a lot of help in learning how to work with my son's handicap, and I've learned about a variety of networks, such as spouse-abuse network and the Social Services programs at the Human Resources Center. Those are the only things that have enabled me to keep going. Now they're all getting cut back in their funding because someone has decided they don't provide a useful service.

My morning begins at five o'clock and I go all day long and keep going until I fall into bed at midnight or one o'clock in the morning and do that day after day after day. It doesn't sound like much, but anything that helps me cope with it is a useful service.

I suppose someone could also decide that the Comprehensive Developmental Center wasn't useful, but I know what it means to Brandon and to me. Without it I would have to pay about $7,000 a year, and that's just for the normal evaluation and a checkup maybe once or twice a month.

They screen the children, they do evaluations, and everything is integrated. They have physical therapists, occupational therapists, child psychologists, and speech pathologists, and they can do really intensive evaluations and make referrals to community services. And they do home training programs for the parents. If the child needs adaptive equipment or surgery, they arrange for that. They take you in and make you part of the family.

Brandon is four years old now. He's covered by Medicaid, but if Medicaid should ever drop him for any reason, I don't know what I'd do. He receives the services of a physical therapist, the social services agencies, the occupational therapist, the orthopedic surgeon, and the child psychologist. The child psychologist used to meet with us as least twice a week, and more often than that during the first three months. The services from CDC are just tremendous.

I've been trained to give him physical therapy. I work with him every day to help him with movement, with learning, and how to feed and dress himself. Essentially what I do is go through every single motion with him. To teach him to pick up a fork, you take his arm and put his fingers on the fork and teach him to pick it up. It's a kind of programming, and it takes a lot of time. I've got it down now so it's just part of the daily routine, but at first it was more complicated, because it required keeping written records for CDC to measure progress.

I took Brandon out of the CDC program at the end of the summer of 1982, not for financial reasons, but mainly because it was time to move on. We needed to open a slot so somebody else could get help and I was pretty well trained. I can still call them for help, though, and he still has the services of an independent physical therapist.

All of this has been taken care of by Medicaid, so far. Last

91

year he went through surgery three different times in an eight-month period. We were trying to figure it out one day—the surgery, the hospital costs, the orthopedic surgeon's fee, the psychologist, the adaptive equipment, the physical therapist—and we concluded that Brandon was receiving about $30,000 a year in services from CDC.

Now, of course, he's not receiving such extensive services, but every day, it seems there's something in the paper about more cuts that they want to make or about redefining the guidelines or changing the regulations and the eligibility. I have no idea what's going to happen. All I can do is sit here and hope it doesn't; and I write to my congressman.

I don't enjoy the uncertainty, but I enjoy Montana and I'm glad I was born here. In Montana you can do a lot with your children without spending a lot of money. There are places to swim without having to go to a pool. You can go skiing and sledding and ice skating. Nature itself keeps the kids entertained. All you have to do is go along and chaperone them.

I noticed that with the day-care program, the people who run it rely on Montana's variety. They can take the children out on nature hikes, up in the mountains, or field trips. It takes very little time to get out of town. And a city the size of Missoula is not impossible to get around, so they can go to places like the fire stations, the bottling plants, the radio stations. In a bigger city that would be trickier, with the traffic and so on.

When we first moved here, we lived in a little trailer, right down by the river. Now we've moved out of there, but the kids must have formed some sort of attachment to that place. They always want to go back down there. We go down and skip rocks. I taught Keenen how to skip them, and then Aria and

Brandon. Well, I'm not very good. Keenen is actually better than I am by now, but I got the idea across.

If there's money for gas we drive up the Rattlesnake or through Grant Creek; we take little scenic drives. They're very soothing for me, and the children really like it too. Or we go out to the mall and wander around and visit the second hand shops. You can find relaxation here in the little things.

I want to stay in Montana. Where is it going to be any better? When I receive my degree in physical therapy—if I ever do!—a big city would be my best bet for job opportunities and for more money, but I would feel stifled. In Montana, even in Billings, how long does it take to get out to the country? It takes maybe half an hour on a really bad day.

I need the horizons and to be able to get out and look all around and not see people. There's a lot to be said about the healing powers of nature and to be away from throngs of people, and to be able to see the sun shine, when it does. Of course, Missoula kind of limits that.

It worries me, this smog problem. From what I've read, though, it doesn't seem to be anything new. The city is situated in a valley that just seems to trap the clouds and holds everything here under that cloud cover. I've read articles from the 1800s, when there weren't as many people here as there are now, and they mainly relied on wood for heat and there were problems with the smoke being trapped in the valley. They were trying to figure out what to do about it. But then, of course, the mills came in. Just by developing the resources, it contributes to the problem, but if you don't develop the resources, then there are no jobs. I can see the dilemma.

Montana's attraction is its wide open spaces. But if you want Montana to grow, to be healthy, you have to bring people in, right? But to bring people in, there have to be jobs and in

order for there to be jobs, there has to be industry of some kind. But you start putting too much of that in Montana and you'll destroy it. About all I can say is, keep the population small so the demands on the resources aren't too great.

I can remember Seeley as a really clean, nice little town. Then the oil boom hit, and the town has sprawled in every direction, and there's not enough planning. If you have to have expansion, I would say you somehow have to try to get qualified people to do long-range planning. It's just like nuclear energy. They were so gung ho for that, never worrying about the waste. So what do we do now, sit here and hold it for the next billion years or dump it in the ocean? Things have to be planned for, or otherwise it's just one shock after another.

It's not hard to feel caught in a situation that's beyond our control. Most of the jobs in this part of Montana are in the timber industry. With a recession like this one, thousands of people are thrown out of work. That was one reason I was really upset when I was told I had to get a job. With all of these men out of work and scrounging for whatever they could find —and their wives out looking for work too, there were not that many jobs.

I was raised out in the country on a farm. I had a pretty rural background—it was about seventeen miles to school— and in many ways a pretty idyllic childhood. There were four of us: one older brother and myself and a younger brother and a cousin that my parents took in. We were well taken care of. Of course a lot of times I felt really abused, because nobody wants to go pull chicken eggs out from under the chickens.

There were times, of course, when I would rather have been living in town, but all kids go through that. Nobody is ever really happy where they are when they are growing up. Today I don't know that I would ever want to go back way out in the country, but there are lots of little towns in Montana where your children have the freedom to grow and gain responsibility because you don't have to be checking on them all the time. All you have to do is check with one or two people and you can track them down. I think small towns build character.

And there are a lot of people who are willing to reach out and help their neighbor. You've got the helping hand. In fact I could probably go back to my parents' farm and live there and raise my kids, but it would be just an existence. I'm getting a little bit old to have my parents support me, though they do try to help me out as much as they can with food supplies. But I go down and help them out during the summer, too. In that way, I try to pay them back. But going to live there— I still wouldn't be educated.

I get scared of huge money problems, of owing money, and that really irritates me, because money has never been a big thing in my life. I either had it or I didn't and if I didn't I made do. But when you have children it suddenly seems so important. Any major medical problem can turn into a disaster. And if anything happened to me it would be terrible. Even minor things can be disastrous. There's no security. What happens if my car does a job on me? Last week there was something wrong with the wiring. All the wires under the hood burned out. I had it rewired and the same thing happened again. My whole paycheck went for that, so I had to stagger my other payments. Mountain Bell doesn't wait very easily.

When I was married, my husband could provide for the children financially—it was nip and tuck, but we made ends meet—but he couldn't provide for them emotionally. As far as I'm concerned he couldn't even meet the demands that were placed on him in a normal family situation. He could not deal with anger. He would just explode. After the divorce he came up to Missoula about four times, and the violence continued, and finally I had to file assault charges against him.

So it's clear to me that we may not be as well off financially but we're better off emotionally. My children may have to do without lots of things but they're going to know they're loved. And in a lot of ways it has made me stronger, going through what I've been through. If I ever do finish school and get out there in the working world I am going to be better equipped to deal with it. I'll be better able to understand people—all kinds of people.

I think of one girl in particular. She has two children, and just in order to get out of the house, she will leave the children alone. She has no money to pay a babysitter. She hates being obligated, having other people take care of her children, so she won't ask for help and she leaves the children there by themselves. She's beginning to use a lot of alcohol and other drugs, simply because she's so depressed. Her ex-husband is in the state penitentiary. He doesn't pay child support. Things are pressing her up against the wall; she's desperate and she's either going to fight or she's going to reach the point after awhile where she just can't fight any more. Some of the welfare people never understand that.

People give up in different ways. They stop looking for higher education; they stop bettering themselves; they just kind of "sink back" and go along in this world leading tedious and humdrum lives, and it reflects in turn on their children. They grow up hohum, and that's sad.

I have a lot of hope that someday I will finish school, and that I will be able to get a job somewhere that I like, and be able to buy a house and settle down with the children and be able to have them go to one school and to know that we aren't going to be moving all over the country. Perhaps I'd even like to be married again, but not now.

I want to be self-sufficient, even though I don't think people are ever totally independent. I'd like to reach the point where I know my kids won't be deprived of essentials, and to have time for a bit of a social life and relaxation. I would like to have more choices. Now, in the evenings, after I put the kids to bed, I can sit on the couch and stare at the laundry or do it. I can choose between the cleaning that there is never time to do, or the dishes. Maybe once a month, I just sit there and stare at the wall.

Walter Minnick

Walter Minnick is the president and chief operating officer of the Trus Joist Corporation of Boise, Idaho. Trus Joist is a $100 million business with operations throughout the United States and in western Canada. The company makes roof and floor joists for home and office buildings. Minnick has had a varied career as a lawyer, White House staff member during the Nixon administration and now corporate executive. During his years in Idaho, he has been active in plans to redevelop the Boise downtown area.

"WHAT'S THE STORY ON DOWNTOWN BOISE?" you ask. "Why the empty space and the empty stores? What's going to happen?" That's the major issue in Boise, and has been for seventeen years. We started an urban development project in Boise seventeen years ago; ripped out the heart of our downtown and never rebuilt it. It's a hot local issue, and the question is: What do we do now? We've had a downtown redeveloper for the past several years who has been unable to pull off his redevelopment plan, centered around a big, enclosed mall. He hasn't been able to do it, and he's the fourth in a row to fail.

Downtown can be redeveloped, it's just that the concept we've been using is wrong. Trying to sustain a large regional suburban shopping center downtown in an enclosed mall is economically unviable. It's a Los Angeles solution to a Boise problem.

The economics are unfavorable. The cost to build the elaborate superstructure, and of the energy to provide air-conditioning in the summer and the heating in the winter is such that it's totally uneconomic in terms of the kind of retail rental rates tenants would have to pay. It would also worsen our already serious air-pollution problem and impose an impossible burden on our overloaded metropolitan street system, and it's inconsistent with the tenor of the community. The average Boise resident doesn't want a fancy Los Angeles type shopping mall in the middle of his city.

96

So the concept we've been using is inappropriate. But there are other concepts less grandiose and more in tune with the philosophy of the community; we just haven't tried them yet.

I think most Boisians want a mixed-use downtown, not simply a retail center or a financial center. They want entertainment; restaurants; small, high-class specialty shops; and hotels. They want to turn the downtown into a twenty-four-hour activity center, rather than have it just as a place where people commute to work at eight o'clock in the morning and commute out again at five, leaving it a ghost town the other sixteen hours—all of which leads to decay and a dead downtown.

It's hard to get anchor tenants—the big, high volume department stores—if the concept is strictly retail; however, the principal problem, in my opinion, is that the basic development concept has been wrong: too high-priced, too grandiose. It should be scaled down, to mixed use, more open spaces, more specialty shops, fewer department stores, better use of existing buildings, and a lot less costly infrastructure. We also need to hire a proven, experienced urban developer to oversee the project. Transforming a downtown is a terrifically complicated, difficult task, much more so than building a suburban shopping center. We need to put a pro in charge—someone with a real track record of success with this kind of project.

Greater use of existing buildings than is contemplated in the current concept, is important, not only because these buildings have historical value, but because existing structures can, in general, be renovated more cheaply than ripping them down and building new ones. They also add a character to a downtown development that is entirely consistent with the basic feelings of the community. We're a western town, and we should capitalize on our heritage. Doing so would be far more consistent with the true sentiments of the community's residents than building a gleaming new multi-story and modernistic structure to serve the same function.

Boise is, after all, very historic. Fort Boise was a principal stopping place on the Oregon Trail, and Boise was one of the first communities in our part of North America to be settled back in the 1860s, and it was the center of the gold rush of the late 1800s. It's not old by the standards of the East, but by the standards of the West, it's *very* old; and we should treasure and build on that heritage.

I came to Boise from Washington, D.C., in 1974. I'm almost a native, though, because I grew up on a farm across the state line in Washington State, just north of Walla Walla. I wound up in Washington, D.C., for a while because the only way I could stay in law school was to join the army, and the army sent me to the Pentagon.

You see, I went to law school during the Vietnam era when draft deferments were hard to get. I was admitted to Harvard Law school but my local draft board didn't want to let me go. My draft appeal finally worked its way up to the presidential appeals board. If I won, I would be able to finish my first year of law school and then get drafted. If the state of Washington won, I would have to go right away.

I didn't mind going in the army, but I really wanted to finish law school first. So I joined the Reserve Officer Training Corps unit—that was a couple of years before ROTC got thrown off the Harvard campus. This was in the late sixties, which was a very interesting time to be in New England, particularly on the Harvard campus.

After graduation I practiced law very briefly in Portland, Oregon, and then in the summer of 1970, the army called me up for active duty and sent me to Washington, D.C. It was the Nixon administration, but there was a little of the Robert McNamara era left in the Pentagon. I had a few friends from business school who were still there, and I had a background in economics; so I was assigned to the Pentagon to work as an economist on Vietnam.

It was difficult to determine what to do with the Vietnamese economy—assuming Vietnamization was going to work—because it was the only economy in history where the standard of living went *up* when the country went to war. At that time, South Vietnam was maintaining the world's fourth largest standing army—an army equivalent to a U.S. military establishment of about forty million—far larger than our military at the height of World War II. The burden on the local economy was staggering, because essentially the nation's entire male population was in the military and not producing anything for the economy. Yet, everyone was living better than ever before, and we were footing the bill. Vietnam was importing about $800 million a year in goods, and exporting only $15 million, so it had a more severe balance-of-payments deficit than any other country in the world in modern times.

And the problem was that if Vietnamization was going to work, they had to maintain that standing army as we withdrew our troops. Given this military reality, what could we do to help build up their economy during an era when the peace movement was forcing decreases in U.S. economic aid? Which it was. So it was a very interesting problem. We had some good ideas and were making progress, although, after the Tet Offensive, the whole thing rapidly became academic.

Toward the end of my military commitment, I began making plans to go back to my law firm in Portland, but a friend in Washington, who was working as a White House fellow,

kept telling me about the very interesting and important things going on at the White House. Being on the White House staff is an exciting experience for a young person. It is a very rarefied atmosphere, and everybody at the level where the real work is done in the White House is young—nobody over 35. In any administration I suspect it's that way. At that time the heroin problem with troops in Vietnam was endangering public support for the administration's Vietnamization policy, and a lot of voters took a dim view of turning a generation of American soldiers into heroin addicts. John Ehrlichman was given the job of doing something about the problem. On his advice, the president set up a cabinet committee, involving about twenty-five departments and agencies—everything from the CIA, Defense and Justice to Agriculture and the National Institute of Mental Health. Ehrlichman was looking for a staff coordinator, so I was hired.

I spent about two years working on the international drug problem, and after the 1972 election, Ehrlichman asked me to stay on, and at that point I was principally responsible for the study of the drug problem generally, including domestic law-enforcement and the treatment and prevention aspects.

I ran that program from the White House for another year. We pioneered methadone maintenance and youth education programs and cracked down on traffickers worldwide. We masterminded the capture of the leading drug-running feudal warlord in the Golden Triangle of Burma and the destruction of his private army by Thai government irregulars. We indicted the brother of the president of Panama and destroyed clandestine heroin labs in Marseilles. I staffed and stage managed meetings of cabinet members and for a while wrote or suggested virtually everything the president said about drugs. During my time at the White House total government spending on the drug problem increased from $65 milion to $850 million, two-thirds of it for treatment and prevention.

It was a major job, a lot of fun, and 80 hours a week. It would have been a fascinating experience even if Watergate hadn't happened. But Watergate did occur, and while I was there the Administration collapsed That too was . . . interesting. And I was tangentially involved in that, because my first boss, Bud Krogh, went to jail. He was in charge of the "plumbers" unit, and my first two office mates, in the suite of offices I was in, were Howard Hunt and Gordon Liddy, whom I knew quite well. And John Ehrlichman went to jail. I knew a lot of people who turned out to have some serious problems before it was all over.

I didn't go to jail. I did not get disbarred. I was not a subject of investigation. And my name wasn't among those featured in the books or on the CBS evening news. However, I was very much affected by it all. As I watched it all unfold, touching friends and affecting my ability to do my job, I became progressively more dissillusioned with President Nixon to the point that I finally had to quit.

It was Monday after the "Saturday Night Massacre" in October of 1973 [when Nixon, seeking to fire special prosecutor Archibald Cox, fired Attorney General Elliot Richardson and Deputy Attorney General William Ruckelshaus for refusing to carry out his orders]. I had been working with Elliot Richardson, staffing a meeting that was to take place the next week between him and the Mexican attorney general to discuss the growing Mexican heroin problem. All of a sudden Richardson was gone. That was the last straw. I decided that weekend that I couldn't work for President Nixon anymore— for a person so *obviously* lacking in integrity—so I quit. It didn't make the news, but I was the second member of the Nixon White House staff to resign in protest over his handling of Watergate.

I spent six months looking for a job, ending up in Boise, Idaho. I didn't have any connection with Trus Joist Corporation then, and I didn't know anybody here. I was unemployed and I came here because I decided that I wanted to live in Boise. I liked to ski, to backpack, and to fish, and I *loved* the Rocky Mountains. So it was a very conscious choice, based totally on lifestyle, not on career.

I wanted a town larger than Walla Walla, which was about 25,000. I'd lived in Washington, D.C., in Boston and in Portland, and I wanted a place smaller than those cities. I looked very hard for a job here, and finally got one as a management trainee with Trus Joist. After five years and a number of responsibilities, I was made a vice-president, managing five operating divisions. Then the company's president resigned suddenly, and I was asked to take his place. I was thirty-six at the time. It's been very challenging. My marriage survived Watergate, but it didn't survive Trus Joist and three years of the deepest recession in the building materials industry in fifty years. That turned out to be a tougher challenge.

The Northern Rockies region is not as different as people in the East presume. The ignorance there about the character of the West is appalling. The most provincial people in the world are those who have grown up and spent their lives in big cities in the East. They have no conception of the rest of the country. They think we have Indians on horses, and the Pony Express, and people walking around with six-guns; they think we're ignorant and rough. They have no idea that, basically, a city is a city. There are subtle differences of lifestyle and attitude and philosophy, but essentially twentieth-century America is a very homogeneous society, whether it's East or West.

We have four, billion-dollar companies headquartered in Boise—Albertson's, Boise Cascade, Simplot, and Morrison Knudsen—and eight or nine companies like Trus Joist in the hundred-million-dollar range. We have some of the best professional people anywhere and a wide range of cultural activities. So I would say that it's not that different.

The physical environment is different (and better), of course, but there's more difference between urban and suburban, or suburban and rural, than between East and West. There's a far greater difference between upstate New York and New York City than there is between the state of New York and the states of Idaho or Montana. People don't appreciate the sophistication in the West, or the fact that we have urban societies. People think of this as a rural region, when in fact, most people live in towns and cities.

There's a difference in the way government operates, but that difference is more a function of scale than anything else. Idaho and Montana and Wyoming have small populations, and the problems are easier to solve; they aren't as intractible. The number of people involved is equivalent to less than the population of the borough of Queens.

It's very hard to live in Helena or Boise or Cheyenne without getting to know the governor. You get to know the people who are influential, not because you're making an effort to know them, but because they happen to be neighbors and you keep bumping into them. I've been surprised at how many political people I know here, even though I've had almost nothing to do with politics since coming here.

Given the values of the current generation, places such as Boise and Missoula—or any metropolitan area in any of these three states—are second to none as attractive places to live. In fact, that's the principal problem of the region: it's too attractive. There's a danger that over the next twenty years it's going to be ruined as a distinctive place to live by virtue of the inrush of people—that's the number one problem. And it's unfortunate that the governors of all three states, by trying to attract more companies to move here, are bringing about the destruction of what it is that makes these three states distinctive.

Setting limits on growth is very hard, because this is a region that is allergic to planning. You can remove incentives and stop the propagandizing, but it's very hard to put positive bars in place, because that's contrary to the ideology of the local citizenry.

The danger is that Idaho, Montana and Wyoming will become like Colorado, which is still a nice place to live, but within any reasonable radius of Denver, you find the same big-city crime and traffic problems and the same air-quality problems as you'd find in a city the size of Boston.

Three hours after leaving my office on a midsummer afternoon, I can put on my backpack and before nightfall be all alone at a high alpine lake, casting my fly rod. Fishing is still great and there won't be anyone else there all weekend. That's still possible within a three-hour drive of Boise. It's that quality which I cherish more than anything else about our state, and it is in danger of slipping away.

I advocate planning which does not add things simply for the sake of growth. I think the public policy of the region should be to discourage immigration, rather than encourage it —distincentives rather than incentives.

The governor of the state of Idaho shouldn't go to an electronics show in Washington, D.C., and brag about all the things he would do to get the next Hewlett-Packard plant for Boise.

That kind of thing does nothing to cure our economic problems. Our economic problems are national; they have national causes and national solutions.

Because of our dependence on tourism and natural resources, the area is fundamentally more healthy than the country as a whole, as long as the country doesn't drag it down. We do have a mild unemployment problem, but usually the problem is at the other extreme. This area has been growing four or five times faster than the national average, and creating strains on the public sector to provide the necessary service. Growing more slowly would ease the strain. We shouldn't be providing special incentives for growth. We don't need to import electronics and forest product companies. We're already getting them fast enough.

I'm on the executive committee of the Boise Futures Foundation, an active organization that is entirely privately funded, mostly by the business community. That's something we're doing in Boise that I think is quite exciting. The Foundation's purpose is to document the facts on the growth issue. We're not political and don't take partisan positions. Right now we're getting the facts on the air-quality problem in the community— what it is, what can be done about it, what are the limitations.

101

By way of comparison, about the only thing the public sector is doing about air quality is complaining about the EPA and trying to repeal our vehicle emissions inspection law.

At the Boise Futures Foundation, we have studies being done on air quality, transportation capacity, water capacity, energy and public finance. We're attempting to provide a data base that will help raise the level of public consciousness on these issues.

My only real hope on the runaway-population-growth issue, is that our fiscal crisis will help take care of it. We have a public-finance crisis so severe in this state, and such strong ideological obstacles to doing anything about it, that we may hamstring ourselves—providing levels of public services so inferior that no matter what the governor says, the next company won't come to Boise.

When Texas Instruments has us on a list of plant-site possibilities, our declining university system is a negative; when we're spending only a fifth of what we should to maintain our city and county streets, that's a negative; not providing enough police protection is a negative. It's an unfortunate way to constrain growth—and it's not fair to our children—but maybe it's the only kind of constraint our political process has the ability to adapt.

We have an ideological complexion that doesn't allow us to raise taxes. We have a Proposition 13 that has undermined and limited the property tax, which has already been reduced substantially and will grow proportionately smaller in the future.

Our rather myopic philosophy of government invariably says, "Let's get by on the cheap. Less is better." I don't necessarily disagree that less is better, but the problem is, you cut everybody's salaries and eliminate positions by attrition, and you downgrade everything a little. Instead we should be saying: "Okay, there are some governmental functions we aren't going to perform anymore. For the functions we *are* going to perform, we are going to pay enough money to attract quality people and see that those jobs get done right."

Unfortunately, that is not the way the political process works here and in many other places. When you have eight percent inflation, the legislature gives four percent cost-of-living adjustments across the board and everybody is four percent poorer. Competent people drop out to go get jobs with Morrison-Knudsen or somebody else. You're left with public servants who have no choice but to stay and with less-qualified people who come in at the bottom.

Education in Idaho is in a sorry state of affairs at every level. We don't have a tradition here of good education, and, having never had it, there isn't enough appetite for it. I don't know for sure if Idaho ranks last among the states in teachers' salaries, but we're certainly among the bottom four or five.

Most parents here want the average high-school graduate to try Boise State University for a semester or two, or just go get a job. Graduate education? A national class university? God forbid! We don't have that tradition and we have acute financial pressures, so we're cutting back from an inferior base—and without the kind of hue and cry that would go up in Massachusetts or in Oregon.

We have some special problems in Idaho that help diminish the amount of money to be spent on higher education. We're a state that might be able to support one quality school, but we have three universities; so there's a problem of spreading too little money around for too many schools, and each of those schools has a political constituency. In nothern Idaho, people support the University of Idaho; eastern Idaho supports Idaho State; and southwestern Idaho supports Boise State.

The first Idaho university was started in Moscow, which is very far from any centers of population and is in the part of the state that has had the least growth; consequently, another school was started over in eastern Idaho, but the population center of the state has increasingly shifted toward southwestern Idaho. So a junior college has grown over the past twenty years into a third university that is now bigger than the other two—that's Boise State.

All the universities are too small and too poor to compete for the best faculty, and all have financial resources so meager that they are virtually condemned to being second-rate schools. That problem has been exacerbated by the lack of a tradition of quality education. The decision making is being done by a legislature that includes very few people who have ever attended an institution of higher education. Most legislators regard universities with great suspicion, because universities tend to be the centers of all the things they are afraid of.

It's that kind of situation which has led to something like fourteen professors leaving the business school at Boise so far this year. One of those professors, a friend of mine, John Mitchell, is probably Idaho's best-known economist. He's truly talented and a great teacher. But you can't expect a guy who's making $18,000 a year, and who has received real pay cuts for seven or eight straight years, not to go, given the opportunity to work for an out of state bank at three times the money.

The situation is tough everywhere for academia, but nowhere is it tougher than in schools like the three universities we have in Idaho. It's a very depressing picture, and I don't know that there's any easy answer to it. One solution would be to pay state legislators enough that a broader range of men and women could afford to serve. I couldn't serve in the Idaho legislature, because I can't take five months a year off or live on $4,200 a year, or whatever it is they pay legislators; nobody can, unless that person is independently wealthy, retired, or has a job of seasonal nature. That's part of the problem, and I don't see a politically acceptable solution.

The business and professional community ought to be doing more to support education and ought to have the courage to accept its share of the higher taxes that go with it. For the only solution, really, is to tax ourselves more, and that is ideologically very difficult in this state at this time. And, of course, we should consolidate our universities, but that probably won't be done. So I'm afraid we may be doomed to inferior education, particularly at the higher-education level, for at least the foreseeable future.

Do I ever think about going back into government service? Well, I really prefer the private sector. I couldn't put up with the phony lifestyle required of an elected public official. I'm a bit too outspoken and too inflexible to make the necessary, politically expedient compromises on the issues. I don't suffer fools lightly, and you have to do that.

As a very young man, it was something that looked very glamourous and attractive. Now I might consider an administration position, on a short-term basis, where you didn't have to go through all the baloney associated with elections. But I've been there once. I've been at the very center of the government of the United States during a very exciting period of time, and I don't really have a desire to go back and start over in that world. Basically, I'm able to control my enthusiasm for the public sector.

Rubie Sooktis

I WAS BORN ON THE NORTHERN CHEYENNE RESERVATION. Officially, by tribal enrollment, I belong to my mother's people, the Northern Cheyenne Tribe, but unofficially, I also belong to the Southern Cheyennes of Oklahoma through my father. Although I was born and partly raised on what I consider the most beautiful place, the Northern Cheyenne Reservation, I spent a large part of my childhood moving from place to place with my family because of the high unemployment on the reservation during the 1950s. Like migrants, we followed the sugar beet season in Rosebud County. With a little luck, my father and grandfather sometimes remained employed with one of the farmers after the sugar beet season.

Life was hard. The best times I remember were spent with my mother's family. During these years, I learned the culture and history of the Cheyenne people through my grandparents, Dan and Jenny Seminole. I especially remember the times with my grandmother, with whom I spent a great deal of time, as we both often had to walk several miles to the store in Cartersville, a small farming community.

During the late fifties, the United States government devel- oped an American Indian relocation program for the Indian people. When my parents, Charles and Josephine, learned of the program, they decided to move us to Denver, Colorado, where we remained for seven years. It was not easy to move so far away from my grandparents and other relatives, but my grandmother, through a translator, wrote faithfully to us.

The American Indian relocation program was just another termination policy for the Indians. For years and years, the federal government has made attempts to relieve itself of its trust responsibilities to American Indians. And in the fifties the Eisenhower administration adopted the relocation program, which was intended to move Indians away from reservations.

Once an Indian family arrived in the city of their choice, the Bureau of Indian Affairs would assist the head of the family in finding employment. They helped us find housing and funded our first home furnishings. So began our urban life in Denver with members of many other Indian tribes. The reloca- tion program was really the beginning of the urban Indian centers that the big cities still have.

After years of moving around, the move to Denver wasn't exactly like being uprooted for me. At eight years old I had already gone through a lot of schools and had left places I didn't want to leave and gone to places I didn't want to go. So it wasn't a strange process, not as strange as when I first went to school. We were living in Rosebud, a town north of the reserva- tion. There's a little one-room grade school there—one teacher with eight grades. I remember that first day; I didn't speak one word of English. I had my older sister, Esther, and an older brother, Butch, going to the same school along with an older cousin, Johnny. I stayed around my cousin, because we were in the same class and he could translate for me. During recess there was a commotion outside (I'd stayed in because my cousin had to stay). Outside they had found a bull snake crawling into the school. The sugar beet season was coming in, so there were also Mexican-Americans there, and of course their children didn't speak any English either. I think it may have been more traumatic for the teacher than it was for us.

When I was fifteen, my folks brought us back home to Birney, Montana, the smallest community on the reservation. It was time we settled down, they said. It was quite a change, moving from metropolitan Denver to a tiny village. I certainly was happy to return to my grandparents, aunts, uncles, and other relatives, but we moved from a three-bedroom house to a two-room log cabin and that, you know, is quite a difference.

It took a little time to readjust to not having the conveniences of more than one television station and good radio reception. I missed a lot of things, especially the museums. But I didn't miss the noise or the crowds of a big city. Birney was a special place for all of us, and we quickly got involved again with summer swimming in the Tongue River and gathering with our friends at the white bridge and at the well.

We expected it would be a difficult time for my father. It was always difficult, finding work, but the reservation was in a little better situation than it was when we left for Denver. The Catholics had been expanding their educational program. The Catholics and the Mennonites are the two oldest denominations on the reservations, and the Catholics were expanding programs so that they could provide employment to the Cheyennes. They had a factory where they made plastic figures, and it provided a lot of work.

After a couple of years, my dad and mother started working for St. Labre, which is the name of the church. But then we began moving again, to Hardin and to Billings. Then we came back to the reservation. It was always for employment.

Rubie Sooktis, a member of the Northern Cheyenne tribe, lives in Lame Deer, Montana and is a writer, editor, photographer and film maker. She has served on the Northern Cheyenne Council of Forty-Four (the tribal government's governing body) and has been active in efforts by the tribe to control its mineral resources and to strengthen tribal sovereignty.

My father applied for a job on the reservation as an ambulance driver with the Public Health Service, but the job was not made available, so he decided, "Well, I'm going to take my years passed before I actually became a photographer. I ended up doing a lot of other things. I was trained in visual arts, and of course it had a lot to do with media discipline, which was family to California." So we went on their relocation program again—this was in 1964—and ended up on Los Angeles. And ten days after we got there, my father got the ambulance driver job. So they sent us back to the reservation, to Lame Deer, where I still live today. We finally settled down.

On the reservation, there was work for me as a young woman, but all I wanted to do was to fulfill the dreams I had as a child. I wanted to be a photographer, I dreamed of being a writer and a teacher, and I wanted to get into filmmaking.

My aunt Eva inspired my fascination with photography. She had a little Brownie camera and took a lot of family pictures. I had always wondered how in the world this little thing could capture the images, and I was even more fascinated about how they were put on paper.

I didn't know how to read or write until I got into school, of course, and my grandparents would say, "Learn how to read and write so you can translate for us sometimes." So as a result of this, I wanted nothing more than to be a writer someday.

Living off and on the reservation, we had the chance to go to the movie houses almost on a regular basis. I can remember the first movie I saw, when I still didn't understand English. It was *Jumping Jacks* with Dean Martin and Jerry Lewis. Showing with it were *King Kong*, newsreels, and cartoons. Again, I was fascinated by the images on the screen. So that experience influenced what I wanted to do.

I had to leave the reservation again after high school to pursue my education. I went to Seattle and learned how to be a photographer. Then I was able to go to New Hampshire to learn more about photography. So when I came back I was ready to pursue my interests on the reservation. But several very useful when I later became the tribal editor. I was able to satisfy my curiosity about teaching by working with the

Northern Cheyenne Head Start program. I did that for a couple of years, and then I left and became tribal editor for the Northern Cheyennes and learned how to operate a press. And it was all building from my training.

While I was working as an editor for the tribe in 1972, they signed their first major mineral leases. Some of my friends were extremely concerned about it. I learned about the dark side of coal development—mining the land, the influx of people, the potential to turn the reservation inside out.

That was the beginning, not only of my own concern about natural resources, but also of taking my rights very seriously. But more importantly it was the beginning of my writing. There were two people especially—the late Dave Robinson, former director of the Northern Cheyenne Landowners Association, and Mr. Robert Bailey—who were concerned and were discussing programs they wanted so that the people would be better informed about coal development. As the two of them discussed their ideas, I'd sit there wondering what I could contribute to the tribe.

I guess I wanted to contribute as a writer and that was the turning point. I began to plan my life as a writer. Since then I've been involved with the Northern Cheyennes' natural resource issues. I've been a very strong supporter of the struggles, the legal battles. I just wholeheartedly support the whole effort.

I've watched many things grow out of that natural resource struggle. I've watched the tribe take their trustee—the Interior Department—to task on coal leases and permits. They said, "It's time the coal leases were suspended." That stopped the coal development at our front door, and it stopped people from moving in.

I've seen the tribe develop both an effective coal research program—the Northern Cheyenne Research Project—and the

Northern Cheyenne Land Owners' Association, which dealt with the land owners on the reservation and fought for their rights. And I've seen a lot of people—native Americans and non-native Americans—come to the reservation to assist the tribe with their expertise. I've seen a lot of good things.

All of this has contributed to my own education. In 1976 I completed my first paper dealing with the cultural development of the Northern Cheyennes. Then I got involved in the tribe's communications commission and co-authored a film script about the Cheyenne land. It was based in history, on a specific event, but the struggle was the same. They fought for their land, struggled for it, and at the end, they got it. The film script was completed in 1978. Then, that fall, I was elected to the Northern Cheyenne tribal council.

Traditionally there were no women on the Council of Forty-Four. That began to change after the tribe adopted the Indian Reorganization Act in 1935, which incorporated the Anglo philosophy of electing your officials and developing your government and your economic base and so forth. In the 1940s, Bessie Harris was elected to the council—the first Cheyenne woman to serve. She spoke Cheyenne and was a very articulate individual.

But I must add that the Northern Cheyenne people do not discriminate against each other. There's no struggle between the sexes. There's a very definite need for everybody's ability within the tribe—for the tribe's benefit and for its whole being. That might seem strange to a culture where one of the sexes is dominant, but the Northern Cheyennes have had both male and female spiritual people and medicine people of both sexes, and the ceremonies—even the ceremonies we have today— require both men and women in order to be complete.

Land ownership is a very complex issue. To understand it, you have to look at the Indian General Allotment Act—it was also called the Dawes Act—of 1887. The Dawes Act gave the Indian people individual allotments, depending on their age; some got 80 acres, some got 160 acres. These allotments were to be held in trust for twenty-five years. After that they would be out of trust. The individual allotments would fall under the state for taxation, and the holders of the allotments would have some of the rights of ownership, including the "power of alienation," meaning the right to confer title.

The Northern Cheyenne Reservation was established in 1884, but the tribe was slow in being reached by the policies of the federal government. The Northern Cheyennes finally received their allotments in 1926, and I think the trust period was fifty years, so the question of surface rights in the early 1970s was very complex. And the question of mineral rights was unsettled until a few years ago when the Supreme Court ruled in favor of maintaining the mineral rights in common, which means that the tribe as a whole now owns the minerals.

I can't say that the whole tribe is pro-development or anti-development. I will say, though, that the dilemma is clear. It's a dilemma not only for the Northern Cheyennes but for the other Indian tribes with valuable minerals.

The present-day Cheyenne experiences the need to be a Cheyenne—a traditional Cheyenne—and pursues that goal, and yet at the same time he's caught up in the material world, which means having to have enough money to pay for basic needs. He must have work. Development of resources means work and income for the tribe. At the same time, the traditional, spiritual strengths of the Cheyennes are tied to the land.

I know it's a very terrible dilemma. Our leaders from one hundred years ago, or even fifty years ago, didn't have this monetary, material pressure. The Northern Cheyennes had the buffalo, which provided a lot of their nutritional and household needs; nature provided most of their general needs. They could exist without the pressure to find work. They worked, but it was not for monetary compensation.

There have been many attempts at developing the reservation economy in other ways. In the early days of the reservation, they taught farming and ranching skills, and the Northern Cheyennes developed their cattle herd to about 15,000 head, I believe, and their horses to 3,000 head.

It took them about twenty-five years to develop those herds, and then, in the early 1930s, I believe, the Bureau of Indian Affairs decided that the reservation was being overgrazed. The cattle and the horses were individually owned, but the BIA said, "We're going to shoot your horses and your cows for six dollars until we cut the size of the herds down." So they did that—treated the herds as commonly owned by the tribe and killed the cows for six dollars a head. That was the end of the only successful economic development in our recent history.

Since then there have been other attempts to develop an economic base on the reservation. There was the plastic factory at St. Labre, but it's no longer there. And the federal government's Economic Development Agency has supported some big white elephants on other reservations, but not on ours. Our neighbors—the Crow Reservation—have this big beautiful motel which was a gift from the EDA. It doesn't make money, but it's there.

The Reagan administration's cuts have hurt, but there has never been a favorable administration to the Indian people at any time. The Economic Development Agency, for example, has always given people enough to begin, but never enough to continue. That's been the story of our federal funding. So Reagan is just another in a long line. He's a little more diffi-cult—a little more like Eisenhower—but he's just another.

To build an economic base, the tribe will need to develop regulatory agencies that can protect our interests, not only from the corporations, but also protect our hunting and fishing rights and our rights on the reservation as a whole.

The tribal government since 1935 has developed a political base very well. It has worked through the different Indian organizations and with the federal government. But the economic base has yet to be developed, and, going back to the termination idea, there's the question: What is the economic well-being of the tribe? What does economic success do to its relationship to the federal government? Those are still questions down the road. Many tribes have a potential for developing an economic base, but a lot of things have to be dealt with. Some tribes in Washington State and the Menominee tribe were terminated because they built a good economic base, and of course the federal relationship affects the tribal economy. Federal agencies, people like James Watt, just take the native Americans so lightly.

I worry about that, but looking down the road, I think I'm more optimistic than pessimistic, for two important reasons: Number one, in spite of all the hardships we've had since the reservation began, in trying to live under all the different federal policies, we were able to maintain our Cheyenne way of life. Number two, more recently, we have developed our human resources. The tribe has its own educated individuals. I'm optimistic because of that educational development and the ability of the Cheyenne people to maintain their Cheyenne world.

I see these as reasons that the Cheyennes' future will be sensitive to their cultural, political, and economic needs. That is the kind of future I would like to see, and I want to be a part of it, as a writer.

Tyler Dodge

THE LAND IS WORTHLESS WITHOUT WATER. Water is needed for domestic wells, stock wells, irrigation, and for housing subdivisions. Your land is no good if you can't count on your water supply. We've had big regional battles about the water issue and I think they'll continue. We'd be in a real firestorm right now, I think, if the demand for energy hadn't slowed down.

I think it's imperative to get a few things organized before demand picks up again. The surplus of oil and natural gas won't last. If the economy turns around, energy will be a bigger problem than ever. And if we don't do some planning—anticipating water needs, for example, and how to provide for the people that energy development will bring in—we'll be in another crisis situation. And guess who will lose? Agriculture.

I don't know that we need new legislation or an amendment to the state Industrial Siting Act. We have most of the legislation we need in place, but it needs fine-tuning. My fear is that in a panic situation we're going to act just like the federal government: throw a lot of money at a problem; throw out big chunks of money to support large projects and forget all about the small projects that are probably more efficient and more appropriate. The small projects don't create good jobs for bureaucrats, and they don't make good newspaper headlines. A press release about a billion-dollar project gets attention. You don't get much press when you decide to capture a couple of thousand-acre-feet of water to supplement a marginal irrigation district or support a small town.

But we don't need complicated engineering projects based on pump-storage reservoirs and networks of pipelines with enormous annual maintenance costs. There are a lot of irrigation districts in the state—this being one of them—where you could take far less money and just do some simple things like upgrade headgates and put in some pipeline. Little $10,000 projects here and there would greatly increase productivity and return more per dollar than you will ever see from some of those big projects.

People here shouldn't forget that when this state was settled, the best land—the land that was the easiest to manage and the most productive—was the first land to be taken up, as with every other state. That's where the good water is. Unfortunately, when you build a big project sometimes it's that land that gets covered up first, as in the case of the Grayrocks Dam, and you cover land that is far more productive than the land you plan to use the dam to pump water to.

How do we develop sensible thinking about water? Boy, I don't know. The Little Big Horn project is a classic example of not doing things sensibly. Little Big Horn is a stream that originates in Wyoming and runs into Montana through the Crow Indian Reservation. There's a fair amount of water available. Very little is used for irrigation in Wyoming—only one or two small ditches, I think. But it does go through a scenic canyon, so you're going to get objections if you do anything with it.

Tyler Dodge operates a ranch near Wheatland, Wyoming. He spent several years as a ski resort operator and real estate developer in Colorado before moving back to his native Wheatland in the early 70s. He is a founder and long-time chairman of the Laramie River Conservation Council, a rancher-conservationist group organized to oppose the Laramie River Station, a mas-sive, 2,000 megawatt power plant slated to be built in Wheat-land in 1973 by the Basin Electric Power Cooperative. As a result of the Council's work, Basin Electric reduced the plant to 1,500 megawatts and modified it to protect wildlife and water supplies and to reduce its impact on Wheatland. The plant was completed in 1982.

Some people in Sheridan wanted to develop it. They had an opportunity to sell the water to ETSI, the coal slurry pipeline company. And they worked out a pretty good plan for diverting that water out of the canyon in such a way that it wouldn't tear up the canyon.

Before this happened, the pipeline company had gotten permission to drill wells out here to tap the water in the Madison aquifer. But the Madison is kind of an unknown quantity. There's a lot of water there, but every time the company does a study, it comes back with a little lower figure on the recharge rate. So a furor developed over the potential drawdown—the fear that ETSI would be jeopardizing the water supply of towns in Wyoming and South Dakota. The city of Douglas, for example, gets its main water supply from the Madison. When ETSI got its permit, I suppose 99 percent of the people of Douglas didn't know that.

The people who wanted to divert the Little Big Horn ran up against a faction in the northern part of the state that said, "No, you can't do that; we'll fight you all the way; we don't want anybody touching the water in the Little Big Horn or making money from it." At that time, however, the Little Big Horn people were going to do all the development with private money—no state or federal money; it wasn't going to cost the taxpayers anything. But the opposition was strong enough that the project was killed in the legislature. The permit to export the water was denied, so they couldn't sell it to a coal slurry outfit. Well, what happens next? The water goes on down to South Dakota. And now they're talking about pumping it back into Wyoming—at a tremendous cost.

Logical decisions about this thing were impossible, because there was so much emotion. But it should have been possible to do hydrological studies and determine flow and divvy it up.

And the Little Big Horn people were going to build some storage to reserve some water for the cities, if the cities wanted to tap on the pipeline, at a pretty good rate. But they didn't get to do it. Well, now the Little Big Horn people have come back to the state of Wyoming with a $600 million deal, and they're saying, "Hey, we want some help developing this thing." The state is probably going to do it, which means the taxpapers will end up paying for the project after all, and in the meantime the water goes down the river to South Dakota and they pump it back.

I don't want to see us arguing over whose water is whose. Interstate water fights cost all of us. We fight with Colorado and Nebraska; we fight with Montana. The attorneys are getting rich, but they're not generating another drop of water. People need to look at all the costs involved.

For instance, in our fight to block construction of the Missouri Basin Power Project's Laramie River Power Station, there were many important issues—water was the big one, of course—but we were often forced to spend almost all of our time developing our credibility, with very little time left over for the issues. When we went down to the Public Service Commission hearing, for example, we, the Laramie River Conservation Council, had to spend a day and a half trying to prove our standing as parties in the hearing.

We had two young lawyers from Sheridan representing us; the MBPP had fifteen lawyers. Finally one of our lawyers, Tom Toner, jumped up and said: "Hey, just a minute; look around in here. Fifteen lawyers, and only one of them is from Wyoming. And you're talking about *our* standing!" Well, that helped to turn it around, but it was after a day and a half of arguments. What a waste of time and money.

I suppose we'd do a lot of things differently, if we had to

do it again. For one thing, we didn't know all that much about fighting a battle for public opinion. Folks thought the project was going to bring an absolute bonanza to this community, and they were scared to death that we were trying to kill that.

Well, it wasn't the tremendous bonanza they expected. Some of the local business people did fairly well, and during construction, the project helped keep local young men and women from migrating away in search of jobs. But there weren't many long-term local residents out there on the permanent workforce.

The boom associated with building the plant is gone; now it's the withdrawal and we're off the fix. We've had problems that were foreseen and might have been avoided.

From the point of view of someone in agriculture, living outside the town itself, we subsidized the project to a great extent because of the artificial inflation—there was inflation all over the country, of course, but ours was accelerated here by the effects of the project. It cost us a lot of money in that respect, and it cost us some of our suppliers: they went out of business. It also cost us the inconvenience of having to compete with an overloaded service sector, which was overloaded partly because it couldn't get the help it needed to deal with increased demand for services. For a period of four years it was really tough to get help at any price. The good agricultural help went out to work on the project, or in the service sector.

But it didn't cost us as much as it cost the town of Wheatland itself. The town is really paying through the nose now, because when this started, the town of Wheatland had no debt, and the city tax was very low. Basically all the streets were paved and water service was really cheap. Some places were metered and some weren't. Garbage collection used to be free, twice a week. The city had its own little electric power plant.

It marked up the price of electricity from time to time and that paid for paving the streets, for the parks, and for running the town generally.

In order to take care of the boom, MBPP built, with the town's approval, the Black Mountain trailer housing project, and it was probably the right thing to do. But the town had to increase the size of the sewer system all the way through town, and that meant tearing up about two and a half miles of street to do that. When they pulled the streets up, of course, they had to go back and repave them. They had to run water lines out there and electricity, and in order to do that they had to put in a new substation. To get water they had to drill new wells and put up a new water tower.

They did some of this with grant money, but the town is on the line for a tremendous amount of debt—and it's more than a matter of money. During the construction period, Wheatland changed a tremendous amount. In two years, the town more than doubled in size and attitudes changed about shopping and about recreation. It used to be that a lot of the social life in Wheatland was folks from the country dropping into bars to have a drink. It's gotten to where a lot of people won't do that anymore, and the prices in town have become so high that a lot of the local folks have started trading out of town. At the same time the merchants discovered they had to be more careful about charge accounts. There was not the tight little community feeling that there used to be.

I'm not saying that it isn't swinging back the other way, now that this boom has tapered off, but the community has changed. It's something you can't always put your finger on, but it's there. The records of the Southeast Mental Health Center office here and the sheriff's calls and police calls verify that. Alcoholism, violence, depression, and divorce are all way up, among the long-time residents. I believe that's because having more people created more stress for everyone.

These problems are tapering off some, I'm sure, but not as much as you would think, because we went into a general recession in this country at about the same time that this project peaked. Consequently, a lot of the people who would normally have pulled out and headed for the next job—found there were no jobs to go to. So they stayed here and went on unemployment and kept their kids in school here.

You lose community stability. People talk about how they used to know everyone in Wheatland and now they walk downtown and they don't know a soul. When our twins were in the fifth grade, we discovered at the end of the school year that there had been a sixty percent turnover in their class. This is one of the things you can't quantify. Sure, you can go into a hearing and argue for more school rooms, more teachers, more athletics. You can throw dollars at these things and get them done, but you can't quantify what happens to the quality of education when you have this kind of turnover.

Back in 1974 when the Laramie River plant was in the early planning and permit stage, several of us got together and tried to figure out what to do, and organized what became the Laramie River Conservation Council. We decided to have a big public meeting, to try to get the Wheatland community and the rest of Platte County aware of the pros and cons of this big proposed power project, and some way or another I got trapped into being chairman of the deal and never got rid of the job.

So we held the meeting and about 300 people showed up. We had a panel, with a legislator from Gillette and a fellow from Rock Springs to talk about their problems with development booms, and a representative from the power company and a moderator. Everybody was given time to speak and a chance to rebut, and then there were questions from the audience. It got people talking and they all had opinions when it was over—but I'm not sure it convinced anyone that the project wouldn't be a blessing.

Small towns have a "have-not" syndrome. People think that because they live in a small town, they're deprived. They think if something big comes in, it has to be better. I remember one fellow here in Wheatland—somebody who doesn't share that view—saying sarcastically to me after the meeting:

"Well, you know, maybe if this thing comes in, and it's successful, then we could be as successful as Cheyenne. That would be great. And if it's really successful, we could be like Denver! And the epitome of success would be to be like New York City!"

Unfortunately, most people didn't share that skepticism. But in the course of going through various hearings, some of us began to work together for the first time. Our members belonged to several different water organizations—the Wheatland Irrigation District and the Middle Laramie River Water Users and the Lower Laramie River Water Users and the Upper Laramie River Water Users—and for the first time in almost a hundred years of water history in the Laramie River, we were all sitting on the same side of the table for a change, instead of fighting among ourselves.

It all came to a head, finally, after the state of Nebraska filed suit against the project. The plant was already under construction by then—I suppose they had the first unit a fourth of the way up, and they were building the dam. Nebraska sued because they had decided that this plant was going to use some water that legally belonged to them. They had a variety of hydrological and other studies and concluded that the dam was going to considerably reduce the flow in the North Platte River.

That's when the wildlife people got involved. They joined

the suit because they decided that if the Platte River flow was reduced, it would deteriorate the habitat of the whooping crane. Some other folks got into the suit on basically the same basis—that the project would deteriorate the water fowl habitat, and so forth. The point being that less water means less habitat.

In terms of public opinion here, it hurt us to get the whooping cranes involved. It's very unfortunate that it took the Endangered Species Act for anyone to get a hook, or a lever, on the water issue. The water issue should have been decided on water, not on the Endangered Species Act; but that was the hook. Basin had failed to consider the downstream effects and had ignored everything beyond the state line. They ignored the whooping crane habitat, and when the whooping cranes were brought into the suit, that was the hook that finally got an injunction and actually stopped construction on the dam for a week or so. And boy, that's when things started happening. For the first time, Basin Electric wanted to talk to us. I mean they were ready to negotiate, and we wound up with a settlement.

The problem was that there were so many downstream parties involved in that suit. Many people still believe that those of us here unwittingly helped Nebraska acquire more water; but our point was that Basin needed a certain amount of water to run their plant, yet they were guaranteeing downstream flow rates in an effort to get Nebraska off their back. The water could only come from one place—from our watershed, which was our traditional water supply. Our interest in that case was to try to limit Basin from letting any more water go downstream than was necessary and from expanding the plant beyond the reasonable water supply. For whatever it's worth, we succeeded in limiting the size of the power plant by limiting the amount of water it could use.

But there's no way to explain how contorted these water issues can be on a project. I imagine that the local agricultural community spent over $100,000 on legal fees and expert witnesses and whatnot just to maintain the status quo—that is, not to gain any new water supply but just to save what we already had. Supposedly, when you've got senior water rights, you're protected by law, but that's just a smokescreen; it's not true unless you go into a hearing on equal terms. The sponsors of a multi-million-dollar project come in with plans and proposals and expert witnesses and all the legal help they need. To rebut them costs money. Protecting water rights is expensive, and it's going to get tougher and tougher.

Given the energy resources in this area, there's no question that there's going to be continuing, tremendous pressure to use our land and water—especially water—in connection with developing those energy resources. We need to be able to put the burden of proof on the entity that wants to use or divert water. We've been trying to do that, but we haven't been successful because we need some legislative changes. As things stand, they can simply take the position that they aren't going to hurt anybody, and then the burden is on us to prove that they are.

I believe there needs to be a way to take a more objective look at plant siting decisions. I still feel that the Laramie River power plant would make sense for one unit. The rest of it should have been over on the Missouri River somewhere, because that's where the participants are—the consumers, the load center, and the money. It doesn't make sense to use two hundred megawatts of this plant for the city of Lincoln, Nebraska, and there's another group of cities and towns that tap probably a fourth of its capacity or more and they're all located right along the banks of the Missouri.

It would have made more sense to put this plant at their alternate site—Pierre, South Dakota—and load Wyoming coal on unit trains and send it 150 or 200 miles to that location. There's no question that they had the water supply there. They just didn't want to pay the freight rates to the railroad.

The fight against the plant demonstrated, too, the need for better planning on the part of the companies building these projects. In order to get the attention of a behemoth, you have to keep raising every embarrassing issue you can think of. Our primary issue was water, but we were still interested in social issues—the impact on our schools, for example—and in environmental issues. We insisted that the plant be equipped with scrubbers, for example. Basin was unhappy about putting scrubbers on at all, but the support of the local population was overwhelming. They wanted the plant, but they wanted it clean. They didn't want dirt coming out of the stacks. That was a popular issue.

Well, they built the first two units with wet scrubbers. I've forgotten now just how much water a wet scrubber requires, but it's substantial. Then the Nebraska agreement limited their water supply, and they squawked and yelled and carried on because they wouldn't have enough water to put a wet scrubber on the third unit. But they went ahead and put a dry scrubber on it. And guess what has happened? The dry scrubber works better and more reliably and requires fewer maintenance people. But we won't get a consulting fee from Basin, even though we forced them to improve the design of the plant; and we won't get any thanks for pressuring them into changing the design of the dam, either. The base was unstable—sitting on 150 feet of unconsolidated sand and gravel—and they weren't going to do anything about. Even if the dam didn't let go, if it were to leak substantially it would destroy their water supply.

One thing you learn from something like this is that it's imperative for the existing water users to stop this fighting among the different groups and then to go on and stop the states fighting among themselves. If the point is to try to protect agricultural water, you can't let state lines get in the way.

Another thing you need is a pretty thick skin. They put the squeeze on some of our members at the bank; in fact, they called my notes. I had to change banks. Fortunately I was able to change banks locally—they didn't all act together—but that kind of pressure made it difficult for us to get people to stand up and voice their opnions. Frequently people would say they believed in what we were doing and they would help us, but didn't want their names put on it. They would just give us a check. We needed money and we were grateful for any kind of support, but we needed people to speak up, too.

A lot of efforts were made to discredit us. The local newspaper, for example, was in favor of the power plant; it meant a lot of advertising revenue, because there were more little businesses around town. So it was really difficult for us to get our message across. To take one example, when the town was getting ready to sign a contract on a loan to build the new housing subdivision, I wrote a letter to the editor, pointing out that when the boom tapered off and the subdivision emptied out there might not be enough revenue to pay off the loan. It was supposed to be paid off by tax fees—monthly fees on the water and sewer and so on—and they might have trouble if there weren't enough people using those services to generate the revenue. Basin had guaranteed the loan; most people had heard that, but what they didn't know was that Basin would guarantee it only if every other method of paying it off had been exhausted. First the town would have to jack its tax levies up to the limit, to make good on those notes.

Well, I pointed this out in my letter to the editor. The facts had been spelled out in a hearing in Cheyenne, but the editor called me and asked if I wanted to change the letter—said he didn't know if he could print it or not, and didn't have time to check it. He called me on a Tuesday morning and his deadline was Tuesday noon. The paper came out Wednesday. He had a front-page rebuttal by Basin to my letter.

As for getting other press coverage, one of our toughest problems was that we were naive politically and naive in terms of public relations. We spent half our time trying to convince people we weren't just a bunch of rabid environmentalists and just out to stop the power plant for the fun of it. Probably the worst thing we could have done was to call ourselves the Laramie River Conservation Council. The name just carried a connotation, and people kept coming up with the wildest ideas —that we were a front for the Sierra Club, things like that. We spent a lot of time trying to explain to people who we were and what we were doing.

This was the first time I'd done anything of this kind. It was absolutely the furthest thing from my interests, to get involved in this thing. I would probably not do it again, because when you get into something like this, you put everything else aside. It's about all you get done, and I just can't afford that.

When all is said and done, I think the health of this community is still going to depend on the health of the agricultural community. They've been trying to draw some more light industry in, to fill some gaps—to fill up the housing—which is fine, but I don't think anyone has any real optimism about that.

Agriculture is in real trouble, and in a little town like this, it is really the financial base for the local banks and businesses. It's the first time in my life where I've seen everything so bad. In years past, cattle might be bad but the wheat would be good, or the sugar beets, or the beans, or *something*. But this is the first time I've ever seen every commodity selling way below production cost. And what that means is that the banker isn't seeing the repayment of loans that he needs. If he has a sugar-beet man in trouble, he doesn't have a cattle rancher in there paying his note off. It's a tough situation.

And it's beyond the control of the community; it's a nation-wide problem. Our whole economy is not going to straighten out until we get the agricultural economy straightened out.

I don't think people realize that there are only three places where new wealth is generated. The folks downtown here didn't realize it, and they should have. You generate new wealth in fishing, minerals, and agriculture and that's considering timber as part of agriculture. Those are the only areas where new wealth is generated. I'm not sure how the economists figure this out, but they claim that every agricultural dollar brought into a small town will generate seven more dollars in trade.

I don't think the Agriculture Department in Washington has much control over the situation. It's an economic situation, and I think the Federal Reserve Board has more to say about what happens to farmers than Secretary Block does. And the State Department kills us with these on-again, off-again grain embargoes that make us an unreliable trading partner. We've shut off the Russians and the Japanese and whoever we felt like, just to keep food cheap in this country.

Unfortunately, it isn't keeping food cheap. At the production end, commodities are at a historical, all-time low, when you factor in inflation. But that's not so at the retail end, where there's a tremendous amount of slippage. Right now I can sell a fat heifer for grade and choice cuts at 90 cents, maybe 89 cents a pound, and that's the price hanging in the cooler. At retail, the average cut is over $2.50—that's what's wrong.

At our end, when you adjust for inflation, we're selling as cheap as we were in the bottom of the Depression, but we have capitalization costs they didn't have then. My great-grandfather, my grandfather and my dad did a great job, but they had some advantages. They had really cheap labor, and they had free land, in some cases. My great-grandfather started free. It was still almost free when my dad took over, and there were literally no energy requirements, because labor was so cheap. They had no equipment either. We got our first truck on the ranch during the war, in about 1943 or 1944, when I was in high school.

My great-grandfather came from Michigan, initially. When he was twelve, he went to Denver with a bull team—just out and back on a trip. Then, when he married, he moved to Nebraska and had a little farm there. Then they decided to move to Colorado and wound up working west of Fort Collins in an old mining town called Teller City. It was a silver boom town, and when the silver played out, they left and moved to Laramie and then out here on the headwaters of Duck Creek, where they squatted a couple of places and built a shack. Then they would sell their improvements and move and do it again.

After that, my great-grandfather got an itch to go to California, and they threw all their stuff in a wagon and went. They were out there for about two years, in the 1880s. When they came back they settled on the Big Laramie River and homesteaded. My grandfather started putting a ranch together in 1887; then my dad added to it, and eventually he sold it. I had to start over—I'm not on the old home place, because I didn't inherit any land.

Before I got into ranching I worked in Colorado about fifteen years, in construction and ski areas and speculating on land. We came back here and started buying some farms in 1973 because living in the recreational areas of Colorado wasn't the real world. We didn't want to bring the kids up in that kind of atmosphere, and then I've always had a crazy idea that agriculture is my interest and my background.

We've put together a little over 6,000 acres. It's pretty tough to talk about further expansion right now: everybody's pulling their necks in, trying to survive. Nothing is appreciating any more. Operating expenses are eating us up, and unless commodities get back to where they were paying their way, it's going to be hard to stay alive, if you've got any debt at all.

I'm still trying to put our operation together. When we took this place over, it didn't have much for buildings, the fences were in bad shape and the ditches and gates, which hadn't been used for four or five years, were unusable. When we decided to build a house we had to put a road in and a power line and a telephone line, and rebuild the sprinkler irrigation system and fix every headgate and clean every ditch.

Of course at the same time we were still running a feed lot and farming too, over on the flats. What I'd hoped to do was get all these farms sold and moved over here in one place, creating a pretty compact, efficient operation. But a lot of work still has to be done before we get to that.

We don't have this ranch stocked with cattle yet—it was overgrazed when we bought it, so I wasn't in any hurry. Last summer we had about 400 yearlings and a couple hundred head of mother cows. We wintered about 200 cows, and the calves we moved to the feed lot. I think if we get into shape, it would run 500 mother cows and carry most of the calves and yearlings. It has the potential, let's put it that way.

Given the fact that we're starting this late in life, we may not have the energy. I'm forty-nine now. That's old when you start doing things it normally takes a couple of generations to do. We'd like to get it done as soon as possible. I'd hope that in another two years, we'd have everything put together.

We're not typical of what's happening in ranching. Generally the ranches keep getting bigger and they're more likely to be absentee-owned. My great grandfather and grandfather ended up working 24,000 acres. That ranch is now owned by an absentee. They summer some cattle there, with a manager taking care of them, but then, about the end of September, they pull the cattle out and lock it up and nobody is there the rest of the year. That's what has happened to a lot of these places. With some, the owner builds a house on the ranch and comes there quite a bit of the time, but he doesn't oversee the operation himself, because his business interests are elsewhere. The ranch shelters him from taxes.

What used to be my cousin's place has become the "Flying X," a kind of a club deal, where they sell memberships—they're dividing that ranch into 2,000 memberships, and each member gets a place to park a trailer house.

But I don't know where you draw the line on corporate ownership. We get a lot of Nebraska television, and I just saw where Nebraska passed a constitutional amendment prohibiting corporate ownership. I don't know the details, but I think that that would have to be done very carefully, or it could backfire down the road a ways. I could see it strangling initiative. If we wanted to incorporate my family and I wouldn't want to find ourselves barred from doing that.

I suppose you could get around that by very carefully defining "corporate," but you get into having to close every loophole and then it gets out on the floor of the legislature and who knows what will happen. Sometimes we're accused of being too conservative, but really if it's not in too bad of shape you ought to leave it alone. Yes, the money gets poured in here by people looking for tax write-offs, but I don't care who it is, nobody's going to go on forever without something.

Look at the Hunts. They had literally millions of acres. Everywhere you looked, they had big ranches. They got in trouble and they dumped it and took off. Look at the Gates (of Gates Rubber)—they thought it would be a hot deal to get into agriculture on a corporate scale, and they went out to Colorado and drilled all those wells and put in all those sprinklers for irrigation, and lost their shirts. They only lasted about five years. And, boy, that land went back out on the market and now it's all spread out among family farmers.

I'm not sure you have to prohibit large-scale corporate agriculture. Economics may take care of it, or part of it, anyway. With the complexity of irrigated agriculture, whatever you gain in economy of scale, you lose in the inefficiency of your people when you get that big. In the long run, the modest-sized family farm has a future, but it's the short run that worries me.

Moreover, while I am convinced that the medium-sized family unit can compete with corporate farms in the production end, particularly in irrigated agriculture, there is a trend toward corporate control of the markets. If multinational corporations continue acquiring monopolies of the marketing structure and the goods and services required for agriculture, the small- to medium-sized producer is finished.

Jim Murry

MONTANA HAS BEEN ONE OF THE MOST HIGHLY UNIONIZED STATES IN AMERICA. The trends in our economy—the apparent death of the copper industry, and what's happening with the Milwaukee Railroad, and the timber industry—indicate that some changes need to be made in the Montana labor movement. But we have the ability to hang in, over the long haul; that's part of our tradition and our history. I'm sure that the Montana labor movement is going to be there, because of our determination and because we play such an important role in this state—its history, its economics, its politics, its society and its government. We're not going to let our friends go under—the family farmers, the coalitions we've formed with church groups and among low-income people and women's groups, the Democratic party, and people in the environmental movement—and they feel the same way about us, I believe, as we do about them.

We're kind of like an extended family. It's different from other states in the region. There's a lot of good folks in Idaho like in Montana—you can hardly tell us apart—but I'm not sure that people in the other western states—Oregon, Washington, Wyoming, the Dakotas—would have had the patience to

Jim Murry, as the executive secretary of the Montana AFL-CIO, operates the most powerful labor organization in the Northern Rockies. He was first elected to that position in 1968 and has been reelected seven times. He was born in Billings and grew up in a strongly pro-labor family in Laurel, a major oil refining center near Billings. He now lives in Helena.

do what we've done. We've taken seventy-five to one hundred years to build the coalitions we have today.

The coalitions in Montana have come together, not so much because of structure, but because of the personalities of

121

the people in this state. Family farmers and workers have gotten together to talk about their problems and to act together politically, in the legislature, with poor people and minority groups; and you see a closer relationship with the Indian community in Montana. If people in other states expect to put that together in a year, it's not going to happen, because you don't quickly develop the kind of confidence in each other that we have here.

Montana is unique. You look around: we're an island here. There are states with right-to-work laws bordering us, and states with very regressive tax systems. There are good, strong labor movements in those states and good coalitions, but they're not like Montana's.

It's been a part of me all my life. As a kid I grew up listening to this same kind of talk with every meal, and we talked about it before we went to bed at night. There was always a struggle; we always had a mission. It was our family against the world.

I was born in 1935 and grew up in Laurel, about fifteen miles west of Billings. It was a tough old town: railroad repair shops, the refinery, trains coming and going all day and all night. My dad was a trade unionist. He organized a local union that I'm still a member of today: Pioneer Local 2-443 of the Oil, Chemical and Atomic Workers Union.

I was always exposed to progressive thinking, because my folks were involved in both the trade union movement and the farm co-op movement. So I grew up with the feeling that we were really brothers and sisters in that whole larger movement.

That's a feeling that is very pronounced in the state of Montana, because that old farmer-labor coalition goes back to the 1860s, immediately following the first constitutional convention in Helena, when a bunch of farmers and workers got together in Butte and concluded that they'd been screwed in that convention; they really didn't get a chance to participate, because the vested interests drafted the constitution. So Montana has historically had a very meaningful farm-labor coalition.

I got my first union card when I was fifteen, joining Local 98 of the Laborers' Union in Billings, and I've been a lifelong member of the Farmers Union. I pay dues today and have been a member there longer than I've been a member of the trade union movement.

My parents had a farming and ranching background. My mother's maiden name was Cowan; her people came from Georgia and Kentucky, and they were some of the first people in the Gallatin Valley. The Cowans were part of the Georgians who discovered gold over on Last Chance Gulch. My dad's ancestors came up into Wyoming from Texas, with the cattle. And on both sides of my family, we're part Indian: Cherokee, Sioux, and some Blackfeet. People think an Irishman by the name of Jim Murry must have been imported from New York or Chicago, so it always kind of tickles me to talk about my background, because we've been here a long, long while.

As I said, my dad was instrumental in organizing the oil workers' union, and I worked in the refinery in Laurel for ten years and became active in Local 2-443. But the first time I ran for the presidency of that union, I got four votes out of 178. That's still a record in that local. It was a good thing, because it taught me something about humility.

It was a very militant local. The old-timers were articulate and well read. My dad had a fourth-grade education, but he read all the time. So then I came along, and I was a hell-raiser; I'd get drunk, get into barroom brawls, and get thrown in jail. Well, the other members of the local did that sort of stuff too, but you can't run a local union from a bar stool. That is sacred to us and I had to learn about that the hard way. There are no easy lessons in the labor movement.

I came here to Helena in 1966, to work as the state AFL-CIO political education director; then I became the executive secretary of the Montana AFL-CIO in 1968.

Arlene and I were married in 1954, when we were both nineteen, and after bumming around for two years, we came back to Montana, in 1956. We've been here about twenty years now, and I guess it wasn't until we bought our second home that I finally resigned myself to the idea that we probably weren't going to be leaving.

Four generations of our family lived in the same house in Laurel at the same time. The roots were very deep there, and even now, some friends ask me when I am going to come home: "You've been gone almost twenty years—aren't you going to come home pretty quick?"

I have very strong ties in Montana. I've had some opportunities to leave and work elsewhere in the labor movement, but there's something that won't let me go. This region is such an important place to be. I would always justify not leaving on the basis of, "Well, we've got this crisis that we have to take care of." Of course, when that was taken care of, there were plenty more coming up. Now I'm forty-eight years old, and I think there's no place like it and no people like the people here.

Drive down the interstates and you can see people sleeping under these overpasses. Go to the Safeway warehouse here, and you will see people going through the garbage dumpsters every night, looking for food for their families. Our economic problems are being magnified by what Ronald Reagan is doing to us, and it's bringing the labor movement back together and creating coalitions. For a while we kind of grew apart, because

we didn't have to be together. People moved away from that us-against-the-world point of view when times got pretty good for a while, but now we're getting back to it.

I spend a lot of time going to schools, talking to people about the labor movement, and they'll say, "Why do you do this? To make a lot of money, to drive a nice car? Is that why?" In other words, "Are you like a public relations man for a corporation?"

I tell them I've been asked that question in different ways all my life. When I was a little kid in Laurel, people would ask, "Why are you boys always defending the labor movement?"

Well, when I was a little kid, there wasn't a union at the plant where my dad worked, and things were pretty tough there. For one thing, not many people retired there; they died instead—got killed on the job or suffered heart attacks or got cancer. And my dad didn't have any time to spend with us. He worked long hours, every day, seven days a week. Then they formed the union, and there was more job security for him, and he could afford to be a better husband and father. We got to go to some ballgames—not a lot of them, but some—and we went fishing together a few times, ate in a restaurant a couple of times, things like that. And life was really a lot better. We never did get rugs on the floor, but life was better and we felt better about each other.

I'll tell you, I'm a trade unionist because the American trade union movement—even with all the mistakes we've made —has done more to bring about needed social change than any other group in America. There isn't anybody with a better track record than we have, and it's pretty neat to be a part of that.

I know that during good times we have a tendency to get pretty laid back. I think it's human nature to get wrapped up in caring about material things, and there's nothing so wrong with the idea that everyone should be able to live decently, to eat well, to have a nice home, to send their kids to good schools—God, we've fought for those things all our lives. That's what the movement has been about. But when the going gets pretty easy we get laid back. We become a little insensitive.

Historically the labor movement responds best when times are toughest. The labor movement is responding like that now. We're not 100 percent in agreement with each other about which way to go or what we're going to do. We argue all the time, and that's a great thing about the labor movement. But I know this: the American trade union movement is going to be in the forefront of leading this country back on track again, and there will be a lot of folks who won't give the labor movement the credit it's going to deserve.

This is a huge state. You spend a lot of time on the road, and in order to get together—to communicate, to build coalitions—you have to be willing to go maybe four or five months without a day off. Sometimes it'll take all day Saturday and all night to get to a meeting on Sunday, to talk with friends.

I guess that's where the confidence in each other comes from. We have a pretty good idea of who our friends are. Within our circle of friends we have differences, but we know we're not going to hurt each other. Up there in the legislature we may disagree on an environmental issue but we know we're not adversaries. We might disagree, but we know the importance of keeping that unit together; that makes Montana unique. But I think it goes back to what I was saying before about building coalitions. Coalitions turn on personalities. Forming a coalition with the idea that you scratch my back and I'll scratch yours doesn't work. Coalitions work because you like each other.

Extremism begets extremism. We've had some pretty tough battles with corporate Montana. A lot of corporations operating in Montana have been owned by out-of-state companies, and Montana has been a place to exploit. These corporations tried to hurt us. They treated us badly. They abused workers; they weren't very responsible to communities; and they came in and said, "We're going to do this, and you take what we're willing to give you."

And we said, "No, that isn't good enough. We're going to fight."

So that established a very combative kind of environment here. We still have it. God, we're just hell for confrontation here, all over the state, at every level. You see it in the schools. I remember playing American Legion baseball, playing for the state championship, and we took second place; and the Laurel Legion wouldn't feed us after the game, because we took second place. They sent us to take first place. We went to win.

It's not a hobby. We don't fight because it's a fashionable thing to do. We believe all of this, with all our hearts, and we go to win. In a place like Montana, you don't have many people with the kinds of high incomes you find in some other parts of the country. It's kind of like Israel: you find a lot of people who are pretty much the same. So we don't get soft and forget; we don't allow that to happen to us.

I don't care if it's a ballgame or what: we go there to win. When we go to the legislature, we don't just go there to play the game. We work very hard, seventeen to eighteen hours every day of that session. We put everything else aside and we go to win. Anyone who grew up in Butte or Anaconda, or on the south side of Laurel, knows that.

Do I think the fight is still against the corporations? Well, if we'd had this discussion four or five years ago, I might have

struggled with the answer to that question. But we just had Atlantic Richfield come in and buy the old Anaconda Company, and they treated people very badly. They just shut that company down, and they sent the ore to Japan to be refined and smelted and shipped back. People in Butte and Anaconda are very upset about that. And we saw the Milwaukee Railroad shut down because of mismanagement where hundreds of people in Montana lost their jobs.

The economic development committee that Governor Schwinden appointed interviewed the business community and concluded that we ought to have a sales tax to replace the corporate income tax. They said we should have an appointed public service commission, because ours had too much of a consumer bias, and said we should have right-to-work in Montana because the Montana labor movement was too goddam combative. And if we didn't do these things, we wouldn't be able to develop our economy, and so on. Well, we fought a hell of a battle against the corporate boys, and we won.

Looking ahead, we're very concerned about the role of the federal government in Montana, and in the region, because we've been very dependent on the federal government for everything from building highways to feeding hungry people to making sure we have a decent education program for our kids. We were getting back from Washington about $3.75 for every dollar we spent in taxes. That was good for us, but it was also a good investment for the federal government. Well, that income source for the state has dried up. All of a sudden, more and more responsibility has been imposed on the state, but the state legislature is very reluctant to raise taxes because there has been a political tone established that says the problem is too much government.

That's the paradox. Those legislators are caught in it. By refusing to pass tax increases to make up for the cuts in federal programs, they pass the responsibility on to the local communities. I don't know how far that's going to go, but if this trend continues, you can see that the big drain is going to be at the local level: the schools, the parks, other community resources. It's going to have a tremendous impact.

The other thing we're concerned about is that we're losing our heavy industry in this state. The mining industry is coming down. We're losing jobs in the mines and the smelters, and jobs in the railroads and in the timber industry, which has played such a key role in the development of Montana's economy. A lot of marginal operators have gone under during this recession. They're not coming back. We'll see fewer and fewer companies controlling that part of our economy.

We hear a lot about the reindustrialization of America. Well, that's going to be a long time coming. I guess I don't see new smelters being built from the ground up, because we've exported our steel mills, thanks to the multinational corporations. So, for the immediate future at least, I think that in Montana we're looking at fewer and fewer of those heavy-industry jobs that pay so well. We're looking at more lower-paying, less secure jobs.

We're not happy with that. We don't mind Montana's resources being used; we've never opposed that. What we do oppose is the total exploitation of the state, and the abandoning of workers and communities when hard times hit the economy. That's what corporations do; now the federal government is doing it too.

We support the current emphasis on in-state investment of state funds, and we hope it will be a major factor in helping the state's economy grow by maybe 10 percent. The "Build Montana" program that went through the legislature, I-95 kinds of things (an initiative targeting the investment of Montana money to create jobs in the state) has given us an opportunity to do some exciting things by involving the whole community in some decision making that has been pretty much reserved for the financial community in the past.

We think that's a good idea. But, in the final analysis, it's what goes on in Washington, D.C., that determines whether the commerce of this country moves again. If we continue with the economic concepts of the Reagan administration we're going to continue to be, not only in trouble here, but held out to be exploited and used by out-of-state interests as we have been in the past. That's what we have to be on guard against.

When you have a lot of people out of work and struggling to provide for their families, sometimes they feel pretty well locked into accepting whatever they get. They don't see any alternative, but I see the role of the labor movement as one of creating alternatives. We're going to have to work very hard in our organizing activities, not just in convincing workers of the necessity of having a union, but in bringing together all these coalitions we've talked about, and in getting support all over the state and the region for alternatives to Reagonomics.

Lee Metcalf was a master, an absolute master, at that. He saw the necessity of coalitions. He knew there was no single group, no two groups, strong enough to fight those forces.

If you go over to Butte, or to Anaconda, you'll hear the unions being held responsible for Arco selling out. The company has admitted that that wasn't the reason, but they do a subliminal kind of thing that helps people draw the conclusion that somehow it *is* the reason. There's nothing unusual about that—it's a political tactic that corporations have always used—but it works if you let your coalitions get slack.

It has to do with political tone, in an area and in the nation.

During the 1980 elections, a political tone was set in this nation that somehow government was bad, and that it had been playing too great a role in our lives, and that without that interference, business would boom and everything would be fine. And that tone also said that we had too many folks on welfare, folks who didn't want to work, and if we would just let the free market work, everything would be all right.

A lot of people bought into that, and the conservative political community began succeeding in isolating people in the progressive community. All of a sudden, environmentalists weren't liked. The polls show that everyone in the country is concerned about the environment, right? But the polls also show that no one likes an environmentalist. How can that be? A bunch of folks succeeded in systematically isolating the environmental movement and painting all environmentalists with the same brush: they're irresponsible. And sometimes environmentalists did things that contributed to that image.

The same thing happened to women's groups, with the leadership of those groups sometimes helping to reinforce that image; and the image of poor people was perceived to be that they wanted to be that way. A few of us in the labor movement said: "We're going to be in big trouble if they're successful doing this, because they're going to be doing the same thing to unions."

A few years ago there were all kinds of labor-management groups getting together around the country. You remember the pitch: We have so much in common, we should be working together. You don't see many of those groups meeting today. That's not any great surprise, is it? Because now the business community is working on isolating the trade union movement. That's how we get blamed for what's happened in Butte and Anaconda.

What we need to do is set a political tone of our own, through our coalitions and through working together. Our political tone says, for instance, that every kid gets a decent education. The trade union movement was at the very beginning of the campaign for universal public schools, something like 150 years ago, and the political tone that they helped set then was that kids should get to go to school, regardless of what their parents did for a living or where they went to church. There were good reasons for that campaign. Employers were using child labor in the mines and the mills. Older workers couldn't support their families. Child labor pitted children against fathers and mothers.

I didn't pay much attention to my kids for years because I was gone all the time and Arlene was raising them. Just last year I found out what it costs kids today to participate in school athletics, and I'm still very angry. A pair of basketball shoes costs about $75, and then the rest of the gear costs maybe another $35. So a kid up on Rodney Street—an Indian kid for instance—doesn't get to play ball. Only the sons and daughters of families like ours can play.

I'm upset about that, because I know that athletics provides a way out—a way out of the ghetto. It opened the way for a lot of my friends to go to college. They could not have gone any other way. If they worked really hard and disciplined themselves and played, despite broken hands and broken jaws and broken ribs, they could go to college.

The fight for access to education isn't over. And when we're looking to the future, it's that kind of problem we're looking at.

A lot of folks here are in a lot of trouble. Some people have lost their cars and their homes, people like the men and women who worked at the Evans Products Company plant in Missoula. Some of them have worked in the plants for twenty or twenty-five years, and they're forty-five or fifty years old now, and they were making maybe $25,000 to $30,000 a year, and all of a sudden they've lost their jobs and there's no place to go.

There's a misconception that there are no poor people in Montana. Well, there are, but Montanans are so proud, they don't like to admit they're poor. In fact, they don't even know they're poor. I didn't know I was a poor kid. We had an outdoor toilet, we didn't have a car, I walked a long way to school, but I thought we were pretty well off because my dad told me so. We didn't get to go on vacations because we never had the money, but we never admitted that. We were always going to go next year, or sometime in the future. We never did, but the whole family knew we were going to some day.

During one legislative session, when I didn't get home until 10:00 or 11:00 at night, I'd get five to seven calls a week. People would give their names. "You don't know me," they'd say, "and I don't like to bother you at home, but I'm really in a lot of trouble, and I don't know what I'm going to do. I worked at such-and-such a place and I was never on unemployment compensation, but the plant shut down and I'm laid off. We've lost everything, and I don't know how I'm going to feed my kids." It would just make my heart hurt. It was a last-ditch effort, asking me if there was something I could do to help. It was always a very confidential kind of thing. They were too proud to admit, in public, what was happening to them, and I'd agonize over it.

Sometimes you pick up the newspaper and you see where somebody has committed suicide or killed somebody in his family. The suicide rate here has gone up, as well as spouse abuse and child abuse; and alcohol and drug problems have increased. There are mental and emotional health problems, and we'll feel the impact of this the rest of our lives.

We have a very deeply ingrained work ethic here where we say: "God won't like you if you don't work hard." It says you have to hurt a little to make it worthwhile. That's crazy, but that's the way we are. That's why I work as hard as I do, because I'm always paying back by working harder than anybody in the labor movement. I don't take days off. *That's* a puritanical work ethic. That's what it's all about; it's all about the south side of Laurel.

I don't know my kids very well, and that's a hard thing for a father to admit. One day we were standing on the deck and I said to my wife, "You know, I wonder what the hell's wrong with our kids?" She said "What do you mean?" I said, "Well, God, they've been exposed to senators and governors and legislators and people who are really deep thinkers who come to our house and talk. And the kids don't want to go to school. I don't understand that."

"You don't understand that?"

"No, I don't know why that is."

"My God!" she says. "All their lives they have been told, either directly or indirectly, that the only good people in the world are workers. You don't have a friend in this neighborhood. The fellow who lives over there—he's a retired military guy, and you tell the kids he's weird. And over here's another one who's the head of a state agency and you always fought with him because you said he didn't have a social conscience, and you tell the kids that." She went around the whole neighborhood that way, and I said, "God, you're right. Is that the reason for it?" And she said, "It certainly is. You know, you just made it very clear that it wouldn't be acceptable for them to be any other way. You've made them what they are."

And I'm not so sure they're happy with that. I did some things that may have stunted their growth. The work ethic that says you've got to hurt real bad—that's a crazy way to be. But I don't know what to do about it. That's the way I grew up.

I've thought about it. One day I dropped one of our boys off in front of the bank and there was a bunch of Indian kids hanging around there, and he says, "Hey, Dad, drive me around the corner." And I says, "Why's that?" and he says, "God, I get out here and I'm going to have to fight every one of those kids." And I said, "Why's that?" He says, "That's just the way it is. Drive around the corner!"

I got to thinking about that later. When I was a kid, I stood on the corner and beat the shit out of the kid who got out of the car, the kid whose father was influential in the community. But I never think of myself as being influential. I just don't think about that, or about being part of the political establishment of Montana. I'm kind of uneasy when people say that. Because I'm not a part of that. But I was the kid knocking the shit out of the kids who got out of the car. I have to conclude that I'll never get over being from the south side of Laurel.

Norman Guth

WHEN YOU TAKE A GROUP OF PEOPLE one hundred miles down the Salmon River, the "River of No Return," as it's called, there are a million things you have to think about. First is the equipment you need—good comfortable equipment. That's something that is pretty much in the eye of the beholder. Some guys want a trip to be an encounter with wilderness where death is a possible outcome, and they're out there to pit their abilities against nature. Comfort is something they just throw to the winds. We don't do that. We use all custom-made equipment that we've developed over the years.

We have a big boat with a forty-inch airtube. You sit in a comfortable chair, and the only time you get wet is when it rains. We fly the equipment in and set it up and have it all ready, so that the minute our people get there we're ready to load them on the boat and go.

Food is the next thing. You need sufficient provisions for thirty people for five or six days, and the facilities to preserve that food. That's another reason for our big boat; we can start out with a thousand pounds of ice. Our airplane load will be nothing but ice. Just that load of ice costs $300. You can go into

Norman Guth represents three generations of Idaho outfittters on the Salmon River working in the River of No Return Wilderness area. His parents, Howard and Doris, started the family business in the early 1940s. Norm grew up in the business and the family tradition entered its third generation in 1980 when his son Marty received his boatman's license and became a guide. The Guths guided President Jimmy Carter and his family down the Middle Fork of the Salmon during the Carter presidency. The Guths live in Salmon, Idaho.

town and buy it for $30, and that's all people think about—they don't think about getting it in there.

Once you get on the trip, you have to have some good help, good people who know the country and can talk intelligently with our guests. When we get in for the evening, my boys all

130

go change clothes. They get on a white shirt to cook supper, and we take a lot of pride in the food. We do all our cooking on mahogany and we serve green salads and home-fresh foods.

We try to feel each group out and do what they want to do. If one boatload of people wants to go hiking, they'll go. If you have elderly people who are not into hiking and climbing, you catch trout and take pictures. Everyone does his own thing. Having somebody who knows the country and its history and can talk about every little creek and where it heads is part of being able to give people a real thorough experience, not just a ride in a boat.

Then, when we get through the river, we have to get back, so we have somebody meet us with a bus, and we try to have it on time. When they get out at the end of the river run, my wife brings a lunch; as soon as lunch is over, they get on the bus. When they get back to Salmon, the airplane is there, waiting to take them to Boise or wherever they're going.

Howard Guth, my dad, started this outfitting business in the early forties. At that time he was working in a shipyard in Washington, and he came to Idaho to get back to the outdoors. His background had always been outdoors. In the early thirties he had a job in a mining camp here, hunting and fishing to furnish food for forty or fifty miners. In those days there were no limits on fish and game. That's how he got acquainted with this part of the country—hunting and fishing—and he loved it.

When he left the shipyard in 1942, he had a little money, but it didn't take him long to lose it in the dude business. He started guiding hunters and fishermen, backpacking into what was at that time the Primitive Area of the Salmon National Forest, which is not the same as the River of No Return Wilder-

ness. Then we bought the Middle Fork Lodge, on the Middle Fork of the Salmon, in 1953, and moved our operation there, and we started running the river—operating float trips as well as hunting trips.

I had the greatest childhood I think anybody could have. As soon as my brother Bill and I were old enough to go on the pack trips, we did. The first time I packed into the Middle Fork, I was about eight years old. I cannot believe the fishing that was there then! Our lives were just recreation year-round. We would hunt and fish all summer and ski all winter.

When we moved into the Middle Fork Lodge in 1953, the only way in and out of there was by air. I was a junior in high school, and I got a job at the airport in Burley so I could learn to fly. I was gas boy, and took my wages out in flying time. When I was a senior in high school, I had my own airplane. I didn't buy a car until I got married, when I was twenty-three years old, but I had an airplane before I was out of high school. It was a family necessity. Where we were, the only other way to get out was a two-day horseback ride, and in the winter you couldn't even do that.

The length of the season varies from year to year. If the ice goes out by the beginning of February, we'll work from then until the end of March doing steelhead fishing. Then there's a short period that I don't do anything, and then about the middle of April I start bear hunting. That carries me into the middle of May. In the middle of June, I'll start floating the Middle Fork, and I carry that right on through to September, when I just get right out of the float boat and into the jet boat and start steelhead fishing again until the beginning of December.

When we started to run the river in 1953, there were about three of us running it—Don Smith, Andy Anderson, and us. You never saw another soul running it.

It stayed pretty much that way until 1958, when the Forest Service built the road to Dagger Falls. The primary purpose of the road was the construction of a fish ladder at Dagger Falls, to help the salmon get over the falls to the spawning grounds. When they built the road, it was supposed to be for that purpose only, and it was to be kept closed off and chained; the only use was to be for maintenance of that fish ladder. They kept it that way for about two months; then the Forest Service opened the road and built a campground at Daggers Falls. Then they extended the road two or three miles further down the river to a big flat, and built a great big campground.

Before that, the use of the river was limited to a very short period of the year, when there was sufficient water flowing in from Dagger Falls or from Marsh Creek. As soon as they opened that road up, anybody with a rubber duckies and a paddle could get into the Middle Fork. By 1970 it got to where there were about thirty-two different companies running river trips, and quite a substantial number of private folks. The state took the first initiative to put some limitations on that, and the Idaho Outfitters Guide Licensing Board, of which I am now a member, put a moratorium on licensing new outfitters. That put a cap on the number of new outfitters that could run the river.

About 1972, the Forest Service said there were too many outfitters on the river. Well, what's new? So they decided they would limit it. They wanted to cut the number to twenty-six— a goal which, incidentally, has never been reached. Then they put limits on the number of trips we could take, and then on the number of people we could take. With thirty-two outfitters in business then when you divided it up, it worked out that we could run one trip every eight days. That didn't have much impact on a lot of outfitters, but it did on us.

I like solitude. I can't stand a whole lot of people and con-fusion. When we were put on a schedule, we had to combine groups. I didn't like that. Before, we'd have five different parties on the river, all on different schedules. The Forest Service rules and regulations tend to do that. You just can't have regulation without putting everybody into the same ticky-tacky box.

The problem really goes back to 1964, when the Forest Service interpreted the Wilderness Act and decided that an individual experience was worth more than a guided experience, and would be a more appropriate use of the wilderness. Since that time, it's just been one battle after another to try to maintain a rational outfitting industry.

They really want to do away with commercial services in the wilderness. Now, they won't say that. They'll say they recognize the need for those services, but time and again over the past twenty years we've had to really get out and scratch to salvage anything.

It's going to come to a head again soon, with the allocation system imposed on us now. You see, during the season we are only allowed forty-four percent of the use of the Middle Fork. The other fifty-six percent is reserved for private use, for the local resident here who gets a permit and goes down the Middle Fork. This is going to become a real sticky issue concerning the present and future value of tourism. If tourism is locked at the present level, or reduced, there's no future as far as diverse wilderness recreation is concerned.

We've had to battle the Forest Service over bidding. They wanted to put everything out on competitive bid and receive the highest "fair market value" for the wilderness, and they thought they would get it with a bid system, because lots of people would bid for access to the river. Well, many of the bidders turned out to be oil companies and other corporations that wanted private retreats.

We could see that we would have no future if we had to bid for our business. It's not like loggers bidding for timber rights; it would be the equivalent, in a sense, of having to put our sawmill up every year. I have an investment and buildings and airplanes and everything else that goes to support it, and if I lose it one time on a bid, I'm dead. I couldn't go to the bank and borrow money to tide me over until the next bidding opportunity.

But it's the allocation system that is going to determine whether wilderness recreation will grow and prosper in the future or start dying. Because there's a limit to what people can pay, and if you can't expand your business, it's going to go down.

Right now the bankruptcy rate in the outfitting business is really high. Guys get into the business and find out it's not as glamorous as it looks. It can be the greatest life in the world, but you have to put beans on the table. The expenses are so high that realizing a profit is really hard, and a lot of years we don't.

You'll never get the timber industry to admit it, but I think probably around eighty percent of the economy of the Salmon area depends on tourism. People just don't want to admit that tourism is as valuable to the local economy as it is. In 1980, I think it was, the timber industry got the Salmon Chamber of Commerce to pass a resolution opposing all wilderness—all

wilderness of any kind, anywhere! I told the Chamber they were just putting their saddle on a dying horse. Of course, since then, with the timber industry in a depression, we've seen the horse die.

The thing they couldn't believe was that all the timber in the River of No Return Wilderness Area would add only one percent to the total allowable Idaho cut. On a full-blown, "log it up" operation it would add about six months to the life of the timber industry.

I'm not one who wants to put the whole state of Idaho in the wilderness either. I think uses have to be balanced, and resources have to be preserved—used but not abused. I think the debate about the balanced use of public land has been a two-edged sword, good some ways and bad some ways. It's bad to focus the attention on it, because publicity, in some cases, causes as much degradation as the thing you were fighting would have caused.

It is necessary to preserve, by statute, some of these places, because if we don't they are going to be all logged and roaded and we are going to totally lose the wilderness environment. It's not just aesthetics, and it's not the best thing costwise, either. Many resources are dependent on wilderness. One of them getting a lot of attention right now is the anadromous fish resource. Here in Idaho we have literally thousands of miles of pristine spawning and rearing water for anadromous fish— fish that ascend rivers from the sea to spawn. We have a lot of problems *getting* them here—although most of the problems related to dams have been resolved.

We have the largest elk herd in the world here in these wilderness areas—the Selway, the Chamberlain—and that resource, in itself, draws a tremendous amount of income to this state. I don't have current figures, but back in 1980 when

I was testifying at the congressional wilderness hearings, one elk taken by a guided hunter was worth a little over $5,300 in direct income generated through outfitters. That didn't count the indirect spinoff, such as hotels and motels, bars, restaurants, airfare, gas, that sort of thing; this was just the income generated through outfitters divided by the number of animals taken.

A lot of people don't realize how many visitors come to float these rivers. About 400 to 500 people stay in Salmon every night during the floating season—in a town with a population of only about 3,000. They're coming off the main Salmon or going on, or coming off the Middle Fork or going on. More than 100 people will start out on each one of those rivers every day, in addition to the Selway, and that really brings a lot of outside income into the local economy.

Also, I think wilderness is like putting resources in the bank. Those resources can be withdrawn some day. You're not going to kid anybody into thinking that if the last tree is in wilderness, that just because there's a law that says you can't go get it, that's going to stop them. They're going to go open it up and go get that timber, minerals, gas, oil, whatever happens to be in there. The wilderness bill doesn't really prohibit those things; it postpones them. So I don't see wilderness as in any way anti-productive. It's not going to have a negative impact on the long-term economy, and I doubt that it will have a negative impact on the short-term economy.

The biggest reward I receive from the outfitting business certainly isn't the money, it's the enjoyment I get from seeing someone else really enjoy that backcountry. If I get a boatload of people who are really taken by the beauty, especially the Middle Fork Canyon, I understand that, because I just never go through that canyon that I'm not on a high. That is the *most* beautiful piece of country in the world.

Lynn Dickey

I'M A PRODUCT OF SMALL-TOWN WYOMING, and I'm a product of homesteaders. I have great-grandparents who moved out here from Minnesota and Iowa, and grandparents who came from Georgia. I've always felt the land in myself and always felt small-town Wyoming in myself. But those feelings haven't always been positive. When I left Buffalo, Wyoming to go to college, I was really ready to leave. I had no particular feeling of attachment. It only took me about six weeks in Illinois to recognize that something was missing. It's flat there, just *flat*. I was used to having the mountains next to me, and I started to have a feeling that if I looked inside myself I could see the Wyoming prairie, too. I still didn't plan to come back, but those things were a part of me.

I had an Uncle Lynn, whom I'm named after, who was a rancher in Gillette and who ran away from home and never finished high school. After several jobs as a ranch hand, he finally managed to lease some land and run a ranch. While I was away at college, he died of cancer, and it was a major blow. In some way, he and his ranching were a part of me, too; it's just that I didn't become aware of these things consciously

Lynn Dickey operates a bookstore in Sheridan, Wyoming, when she is not representing Sheridan County in the state legislature. She has worked as a lobbyist for the Powder River Basin Resource Council, served as the first director of the state's Office of Energy Conservation, and is a former legislative aide to Governor Ed Herschler. She is a native of Buffalo, Wyoming.

until I came back to the state and went to work for the Powder River Basin Resource Council in 1974.

There was a very negative side to being the product of a small town. By the time I went away to college, I wanted to go somewhere where nobody would know me, where I could just start all over and be who I was. I had no idea who that

135

might be. Growing up in Buffalo, I felt I was the product of people's expectations; I felt stifled.

When I got to the University of Illinois and discovered there were as many kids in the freshman class as there were people in the town of Buffalo, I had a wonderful feeling of freedom. Then, after a couple of years, that kind of freedom didn't really matter any more. I have strong memories of flying back at Christmas, seeing the land and the snow on the hills, and reacting—but I didn't understand the reaction. I didn't want to stay there, and I never intended to come back.

When I did come back for a visit in 1974, I had been living in Wichita, and I had decided that what I wanted to be was a citizen activist. I thought I might move to Washington, D.C., because I figured that that was the best place to learn about it.

I hadn't been active in college in the anti-war movement or anything else other than a few small miscellaneous things, but in Kansas I happened to go to a meeting in Burlington (a little farming community about thirty miles from Wichita), and met a group of farmers whose land was being condemned by Kansas Gas and Electric to build a nuclear power plant. They wanted somebody to represent them in Wichita, because that was where the media and the headquarters of Kansas Gas and Electric were, as well as most of the people whose support they felt they needed if they were going to have any power against this huge utility. So I became their Wichita voice.

I had become a general member of Common Cause, too, but the Wichita chapter was in considerable disarray. It needed somebody to get it moving. I'd never done much organizing, but I managed to get the chapter reorganized and involved in some legislative issues. Out of that effort came a feeling that I could get people together, and could bring out in them what they wanted to give to an organization.

In the summer of 1974, I was getting ready to move to Washington, D.C., when I went back to Wyoming for a visit. My mother told me about the Powder River Basin Resource Council, so I went to a meeting and listened to those ranchers and heard what they were trying to do about coal development in the face of the overwhelming forces that were brought to bear on them. They had been organizing for a year or so, and I got a really good feeling for them: that what they were doing was right.

At that meeting, their only staff person quit, and I talked them into hiring me. They had had enough of a negative experience with the last person that they thought they might just not hire anybody, just sort of run it themselves; however, I talked them out of that.

There were times, years ago, when I thought I would probably go back to Illinois to live and work in Chicago, but that's not in me anymore. There's nothing about Wyoming that I don't love, even though a lot of it I'll fight with. More than anything, it's the land and the space, and the country and the sky and the creatures, including people, that choose to be here.

I've always felt that you shouldn't ever let yourself get too attached to any one place or any one thing, if your main goal is to keep on growing, but I'm beginning to feel now that I can hang on to all these attachments and still keep growing. I can keep on loving the cottonwood trees along the Powder River— old, gnarled cottonwood trees—and all the country shaped by the river. But there's something negative about communities in this kind of country. I live in Big Horn, which has a population of about 150, and I've come to the realization that I have a point of view that needs solitude, but if you live in a community, you can't avoid people deciding who you are and who you ought to be. There are those who think this is essential— to raise children, for example—but I still think it's somewhat

negative, in the context of this great space.

On the other hand, there's more than one kind of community. Running a bookstore gives me an opportunity to talk to people here about the things they really care the most about, because that's reflected in the books they buy. Even if I don't get the opportunity to talk to them, just selling them books means sharing something with them.

My partner and I are in the bookshop, not to make a lot of money, but to make a living and to sell books to people. We've had a pretty bad year in terms of sales, but I think we broke even. We've learned to control our inventory and our expenses better than last year, and we've also cut back on our staff. My partner is really good at dealing with people, so I get to hide in the office sometimes and work on the books, which I love.

One of the reasons we made it through the year at the bookshop was that I took a job at the Sheridan College library for about six months. I'd always looked on Sheridan College as a kind of holding operation, where you went if you really didn't want to leave home just yet or if you kind of wanted to go to school a little longer or something, but I discovered a feeling of community in that college with teachers who are really into what they are teaching and students who get very involved.

I don't know as much about the University of Wyoming. I have yet to get much of a feel for it, but I see people who are trying to amass influence around themselves and make big bucks and fight with each other and with other state employees for turf control. Politics gets into colleges in a way that seems almost more backhanded and vicious than with other institutions, except maybe hospitals, which are even worse. Maybe it has something to do with what happens when people think of themselves as professionals—the influence that they should have, the deference they should receive.

It's a subject that can reach the levels of irrationality in small communities. I decided to bring up the issue of a teachers' union meeting that we had in the legislature with school administrators and school boards, and they of course maintained that they were opposed to anything having to do with the teachers' union. So I just said, "Well, okay tell me what you think of this idea: not a teachers' union but just an opportunity for teachers to negotiate like a union if the school administration agrees to it. How do you feel about that?"

Well, a group of otherwise very rational men launched into a series of speeches not remotely related to the question I had asked or to the issue as I perceived it. The closest I can come to characterizing their arguments is to recall my mother's speeches about how I would become addicted to heroin if I ever smoked marijuana. She knew it because she had read it in the *Reader's Digest*. That's how these men responded to me about the teachers' union, and the teachers are just about as irrational about it.

I asked to get on the Education Committee and everyone I talked to said, "Oh, why don't you stay away from that—you can't hardly win, because you get these big issues." But I'm glad I did.

Abortion—well, I get hit by the pro-lifers and the pro-choicers and I'm neither one of those. My life would be so much more simple if I could say I'm one or the other, but I can't. For one thing, whenever anyone asks if I'm pro-life, I'm really tempted to say, "Oh, no—I'm pro-*death*. I'm anti-life. Let's go for killing!" But I don't. I argue with both sides. That's common for me—I don't fall into groups.

Issues change, for one thing. Take the case of the Powder River Basin Resource Council. The whole tenor of industrial and energy development in Wyoming has changed completely since

Powder River started. We're no longer looking at being deluged by a totally unpredictable and uncontrollable influx of new coal mines and power plants. The economy of the nation has changed so much that that situation is not as out of control and unknowable as it was, and the economy of the state is such that there are more people being laid off than hired. You no longer find hordes of people coming to Wyoming because they know they can find jobs here. That means the challenge to an organization like the Powder River Basin Resource Council is more subtle. There are still problems to be dealt with, and there always will be, but dealing with them requires much more than raising people's awareness of a threat.

The Wyoming Outdoor Council seems to have a broader base, and as a result of that it seems more stable to me now. It was quite involved in two major issues in the [1983] legislative session—the wildlife trust fund and the instream flow question. Powder River wasn't involved in either of those at all, and they were probably the two major resource issues of that session.

Water development should probably be at the top of the priority list, but it's just too complicated for people to cope with. As a legislature we really should take that issue and figure out what Wyoming's goals are relative to water. The best we've come up with is to build reservoirs wherever possible, and that's a stupid policy. People have this idea they're supposed to support keeping all the water in the state that we possibly can. Someone ought to try to cut through the politics of it and lay out some alternatives to those of us who are politicians, so that we can focus on the issue and determine what we want.

Wyoming is being dragged into the twentieth century. I wish it were not. I wish we didn't have to have Shakey's Pizza and Holiday Inns; I wish we didn't have to develop half-way houses for drug abusers; I wish we didn't have to have shelters for battered wives and children who are victims of incest; I wish we didn't have to have better highway systems. You see, I'm just a reactionary, in the ultimate sense of the word. I wish we didn't have to keep creating more government programs, but we do, because we have more people and less space for them to occupy, and that will just keep happening.

We're not very good at planning. We have the best wildlife resource in the lower forty-eight. Well, we could choose to let it go, like every other state, and it looks like we might, if we don't put some dollars into the agency that has the job of maintaining that habitat in the face of growth. I don't know if we'll do it, yet I don't know a person who lives here who doesn't love having those animals out there and knowing there are herds of elk they can see. It's part of what we are. But people are so short-sighted. We're not very good at picking the things that are precious to us and figuring out the steps to take to hang on to what we can. We just sort of think they might stay if we ignore them, and if change is going to happen, well, it probably should. We survived the drought, and the dust bowl, and we'll probably survive this too. We're not very good at planning.

I wonder what's going to happen with the whole question of economic growth. One conflict I have—and Barry Goldwater, of all people, kind of clarified it for me—is this: We have this belief that everyone should have a job that earns money, and everyone should be productive, producing either a thing or a service. If we keep these ideas, then we have to have people buying things that they don't need a bit, and we'll gradually run out of our resources, in order to keep producing.

We have to completely change our idea of what being a productive member of society entails. There aren't enough jobs for everybody, and there aren't going to be, under our traditional way of thinking about what people ought to do. I don't know how we're going to deal with that, but someday, perhaps we're going to have to learn how to plan and how to protect what we have, by doing something like deciding that for every person who is working, we need to find a person who is willing *not* to work, and we have to figure out some way to keep that person alive. Something like that has to happen, because we can't keep going the way we are.

Gretchen and Harry Billings

GRETCHEN: WE WERE GONE FROM MONTANA DURING WORLD WAR II, working on the Pacific Coast, and when we came back Harry looked for a weekly newspaper to buy. For various reasons, nothing worked out. But meanwhile he'd heard that the editor of the *People's Voice* was stepping down. It was the perfect job for him—to raise hell every week in a paper that reached all over the state. So he interviewed for it, and got the job.

HARRY: I went to work for the *People's Voice* in March, 1946, and Gretchen joined me in 1948. I was there until 1969, when the paper went out of business. Gretchen had left in the fall of 1967, so she was there for almost twenty years, and I was there for twenty-three years.

GRETCHEN: We had an office in Helena, right across the street from the capitol building. The Educational Co-op Publishing Company owned and published the *People's Voice*; the company was also a printing plant. The object was to have a business establishment that would help support the publication —with full knowledge that it would also have to be supported by contributions, to keep it independent.

HARRY: We were editor and co-editor, reporting to a Board of Directors. They were good people, and absolutely good for nothing. We had all the frustrations of ownership, without owning it.

GRETCHEN: We had subscriptions all over Montana and all over the nation. Sometimes, during political campaigns, it seemed almost as though we had more out-of-state subscriptions than in-state. During a campaign we'd have a press run as high as 12,000. Our general norm was more like 6,000 or 7,000.

HARRY: Our paid circulation did not *nearly* represent the size of the readership—the number of people freeloading on somebody else's copy. We did some checking around, in the railroad clerks' offices, for example, and found that fifteen to twenty people would be reading one copy every week. It was passed around a great deal. It would go up and down the railroads.

GRETCHEN: We felt the mandate was to defend the general welfare, to be the devil's advocate, and to speak for people who had no voice: for prisoners, for civil rights and for people who had no strong organizational structures to defend them.

During our time, there was no group working to promote civil rights legislation in Montana. There were a lot of people who believed in it, but no group working for it.

And in those days the working man in Montana had no voice in the daily press. Almost every paper in the state was still owned or controlled by Anaconda. The small farmer might belong to an organization with an in-house publication, but he had no way to reach the general public—that was what we tried to do.

I started working with Harry because he needed help, and because the money situation was always bad. So at first I came in to do things such as standing behind the press pulling news-

Gretchen and Harry Billings represent a long tradition of independent journalism in western communities. From 1946 until its closure in 1969, they ran the People's Voice, *a fiery, progressive state-wide newsweekly published in Helena, Montana. Now retired, they spend their summers in Montana and their winters in Arizona.*

papers and helping in the bindery. Then I started helping with the subscription list. The work just kept on coming. Harry got more pressed for time—not only doing editorial work, but running the linotype, making up the paper, running the print shop —and began asking me to go over and cover this or that. I'd had no training in journalism, but I'd always been interested in writing, even as a kid. So I'd go find out about things. And do a story or two.

People viewed the *Voice* as being harsh, and I think when people lose their sense of humor they might as well as give up, so I tried to add a little humor, a little bit of spice, to my stories. Then, after I became more acquainted with the structure over in the capitol, I started a column. I thought people needed to know: "Who *are* these guys here in the capitol?"

For whatever reason, my column seemed to have appeal. So Harry kept after me to do it regularly, and without any training, it was somewhat of a strain on me.

Then we began to need more money. One of the sad things about the *Voice* was that we had a good, liberal Board of Directors that was supposed to raise money, but they were all busy people and they didn't. So he gave me another job. I'd go out to cover meetings and conventions and try to write stories and raise money at the same time.

Harry could make enemies faster than I could make friends. I'd be out trying to win them over and he'd be back at the plant, making enemies. When I was out around the state I'd try to get hold of a copy of the latest *Voice* before I went to a meeting, so I'd know what I was going to be faced with when I went in.

HARRY: When I was hired, my predecessor told me in very strong terms thatI'd never win any popularity contests in this seat. Well, I tried to live up to his admonition, and I think I did fairly well.

GRETCHEN: We sought contributions, as I say. Part of my job was to get out and get myself into groups. Sometimes I'd be allowed to say a few words to the massed gathering. Other times . . . well, I'm somebody who knows just exactly how the skunk felt at the Sunday School picnic.

I came out of a protective childhood, and I'd never had a great deal of exposure to anything like that. I had to go through a hardening, and I had to learn how to accept rejection and keep going, and learn how to approach things so that the rejection wouldn't be harsh enough to destroy me.

When I would attend a meeting, for instance, I would intentionally appear late, so that I could sit far back in the group and be able to look over the crowd to see if there was a courageous friend there. Because, you see, we went through the McCarthy era shortly after we got there. It wasn't very darn long before the American Legion began tagging the Red label on us.

HARRY: I kept a wrench on my desk in case the Legion boys came galloping in, which they did one time.

GRETCHEN: It was a very tough time. People became afraid to be identified with the *Voice*. They would go to the post office and slide the paper out of their box and turn it upside down and jam it into their pockets so that the masthead wouldn't show—that type of thing.

It didn't stop with trying to hide the masthead at the post office. We lost subscribers because people were afraid to have the paper come through the mail at all. The local postmaster could identify them. The risk of being smeared was too great, because we were called a Communist or Communist-front publication.

When the *People's Voice* was started, people were poor; they were down. It was the Depression: farmers had nothing and they needed a voice to promote their cause. Labor was on its back during the Depression; then, as they came up on the economic scale, people began to feel protective toward their status. The object of McCarthyism was to terrorize people about their economic status by threatening their political status and by smearing them regarding their patriotic status.

Harry was very bullheaded. He would not compromise, on principle—even for the life and death of the publication. We were for the Missouri Valley Authority and the Columbia Valley Authority, which were to be modeled on the Tennessee Valley Authority. TVA was seen as the opening wedge of socialism or worse in those days. We were for nationalization of the banks and nationalization of basic industries. But we didn't spend much time promoting those ideas in the *Voice*.

HARRY: Except that we damn well advocated nationalization when something particular came up, such as the time when we got ahold of an exhaustive study by the U.S. Senate Interior Committee—at that time headed by a Montana man, Senator Jim Murray*—that showed all these interlocking corporate directors and how this spider web clearly controlled every facet of Montana's economic and industrial life.

GRETCHEN: But we got into bigger trouble for supporting the Farmers' Union, which was Red-baited for some of its stands. Some of the labor people were very edgy about that. It helped break up the farmer-labor coalition at the time, as did civil rights. Labor was interested in any battle that promoted their economic status, but they didn't think we ought to be involved in civil rights battles—didn't think we should put ourselves in the position of getting smeared because of battles like that.

Sometimes we got smeared in public, but more often it was mouth-to-mouth. A friend of our son's worked for the Montana Power Company and told us about how—I don't remember if it was a rate increase fight or what—they called their staff to a meeting in Helena and mentioned, as fact, that the *Voice* was a Communist publication. They had a network in the communities around the state that they used to take on the *Voice*.

*Not to be confused with labor leader Jim Murry.

143

Our kids had a terrible time during the McCarthy era. In school some of the other kids would harass them and say: "Go back to Russia, you dirty little Communists!" They'd come home and ask, "Mom, is Dad a Communist? What's a Communist?"

You know, the era began before Joe McCarthy put his name on it. It began right after the war and got steadily worse, and then, of course, he exploited it more than anyone else had, and now it carries his name. But the time I'm talking about now was before I was working full-time at the *Voice*, when the kids weren't even teenagers yet.

I thought about what to do. Their dad certainly wasn't going to change. One option was to leave him—divorce him and take the kids to Timbuktu; the other was to figure out how to cope with it.

I did a lot of reading aloud to the kids at night after they went to bed—no TV at that time, and Harry was working long hours each day. I'd read a lot of books to them that sometimes I didn't think they would understand, but when I thought they were daydreaming, I'd stop and ask them to tell me what I'd just read, and they did. They were highly intelligent kids.

So I decided I could read them the Bill of Rights, and explain how their father worked under that; and I could read from liberal philosophers, and explain the basic philosophies of their dad. "Dad is deeply, traditionally democratic," (with a small "D") I told them. It just took time and effort, and it seemed to work, because they stabilized.

HARRY: They also organized: three on any one guy who gave their old man a hard time.

GRETCHEN: But it wasn't for very long that that was necessary. And I tried to impress on them the importance of their personal conduct, that they should be proud of the way their dad felt. Because, unlike a lot of people, he had principles and he was willing to fight for them. We have raised three very fine young men. They have done well in life. They're gutsy.

I'd certainly never have stuck with it if it hadn't been for Harry. Many's the time I would have thrown in the towel in a minute. He was more dogged. But we suffered, financially and personally, and the kids suffered. Then, on the other hand, we look back in retrospect, and see we have three strong, beautiful men for sons, and I can't help but believe that those struggles gave them some of the strength and guts that they have.

GRETCHEN: I was born in Whitefish, Montana. My grandparents homesteaded in Plains. My granddad was a railroad man—he was also state representative and senator. My dad was raised in Plains, then he also went with the railroad. He was a train dispatcher. At that time the biggest game in town was the Northern Pacific going through. My mother was a railroad telegrapher, and that's how she met my dad. Early on, my dad was transferred to the Pacific Coast, so I was raised in the Seattle-Tacoma area.

I was one of four girls, and I had very poor health as a child. I spent most of my winters in bed with asthma, so I was constantly being protected. I'd come back to stay with my grandparents in Montana in the summertime, because of my health, and by the end of the summer I would be able to stand up straight, finally, and go back to suffer another winter of asthma.

I didn't go to college. That, of course, was during the Depression, and I wanted to go, but it just seemed to be out of the question. Nobody talked about it—I was never given any encouragement to think about it—and at that time, gals just didn't strike out on their own, especially practicing cowards like me.

144

I did what was expected of me. I was going to go to nursing school, but our family doctor told me I'd never be able to hack it, because of my asthma. So the alternative was to get married. That was what was expected of me; so I got married and came to Montana. We had three kids—three of them in 35 months—and *then* we found out what was causing 'em!

Then, during the war, we went back out to the West Coast. Harry worked as an assistant naval architect and I got a job as assistant ration clerk in one of the shipyards. It was a real job, and, gee, I found out I really could do something—I was amazed that I had any talents besides washing diapers and cooking food.

After the war, we came back and Harry took the job with the *Voice*. I went back to mothering for two and a half years and then answered the call for cheap labor. I suppose if I hadn't done that I might have struck out on my own, because we had three sons who sooner or later would be going to college.

I'm a great believer in the Equal Rights Amendment because I was a victim of the female syndrome: I worked cheap. That's the reason I started at the *Voice*; they needed someone to do the grub work. I went out later to do the fundraising, and if it had had enough money, the board would have hired a man to do that.

I had to use everything that I could bring to bear to try to get acceptance. I was very conscious of how I looked. I believed you could be an independent woman and still be feminine. I was tough and I stuck with what I believed in, but I tried to make it difficult for people to hate me.

There's a basic lesson to be learned: never lose your sense of humor. If you ever find yourself in a position where you think somebody's going to knock your damn head off, find something to laugh at—even if it's only hysterical laughter.

One time I'd done a little lampoon on Bob Corette, the lobbyist for Montana Power Company, and he was furious. He had quite a raging-bull mien about him, and when he saw me at the legislature he came stomping up. I didn't give him a chance to say a thing. I said, "Bob, kiss me, don't scold me!" There were legislators all around us in the lobby, and poor old Bob, he didn't know what the hell to do.

I'm very much in sympathy with the ERA fight today, and have been from the beginning, when people would sneer about "women's lib," coating that phrase with contempt. I know that tactic. Believe me, it was characteristic of every battle we got into. Somebody would come up with the easy derogatory two-word phrase. When you said those words that way, there was supposed to be no more discussion. With that tone they had smothered it; they had buried it and that was supposed to be the end of it. It's been that way with the ERA—smother it under "women's lib."

HARRY: I suppose this is a little self-serving, but I'd like to make the point that the Montana AFL-CIO supported the ERA before the national AFL-CIO reversed itself and went for it. We couldn't do it openly because it was against national AFL-CIO policy, but we made all our facilities available to the gals supporting the ERA. We even figured out how to finance some of the meetings from staff funds, and they were able to use our hall. We were first for ERA, and in fact Jim Murry was one of those who were influential in getting the national AFL-CIO to reverse itself later. That's one of the good points about labor in Montana.

HARRY: Vietnam was what finally destroyed us.
GRETCHEN: The damage we took during the Vietnam War made the McCarthy era look like a Sunday School picnic.

HARRY: We had taken the same stand on Korea. The United States had no damn business getting enmeshed in that affair, and we got tarred and feathered and taken over the coals for the stand we took. I remember a friend coming up to us in the fall of 1952 and saying, "You know the stand you've taken on Korea all these years? The Republicans are going to take that stand and ride it to victory on the first Tuesday in November." And they did. Eisenhower campaigned on a plat-from that if elected he would go immediately to Korea and end the war, which he did. Didn't do us any good. And the same thing happened, only worse, with Vietnam.

GRETCHEN: Oh, my. Emotions ran *so* strong. People would come in and try to convince Harry to change his editorial stand. They'd troop through the office and sit there and argue with him.

Then, when they saw he wasn't going to change his mind, they'd use such arguments as he was going to cause the defeat of Lee Metcalf. Lee Metcalf was a very dear friend of ours and we certainly wanted him to remain in the United States Senate, but it wouldn't have made any difference to Harry—he disagreed with Lee, and said so. So then they'd say, "Well, if you don't care about Lee Metcalf, and you won't change your mind, can't you at least not say anything—just keep quiet!"

After none of those arguments worked, people started withholding their contributions—people in the Democratic party and people in the labor movement.

HARRY: We could cope with attacks on us from the traditional enemies of Montana—Anaconda, the Farm Bureau, the American Legion, that bunch—but we could not cope financially, with our own former close allies dropping us.

GRETCHEN: Some individuals stopped giving their annual contributions—including some that had been fairly substantial. The labor groups would gradually drop their group subscriptions, and all the rapport I'd spent years building up just disappeared. I got terribly tired. I had to have back surgery.

"What in the world would ever cause this?" I said to the doctor.

"Well, stress," he said. "You know, you give at your weakest point. If you had had a weak heart, you would have had a heart attack. But you've got a weak back, so . . ."

"Stress crushing a *disk*?" I said. "I'll certainly never be able to tell any of my friends that, because nobody will believe it."

Anyway, at that point, we hung on quite awhile after the money started going. But I had to give up going out around the state—the pain was intense, and I wasn't getting anywhere.

When I was out scrounging, people would always say, "Well, if you would just take advertising." The policy of the paper was not to take commercial advertising. We were allowed to take ads from non-profits (labor organizations and co-ops, legal advertising, and political ads), and I'd upset people by telling them that if I had my way, we wouldn't take political advertising, either.

You know, some politician would put a tiny ad in the *Voice* and assume that he had bought control of the editorial policy. Or worse still, some of the readers would conclude that we were supporting that politician.

We didn't accept commercial advertising because the corporations—Anaconda, Montana Power—could control too many weekly papers in Montana by buying a $25-a-month ad. Twenty-five dollars a month would buy the soul of an editor.

I'd keep trying to explain to our contributors, "Look. Things are tough. We need money. You say, take advertising. Suppose Bell Telephone buys an ad each week for twenty-five dollars. The phone company goes in for a rate increase. We fight it. The company cancels the ad. You're going to come storming into the office wanting to know why we couldn't keep our mouths shut, telling us it wasn't worth the loss of revenue."

Every summer I'd visit the co-ops in eastern Montana—the rural electrics, the phone co-ops, grain, every kind of co-op. Gradually the co-ops became more centralized. Power moved from the local co-ops to the regionals. The regionals would put pressure on the locals not to support the paper. They'd find whatever lame excuses they needed—the format, maybe.

HARRY: Not everyone in Montana supported the war at that time, but it was tough for a labor paper to oppose it because the national AFL-CIO was very strong for it then. But Lee Metcalf concluded later on that maybe it was a bad deal. The Democratic party here objected very much because we were kicking old Lyndon Johnson all the time.

A lot of people thought that was unpatriotic. You had to stand by your country in times of stress: that old nonsense about "My country, right or wrong," which is nothing but a bunch of words like "Montana water for Montana people." Doesn't mean a damn thing. But, as more people's kids got killed—and they had to find some meaning in it—they turned against us.

GRETCHEN: There was a very dramatic incident in 1968 that illustrates what was happening. The carpenters' union wanted a convention secretary. I'd already left the *Voice* at that time—and that was clearly understood—and I served as the secretary, using a tape recorder and taking notes.

The convention committee called me before them to raise hell with me. I told them I was no longer representing the *Voice*, but that didn't make any difference to them. They kept riding me, and the chairman of the committee said he wanted it clearly understood that unless our attitude changed they were going to boycott the *People's Voice* and ruin it.

By that time I'd had back surgery for a second time. Over the years I had taken all the guff and held my composure, but that time I broke down and bawled, and I told them: "You're no better than the Montana Power Company." They had put themselves on that level. It was a shameful, shattering thing.

HARRY: You know, toward the end of the war, George Meany came out and said, in effect, "If we had to do it all over again, we would take a different stance." It finally got through to him and the national AFL-CIO that we had no business being in Vietnam. But it took years! At least they finally admitted it, and that's something that leaders very rarely ever do.

GRETCHEN: To me there's no second grace in that at all. When I finally quit, it was purely and simply because I had become so bitter. I was suffering physically, and I couldn't allow myself to become a permanently embittered woman. I had to get over that. It took me longer to get over the psychological problem—the sense of futility about it all—than to get over the physical damage.

And then, a long time later—after the publication had been destroyed and there was no more *Voice*—people began telling us how right we were about Vietnam.

I got very bitter because I was so exhausted and my health had turned sour. That was a kind of cumulative, nonproductive, self-destructive thing I had to overcome. But we would go to gatherings in the state once in a while, and I'd find that I just didn't want to go back, because everybody would come around and tell us how dreadfully they missed the *Voice* and how the state needed another *Voice* and how people had tried to get other publications going and how right we were about the war. To me that's no comfort.

HARRY: There have been a couple of attempts to revive the idea, at least, of a statewide paper, but they haven't worked out.

A lot of young people put a lot of work into a paper called *Borrowed Times*, but didn't get much out of it except the pleasure of trying to make a success out of it. *Montana Eagle* had a little bit better financing, but maybe they were *too* energetic, going for too many pages, and having too much overhead on printing costs. I couldn't see how they could possibly ever make it pay.

It's a lot harder to get a paper going today than it would have been to keep the *Voice* alive, but they didn't think about that then.

GRETCHEN: At the time they didn't stop to think about the right and wrong of the war. They thought only about getting Democrats elected. They could see that criticism was going to destroy Lyndon Johnson, and the Democratic party and your once-upon-a-time liberal Farmers' Union and the AFL-CIO went out to silence the opposition because of what it was going to do to the Democrats. All went out together—these same people yelled for Harry's hide—and when he wouldn't give, they just took away the money. Now they're sorry.

HARRY: You want to say, "Where was your check when we needed it?"

GRETCHEN: I can't say that sort of thing to people. I'm just not going to listen to them.

When I went out to try to counter this thing, my first approach was to tell them that if they couldn't stand seeing something they didn't agree with, they shouldn't support the paper, because the purpose of the *Voice* was to be a contentious publication. We were intentionally contentious. Because unless there's controversy, people aren't thinking. I'd say that, and I'd point out that if they did not continue to support the publication, the time would some when it would be gone and they would have no voice in *anything*.

Do you know, people would say to me, "Well, you can say that, Gretchen, but Harry will never give up the *People's Voice*. He'd never leave the *Voice*."

In other words: "Starve to death, Billings!"

HARRY: Well, let's see. I got awfully mad at times at those kinds of things, but we had twenty-three years of almost steady hell-raising—and I guess maybe I got tired, but I sure enjoyed it.

GRETCHEN: Of all the things we tried to do, we didn't win many battles at the *People's Voice*, but we've lived to see things that we fought for—that we were called Communists for—become a reality. And there's some satisfaction in that.

Once in a while the kids would say, "Why do you give your life's blood fighting for these lost causes?" We tried to impress on them, "Can you imagine what the world would be like if nobody fought for causes that were considered far-out and radical?"

The environment—my God, we were dismissed as wild-eyed environmental extremists thirty years ago.

HARRY: The *Voice* brought a lot of those so-called extremists together and helped them understand each other. The late Edmund Freeman who was at the Unversity of Montana for many years, said to me one time, "I think one of the most important functions of the *Voice* is that it is a hub. It draws people together—people of varying liberal views from the farming, labor, and education communities."

Today the cohesiveness of the Left is gone, except for the umbrella effort the AFL-CIO has with some environmental groups. That's the only cohesiveness left that I know about, except for some momentary things.

I don't know whether by the end of this decade there's some hope of getting back into progressive forward motion or not.

149

I can't say I'm optimistic, but I'm not very pessimistic. I go back to when I was a young Socialist, and now as an old Socialist I still believe very strongly that the nation's got to get the ownership and control of its resources and basic industries. There's no doggone way on earth we're going to be able to make this system continue to work unless we have a mixed economy with the major industries being run *for* the people rather than financed *by* the people—directly or through tax money.

GRETCHEN: But we're so far from that! At present, everything is in a holding pattern.

Probably it's a cycle—you get progress, then you have to refine some of those things. People are so conscious of the environment now. Our grandson-in-law—a big rancher out of Gildford—spoke about the fact that he was spraying, and I said, "Well, David, I sure hope you're using masks. I just read an article in *Time* about how farmers are the most susceptible to cancer of anyone." He said he'd read that too, and he said, "The thing is, we didn't know that before. Now it's been ten years since we sprayed, just for that very reason. We are very, very careful."

All right, now that's progress! Because I suppose that at the point in time when environmentalists first started harping about these things, the big farmers wouldn't listen; now they care. Progress came out of some rather dismal periods. We finally got some silicosis compensation legislation after a long fight. We have Medicare. I debated doctors all over the state of Montana about Medicare in 1964.

Now we've got to hold the line. And maybe, for the moment, it's necessary to stabilize, to get things in the best possible functioning order so that we don't destroy all that we've accomplished—even if we can do no more than that at the moment.

T. A. Larson

I WAS BORN ON A FARM IN NORTHEAST NEBRASKA IN 1910 and grew up there. My father made money from the land and got the idea that land would always increase in value, so he bought too much of it and lost his shirt eventually. He and my mother were both immigrants from Sweden; they came over in their teens, with very little education.

My father believed in education—they had five kids, and we all knew we had to have an education. Four of us wound up in the professions, the one girl in the family married a farmer and made more money than the rest of us combined.

My first vote was at the University of Colorado. I went there for my undergraduate work, and had my first opportunity to cast a ballot in 1932. If times had been different, I would have been a Republican—came from a Republican community, and most people seem to inherit their politics—but that was a watershed year when people swung over pretty fast. So many young people just looked at the situation and went along with Franklin D. Roosevelt and stayed with him.

My father was able to support me in my freshman year. After that, I worked my way through, with scholarships and

T. A. Larson is the foremost authority on Wyoming history. He has written and published four books, three of which are definitive works about the history of the state. The fourth book is a compilation and appreciation of Bill Nye's western humor. Larson taught history at the University of Wyoming for thirty-nine years until his retirement in 1975. In 1976 he was elected to the state House of Representatives, as a Democrat. He served for four successive terms, retiring after the 1984 legislative session. He lives in Laramie, Wyoming.

one thing and another. When I was graduated I couldn't find work, so I went on and got my doctorate at the University of Illinois. I finished in 1936, and a job was available on the faculty at the University of Wyoming, so I came on out here and took it, and stayed on the faculty until 1975, when I retired at the age of sixty-five. Then they talked me into running for the legislature the following year, and that's how I got there.

Wyoming history was my field. Actually, I didn't start out that way: I took my doctorate in medieval English history, particularly the relationship of church and state in the fourteenth century. It's always easier to come forward in time than to go backward.

It was an odd situation. This was a fill-in job, a one-year assignment. There were only two people in the history department at that time, and the English history man was going on sabbatical, and they wanted a substitute for him. So I taught English constitutional history and medieval history.

The following year there wasn't a job anywhere that I could find, here or anywhere else, so I made my way to England and did research at the University of London. The next year, the best job I could find was back here, but it carried the requirement that I develop a Wyoming history course on the side, so I did that. The next year, they gave me the opportunity to get on the tenure track, but with the understanding that I teach Wyoming history.

Well, it all worked out eventually. I couldn't find people out here who could read Latin—and you can't do much in medieval history without Latin—but there was a great deal of unused material available on the history of the American West, and I already had some background in that. So I built that up gradually and turned over the medieval and English history to other people and just focused on western America.

This worked out pretty well. I became president of the Western History Association and wrote some books and did a history of Wyoming war years that studied the impact of World War II on the state and how Wyoming contributed to the war effort. This in turn led me to see that there was a need for a one volume history of Wyoming, which I wrote and which has done very well. Then I also wrote a bicentennial history as part of a series of fifty-one books published in 1976—one for each state, including the District of Columbia. I retired at sixty-five because it was mandatory at that time; then I was elected to the legislature and began to serve in the session of 1977.

Because of a constitutional amendment, we now are allowed to meet sixty days in each two-year period, so we meet for forty days in the odd-numbered years to deal with general legislation, and we handle 700 to 800 bills in that period. In the even-numbered years, we hold a twenty-day budget session.

The Appropriations Committee, which I have been lucky to serve on throughout my six years here, meets about thirty to thirty-five days in advance of the convening of the full legislature; we get together, eleven of us (six from the House, five from the Senate), and hold hearings, with the heads of every agency and department coming before us to make their pleas for funding. We study their budgets and prepare appropriations bills which are ready to go when the rest of the legislature

We have a better legislature now than we did before 1970; several factors have contributed: annual sessions, a legislative service office, and the Appropriations Committee, which does much preparatory work. Before we had a legislative service office to do much of the background work, Wyoming's legislature was ranked, in a national survey, pretty close to the bottom. Lobbyists drafted the bills, and the legislature met for only forty days every other year.

Reapportionment—one man, one vote—improved the legislature, too, making it more democratic and representative (cows used to get better representation than people, in some cases). To accomplish this, it was necessary to combine some counties and to do some juggling.

Before, every county had at least one representative, but the average number of people represented by each House member was about 7,000 and Niobrara County (over on the South Dakota-Nebraska border) had less than 3,000 people. Our constitution still says every county is entitled to one legislator, but I and others felt that this wasn't quite right, wasn't consistent with the objective of reapportionment. We tried to combine that county with another with the same kind of constituency—agriculture people—so that they would have what is called virtual representation and would have the opportunity to vote for a legislator even if most of those elected would come from the more populous county.

But the majority of the legislature put in a provision that Niobrara County was to have its own legislator, although the language was placed a little separately so that if the courts threw it out, we could go ahead with the rest of the reapportionment plan without having the whole thing thrown out.

Our Wyoming Supreme Court went with the language of the state constitution, even though everywhere else in the country that big a deviation has not stood up. So the League of Women Voters brought suit, and I and some others contributed some money to help carry that to the United States Supreme Court. We can't imagine that they're going to let that county have twice as much representation per capita as the other counties. The Wyoming Supreme Court did, in fact, find for Niobrara County, allowing it a representative in apparent violation of the one-man, one-vote premise.

I know some people argue the other side, saying that regardless of the principle here, the fact is that the people in Niobrara County can't hope to be adequately represented, appended to a larger county. But I think they'll have more representation, because other counties will pity them and sympathize with them and give them more than they would otherwise get.

But we are looking down the road. This little aberration shouldn't cause too much trouble, but there are population changes in other counties too, and in twenty years, we might not have one-man, one-vote any more. Niobrara County wouldn't be the end of it. If a principle means anything, we have to deal with it.

In the next few years I think we're going to have some real knockdown, drag-out fights over the water issue. Water development is terribly expensive. It's not wise politically to proclaim this from the housetops, but there is no question in my mind that this water can be put to better use downstream, and is being put to better use, in Arizona, California, Mississippi, the Dakotas—places where you have better soil, faster growing seasons, and a lot more people to take care of. So that's probably where the water ought to go—where it's going right now.

We have unused water under our compacts, but the federal government has finally said these projects aren't feasible. The federal government has put in most of our dams and spent well over a half-billion dollars putting them in. They've used up the feasible dam sites, and we're at the point now where it would cost $100 million to $200 million to put in a dam, and there's no possible way you can get the money back out. It's just a big subsidy to somebody—probably to some industry that we don't need. We are entitled to fourteen percent of the water that is going down the Colorado River, at our state line as it leaves, and we haven't been able to use that much because out there in the Green River basin they haven't been able to agree on a dam site. If they could, the only way you could use that water would be to bring in some industry to pay for a good part of that cost —an industry that we could probably get along without.

Let them put the industry downstream where the water is or use the water for people or for growing oranges or something, instead of heaven knows what.

I don't proclaim this view in public because I'm concerned about somebody turning on me and cutting back the appropriation for my county, or for the university. That would concern me very much. We have very large appropriations for the university. We are the only state among the fifty that has just one four-year institution, and we want to be able to hang onto it. We have really been building the university here in the past ten years, since the money has been flowing in from oil and minerals. We have a better salary schedule than any of the bordering states, and we've been supporting buildings and equipment and all sorts of things. But if another part of the state desperately wants $100 million for a dam and I fight it, they are going to get back at me some way. That's the reason I don't talk like that.

I sometimes think that since I'm retired I can say what I damn please and get away with it, but once you represent an area and have a lot of friends employed, you just have to tread carefully and look at your hole card and see what effects your vote is going to have on something else.

The potential exists for a regional solution to the water issue, but the states have fought each other just about as much as they have fought the federal government. We have had a love-hate relationship with the federal government from time immemorial, partly because it's the hand that has fed us and provided most of our employment and our subsidies. Our cattlemen in particular claim they're the only independent people in the world, when actually they've had their subsidies too. It's farcical sometimes.

You ask if there really is a Northern Rockies region, or if it is a figment of somebody's hopes. Well, the regional approach always seems to break down somewhere. We have an Old West Regional Commission to try to develop tourism regionally, the theory being that if you advertise the whole region—five states —people would go from state to state, and I think there is something to be said for that; but as far as regional economic development goes, in the Missouri River basin, for example, they have never got very far with that. We ought to work closely with Idaho and Montana, but we don't. There is a tendency for each state to get pretty independent. They don't learn from each other, and they don't pay attention to what another state does. Each state thinks it is doing it better, so each goes off in an entirely different direction.

If you look at Idaho, Utah, Colorado, Nebraska, South Dakota, Montana, and Wyoming, they have much in common, but they have a dozen different ways of handling the same problem. The people who profit most from all this water business are lawyers. We're paying $80 an hour for our legal talent out of Colorado; we can't even develop our own water experts. I think we have them here, but there's a notion sometimes that we can do better by going to Denver for them.

I think it's true what Father deSmet said, back in the 1840s, that he expected to see the day when the last Indians would kill each other off over the last buffalo. Well, we might wind up killing each other over the last gallon of water.

I think we'd do better by just trying to hold our population

down and by not begging industry to come in here. In 1974 and 1975, they talked about how we were going to get twelve power plants and become a national sacrifice area to support all these liquefaction, gasification, synthetic fuels plants. Since that time, only one big plant has been started in Wyoming. These things haven't come nearly as fast, partly because of our lack of water, and partly because the federal government is not putting up all the front money these corporations want.

We ought to level off on our population at a little over 500,000 and try to make Wyoming more of a tourist place and keep our wildlife going, and our loneliness. We need that in this country. We'll need it more fifty to one hundred years from now. I think less than ten percent of Wyoming has ever been plowed, and I don't think it ever should be plowed. I think the rest of it ought to be left the way it is, as much as possible.

Montana and Idaho are much more agricultural states than we are. Our agricultural income is not that great. The growing of livestock, particularly cattle, is a big industry, and of course, we can graze quite a few animals. We can have maybe a million or so head of cattle sharing the range with antelope and deer. I wouldn't want to see agriculture eliminated, but I might want to take another look at it. Someone proposed, back in the 1950s, that in some areas of the western part of the state we might put the land to more beneficial use by having antelope there rather than sheep, and I might want to consider that, in some places, because it could bring in more income.

We have, at last report, only about 8,500 farm and ranch units in the state. Right after World War II, Governor Hunt had the wild notion that reclamation was going to triple the number of farm and ranch units in the state, but instead, we had 15,500 and we dropped on down to 7,900 or so; we went

the other direction. My goodness, he was an ex-dentist, and he didn't know the first thing about agriculture potential.

We can save ranching, but as far as some of our farming is concerned—well, I think we can save these few little oases that we have. Sugar beets we really don't need; we ought to import our sugar and use Louisiana sugar. The sugar beet industry has always been subsidized. The wool industry has always been subsidized, too, but I can see more reason for subsidizing that. We subsidize a lot of farmers and ranchers with low interest rates, no question about that; some of them get money from the state at six percent to develop pump irrigation, and if it isn't feasible and they lose their shirts, everybody else in the state pays the bill.

You aren't doing the rancher any good lending him money at six percent; you're doing him damage and yourself as well. If you can get fifteen percent investing the state's money somewhere else, why should you subsidize a farmer who will put it into something that won't pay out?

We have to make choices about what we'll do for agriculture. In the 1982 session of the legislature, I voted to support a lamb-processing plant. By the letter of our constitution, it's illegal, but we're going to put $47 million plus into raising the Buffalo Bill Dam, for the benefit of a rather small number of people in Park County, and I don't know why we shouldn't lend $3 million, at a pretty good rate of interest, to a bunch of our ranchers who want to have a lamb-processing plant which I feel would be of more general benefit to our economy. It would be just a loan, so I went for that. If the Supreme Court throws it out as unconstitutional, maybe we ought to change the constitution.

When they drew up the constitution in 1889 and imposed limits on using state funds for this kind of thing, they were battling the railroads. Every little town all over the West was willing to bond itself and give money to the railroads to try to get them to come through town. It was cutthroat competition that the constitution tried to address, but it's a different situation now. I think that as long as we are sensible about it, it might not hurt to lend a little money for some enterprise that would provide a sound market for Wyoming sheep, and also might make it possible for the rest of us to buy lamb chops at a little lower price.

I'm for regional processing of food and other agricultural products so that not everything gets taken out of the region and processed and shipped back to us at high prices. There is that one point in our constitution that seems to make these loans unconstitutional, but I quit some years ago trying to figure out what's constitutional and what isn't. If you look around, you can always find a precedent for anything. Historians are always outmatched by lawyers.

You ask if I'm optimistic or pessimistic about the future of Wyoming, from the perspective of a historian and legislator. Well, down through the years I've noticed that older people are generally of the opinion that the country is going to the dogs.

I'm seventy-two now, and I feel that pretty strongly—not specifically about Wyoming, but about the country. And that makes me cautious, because I can see that that's been a common perception of people my age, all through time. But I do think we've collected more troubles than this country's ever had, and I worry about Wyoming, because it's been my observation that most things that happen in Wyoming are caused by forces outside Wyoming.

Wars have contributed more to change in Wyoming than anything else—wars and the federal subsidies that accompany them, to support minerals extraction, oil, agriculture, the defense industries. So much of our history in Wyoming has depended on federal subsidies.

Not until 1976 did we reach the point where the federal government was putting less money into Wyoming in subsidies than it was taking out in taxation. Wyoming was a have-not state until the 1960s, but thanks largely to the oil cartel and the embargo of 1973, we became a comparatively rich state. But this is new, and possibly temporary. The federal government has always been a great force in Wyoming, and we haven't ever controlled our own destiny.

Marvin and Shirley Martell

MARVIN: I'VE BEEN IN BUTTE FOR ABOUT TWENTY-SIX YEARS, I guess. I'm from North Dakota originally. We moved to Missoula when I was a kid, and then, when I grew up and went hunting for a job, I found one in Butte. Eventually I got a job in the mines, and stayed here and got married.

SHIRLEY: I was born and raised here. My dad was a copper miner. He mined at some of the older mines that are all shut down now. We lived just kitty-corner from the Tebonia mine, in a house that had been my grandfather's and a boarding-house before that. It was a great big old rambling house.

I guess I know just about everybody in town, which makes it nice. We were a small family—just my mother and dad and my brother and me. We went to the old Webster School, an old brick schoolhouse.

My dad would get disgusted with mining every so often and he'd go ranching. He'd raise grain for a while, and then he'd come back into town and go back into the mines.

That was when your time always counted. No matter if you left for a year, you still got credit for the years you worked before. There wasn't the stuff they have today, where if you have a "break in service" you lose credit for the time you worked before, and you start over at the bottom, with no seniority and no credits toward your pension. With my dad, all his years accumulated and he got credit for all of them when he retired.

MARVIN: There was a time, I guess, when you could quit one mine and go to work at another mine the same day, and your seniority would be transferred. The mines were owned by the same company—Anaconda—and sometimes they didn't hold it against a guy for quitting or being fired. That's when times were good around here.

I worked eleven years in the mines, starting at the Leonard Mine, which doesn't even exist anymore. It was right in the middle of where the Berkeley Pit is now. You wouldn't know to look at it. The pit just grew so much it expanded into the old mine workings, and obliterated the old mine, along with part of the town that sat above it, Meaderville. The company bought up the houses and the property. Used to be they bought the property and gave them another house in exchange.

Originally there was a great mixture of nationalities in Butte because of the mines. A lot of that had disappeared before I came here.

SHIRLEY: There's still some of Finntown left, on the upper East Side. The Helsinki Bar is still there, and he's still got the, what do you call them? . . . saunas.

And at one time there were a lot of Mexicans on the East Side. I never paid too much attention to where different ethnic groups lived. I'm not prejudiced. Somebody who's prejudiced might have known exactly where the boundary lines were, but I wasn't afraid to cross the boundary lines, because I didn't pay much attention to the color of a person's skin. I'm different, I guess—I could usually read them through their eyes, more so

Marvin and Shirley Martell

Marvin and Shirley Martell have spent most of their lives in Butte, one of the great mining towns of the modern West. Marvin worked as a copper miner until 1982 when most Butte mines were closed after ARCO purchased the Anaconda Company. Shirley, a native of Butte, was a founder of the Butte Community Union, a local group organized to deal with problems created by the depressed mining economy. In 1983, they moved to Nevada to look for work in the mines.

than what color their skin was. I think a person is a person within themselves. All people are created equal and there's no way to get around it. Everybody has some good in him.

MARVIN: When I first came here in 1953, just about all the mines were running. It was right around Christmas, and each mine had a Christmas tree on top of the gallows frame—the

headframe, where they had the machinery to haul miners and ore up the shaft.

There was a dozen or better gallows frames on the hill then, and every one of them had a Christmas tree on top, all lighted up. It was kind of a sight to see. I don't know what they'll do next Christmas, because they're closing everything down; I don't know if we'll ever see that sight again.

SHIRLEY: That tradition started back when I was a little kid. They usually put the trees up and the lights on the day after Thanksgiving, and kept them up until after New Year's Day. It always gave you the Christmas spirit. They kept the lights up well past New Year's Day for the Serbian Orthodox Christmas around January 6. We have a lot of Serbians here.

MARVIN: They started expanding open-pit mining about 1955. Things really began to change then. Places like Meaderville slowly disappeared and other places where there was a lot of history.

SHIRLEY: People who had lived there all their lives were forced to move out of beautiful homes; people who had lived in one place for fifty years were uprooted. That's a hard thing to see.

Some people tried to fight, but Anaconda was just too big. Some of them sat there, as long as they could, and the company just worked around them. You wouldn't have believed it. They stayed right in their houses until the pit was just about at the back door, and coming around the sides. Then, of course, they had no choice but to go, because they'd blast right underneath them, or so close to them that the blasting would gradually destroy the house.

Imagine if someone came knocking on *your* door: "Listen, you're going to have to get up and move." They did offer money, but money wasn't ever important to Butte people. They had their roots there, and they knew where they were at. That was important.

I think the biggest change came over Butte when Arco bought Anaconda in the early 1970s. I don't know, they just didn't seem to care about the people. At one time, the company cared. The people who started the Anaconda Company cared, because they came from Butte. They belonged here, and they were mining people themselves. Arco was never a mining company; they're oil.

Arco came in about ten years ago, and ten years later they closed down the mines; every mine on the hill is closed. They flooded them, and they closed the smelter in Anaconda and the smelter in Great Falls.

MARVIN: Yeah, I don't know when it was built, but it was a brand new plant, right from the ground up. It was supposed to be one of the most modern plants of its kind. They took their concentrates over there. It was supposed to be pollution-free, too. Arco decided it wasn't feasible to run, I guess, and they closed it.

SHIRLEY: We knew they were union-breakers. I think the people all knew they were, and I know that's what they're trying to do—break the unions. As soon as they get them all broke, I'm sure they will come back in here and mine.

Arco is killing this town. The unions are also killing it, because big businesses wanted to come in here, and Anaconda and the unions wouldn't let them. A glass company, a subsidiary of Ford Motor Company, wanted to come in here to use the slag from the smelter to make glass. They wanted to put up a plant out where the municipal golf course is. This was back when I was in high school, somewhere between 1951 and 1955. The unions and Anaconda wouldn't let them. They didn't want the competition for the jobs.

Three or four years ago, K-Mart bought some property off Continental Drive and put a big sign up—"new home of K-Mart"—and the unions put a stop to that, too. A motel chain, Motel 6, started to build a motel here; already had the ground work set out and the forms down for the concrete. Well, the unions burned the construction shack down, because it was a non-union outfit that was building the motel. And McDonald's has tried to come in, and couldn't—they're non-union too.

There are a few non-union businesses here, but they've come in the past few years. The unions are going to have to do something; they're going to have to let some businesses in here. Something's got to bend somewhere or Butte will break, because everybody shies away from Butte, on account of the unions. We're the strongest union town in the state of Montana.

They still claim we're the richest hill on earth, and I'm sure there's still a lot of minerals worth mining in these hills, but they'll never be mined by union people. There's not going to be anybody here to be in a union. The union officials here in Butte aren't going to have any dues coming in. They're going to have to go somewhere else, and that's the way the companies are going to break the unions.

MARVIN: I've been out of work for fourteen months now. I wasn't working in the mines when I was laid off—I was working at the concentrator. I had eleven years in at that point, that counted; you see, I had a break in service. I started in the mines in 1956 and worked there until 1967. Then we had a long strike which lasted nine months. I couldn't hold out that long, so I went out to Seattle and got a job working for Boeing. I wasn't going to come back, but there was an illness and death in the family, and that brought us back here, and I went back to the mines. But I had to start over again with the company after that break in service.

I don't know when I'll find work. I drew regular unemployment for twenty-two weeks, with an extension, and supplemental unemployment benefits from the union contract with the company—that lasted a year. With all that, we didn't do too bad. Didn't live like kings or anything, but a person got by. Since then, it's not been very well. It's depressing when you run out of everything. They say it's the economy, but there's no demand for copper. The international price is down.

SHIRLEY: But then they transported our copper to the West Coast and shipped it over to Japan for smelting. They said it was more feasible. That's why they closed down the smelter here. I have no idea how it could be cheaper to ship copper to Japan than to smelt it here—to process it there and then ship it back to the United States.

And because it was exported from the United States to Japan, the miners didn't qualify for Trade Adjustment Assistance benefits, which were paid to workers who lost their jobs to imports. Do people feel bitter about that? Definitely.

Run up and down the streets and see all the places that have been repossessed—real nice homes. There's one up in Timberview that somebody picked up for $500 by just paying the taxes on it. Isn't that terrible that someone with a little money to spare can go in and take over somebody else's home and leave those people out in the street?

Some of the banks here are willing to work with you, to see if there's some way to help you out. But there are some banks in Butte that won't help *nobody*—not unless you've got a million dollars backing you up.

So many families here are in the same situation. The men are all very depressed and don't know what to do with themselves. You can only do so much around the house because you don't have the money to buy materials to do something major.

The layoffs either bring families closer together or drive them apart. So many women just dread the idea of having their husbands at home twenty-four hours a day. I know one family in particular I think will probably end up killing each other, and I'm not kidding. I mean there's no harmony there at all. I guess I'm one of the lucky ones, because the past fifteen months have probably been the best time we've had together.

Right after the last strike, when the smelter closed down, I had three daughters get married—one in February, one in March, one in April. It was expensive, but we gave them the best that we could, and we felt that we did very well by them. All three of those girls worked, and they paid for their own wedding gowns, but we provided the receptions. We spent most of what we had. And over the past fifteen months we've gone

through everything we had saved, but we still seem to make it. We do get food stamps, and we only have one daughter left at home now.

I haven't kept anything from Stacy, because she's 16, she's old enough to understand what's happening. But she's very withdrawn. My older kids, they all realized that when a strike came up, you tightened your belt, you know. Stacy is so different, so withdrawn. I can't talk her out of it. I can't talk her out of her mood. Each day I can see her slowly, slowly drift more into this depression state she's in.

Marvin says he feels insecure. He went to a meeting in Helena and felt out of place. He felt like he was the only man in the whole place who was unemployed. When he came back he mentioned something—he said, "It's too bad there isn't some place where all the unemployed men could get together and talk." There are many unemployed Butte miners between the ages of forty-five to fifty-five. I'm sure group sessions would help Marvin to realize he's not the only man in this city who's unemployed. Right now, he feels like a failure. And he has days where he says, "Wouldn't you like to get together with some other people in the same category as us—parents both unemployed and everything?"

I do have some outside income. I take inventory for RGIS —that's Retail Groceries Inventory Service—and I've got five inventories this month. I get paid $4.75 an hour, plus travel pay if I have to go out of town, so that brings in a little bit of income, to try to meet some of the bills. We can't pay much, but we pay something, and I also sell Avon.

Marvin gets a little upset. I don't think it's so much me going out and doing these things; it's just that he has to sit home, and he feels even more that he's a failure because he can't go out and do this stuff.

I told him, "Well, don't you think it's my turn?" You see, some years ago I had open heart surgery. I had a cardiac pacemaker put in. I had to go back because the pacer failed, and I had to have another put in. We went to Salt Lake City three times and I was in the hospital two months, altogether. And when I came home, I couldn't do anything. Most of my children were still at home. Marvin had the responsibility for them, plus wanting to be down at the hospital as much as he could. The company when it was Anaconda gave him the time off.

He did everything. They all stood behind me. So I believe it's about time I stood up to do something for them. They don't look at it that way, and I can't convince Marvin that it's my turn to help out.

I can't see Arco providing any money to train men like Marvin for other jobs, because Arco is not a Montana concern. I think Anaconda would have provided some kind of job training because they were Montana people. If help does come— in the form of department stores or big chains or other businesses coming in—I hope for the sake of Butte that the unions don't step up and say, "Now, you have to be unionized," because if they do, we're done.

Do I think it's more important to have a job than to have a union? Yes. You better believe it. I worked for three dollars an hour today; I had to, because I figured that that three dollars an hour was a lot better than zero. Unions were needed at one time; they served the miners well and they served Butte well, and made it a tougher union town than any place else. But they served their purpose. You can only go so far. When you expect twenty dollars an hour and these companies can move somewhere else and have the same work done for eight dollars or ten dollars an hour, where do you think these companies will go—to Butte, or down the road?

163

MARVIN: Some of the men on layoff would agree with that. I don't imagine all of them would. You've got diehards, you know, in anything. And I don't know if I'm willing to take just anything.

SHIRLEY: I didn't mean just anything. I think people should be paid wages that will meet the economy the way it is, but the unions have to compromise. Some of these unions cost $500 to get into and I think that's outrageous. And then, with some, if you want your name on the book—to get into the hiring hall, so to speak—it costs you ten dollars a month. Just to put your name on the book, and no promise of a job, you're paying ten dollars a month above and beyond your dues. In addition you have to keep up with them.

I've been in several unions, and they never did me any harm. But today, if somebody asked me to join a union, I'd probably tell them no, because I feel as though the unions broke the back of this community. That is why the mine closed.

I don't think there's one person in this whole city who hasn't gone out of Butte to do some shopping, at one of the malls or the discount stores. It's worth spending two or three dollars on gas to get those discounts. Union people go out there because the prices are too high in this union town and the stores are closing.

MARVIN: For a while there was a lot of discussion about using the coal severance tax income to help depressed communities like Butte, but then, all of a sudden, that talk went by the wayside. I think eastern Montana kind of begrudges the fact that we're asking for it, because the coal tax comes from that part of the state, not from our part. But think of the income from our minerals. Some of that is still sitting in banks somewhere, or has been invested. Whatever the legislature decides to do, the money comes from taxes from mining.

We'd like some of that tax money back—money that has been invested in the state of Montana. When the state needed help, we helped. Now we need help.

We aren't begging; we're just asking for what is rightfully ours. The money should be used in job training and industry—bringing industry into the Butte-Anaconda area. Arco paid $1 million to Anaconda, and some of that has been used to help people open businesses—some of them small, employing only one to three people—but that's helping one to three people who were unemployed before.

I've asked about the $500,000 that was given to Butte. It was put into a fund. Some has been loaned out. Harkins Bottling Company got $13,000 to expand, but it did it without hiring anyone, keeping the crew it already had. And money was loaned to start a one-hour, photo-processing shop over here on Harrison Avenue. A Butte man started that up—and he had been unemployed—but it's just a one-man operation, so the money isn't doing much to provide jobs for the unemployed.

I don't know how you go about getting that money. If you're starting a small business, maybe you could, but it isn't doing anything for the laid-off workers of Butte, even though it was supposed to help them.

SHIRLEY: If the unions give a little, and industry gets interested in our terrain, our people, we have to have job training. Just about everybody needs on-the-job training or training through Vo-Tech; just about everybody.

Danielle Jerry

Danielle Jerry worked as a wildlife biologist for the U.S. Forest Service in Idaho's Panhandle National Forest from 1980 to 1983. She holds an undergraduate degree from Vassar College and a graduate degree from Colorado State University. In 1983, she joined the U.S. Fish and Wildlife Service and now works out of Anchorage, Alaska.

WHEN I WAS A CHILD MY FOLKS HAD A PLACE IN THE ADIRON-DACKS, in upstate New York. I loved the outdoors; I was intrigued by animals. My father took us on nature walks because he liked to hunt and fish. He would tell us things: "That duck flying away—he's pretending he has a crippled wing, because he's trying to lure us away from his nest."

My dad got involved with the Adirondacks on the planning level after Governor Rockefeller proposed turning the Adirondacks into a national park. My father wrote to the governor, pointing out that the Adirondacks were already a state park—the largest state park in the nation—and strongly protected by an amendment to the state constitution specifying that the park "shall be forever kept as wild forest lands." My father argued that making the Adirondacks into a national park would create more problems than it could possibly solve.

Governor Rockefeller was big on study commissions, and he decided to set one up to study the Adirondacks, and on the strength of that letter he appointed my father as staff director.

My father claims it was the best job he had ever had. For three years he directed the team responsible for planning the future of the Adirondacks. He hired foresters and wildlife biologists and assorted other planners, and eventully they came up with a plan that went before the legislature and was adopted.

And throughout that time he could go walking through the Adirondacks with wildlife biologists and foresters and game wardens who became his friends. I would talk with them sometimes about their work. While I was in college, I remember one of the foresters tried to convince me to go into forestry, but trees weren't quite interesting enough. They just sat there.

165

I went to college never thinking about majoring in anything else but history. I love the past; I love reading about it, but by my sophomore year I knew I'd never go on with it, because I wasn't interested in teaching immediately, and I couldn't imagine spending so much time doing research in libraries. I liked being outdoors too much.

So I graduated from college, still not knowing quite what I wanted to do—with no background for anything but history —and decided to think about it for a while. I went backpacking all over Europe, and halfway through my stay there, it occurred to me: "What do I really like? I like the outdoors."

I wrote home to tell my parents I was thinking about becoming a wildlife biologist, and when I came back to the United States, with more *chutzpah* than common sense, I applied for entrance to a master's degree program.

I didn't have any of the prerequisites, but I was accepted provisionally at Colorado State. Within a year or so, I had done physics, chemistry—all the background courses—and had gone on and got my master's from the school in three and a half years. Most people can do it in a year and a half to two years, but I had to do the backgrounding first.

My first job was with the Forest Service in northern California. You've heard of old school ties? I always associated that with Ivy League types running the banks and staffing the Congress, but it exists among the land-management types, too. One of the resource officers in Shasta-Trinity National Forest needed to hire a wildlife biologist. Most California people would call up Humboldt or Berkeley, but he was a Colorado State graduate, so he called there instead and asked for a student referral.

I was lucky. It was just a seasonal job, but it generated a lot of publicity for the district—made national TV, in fact.

We were doing prescribed burning for black-tail deer. What that means is that we attempted to duplicate, under controlled conditions, how a forest fire can improve the habitat. Our district was the first to go into this in a big way, and I was the wildlife biologist for the project. So the Forest Service would send out the head honchos to conduct management reviews, and I would meet with them—me, a little GS-5 Seasonal.

Then one of the people I had met in California called me up and recruited me for a Forest Service job in southern California. I wasn't too crazy about working in southern California, and I knew I never wanted to stay there, but the job gave me lots of good experience. In southern California, if you work for the Forest Service, all you have to do is open your mouth and you have ten environmental groups and ten opposing development groups jumping on you. You're very aware of the consequences of what you do.

In the Northern Rockies, people don't pressure the Forest Service—not compared to Region 5. I think federal agencies are a lot better when they're under pressure. It's not that the Forest Service up here is maliciously trying to do anything against the public, but watchdogging is wonderful. I wish there was more of it.

There are terrific opportunities here in the Idaho Panhandle. In the Cleveland National Forest, where I worked in San Diego County, there was only one large ungulate (hoofed mammal), which was the mule deer. Here we have six: elk, white-tailed deer, mule deer, moose, caribou, mountain goat, and an occasional bighorn sheep. Also we have two different kinds of bears.

Some may be pretty small populations, like caribou, but that's beside the point. We have the only woodland caribou in the country. They haven't been totally destroyed, as they have

166

in so many other places. And the grizzly bear—Alaska has a greater grizzly population, and so does Montana, and ours is small, but we still *have* one. It's like a little extra bonus.

I especially like working in the Idaho Panhandle because there's still an opportunity to do something for these species, and in the future, instead of seeing these creatures eliminated from northern Idaho, as they have been in so many other parts of the United States, you might somehow think, "Well, little Danielle Jerry had some impact in keeping them around for a while."

Most wildlife biologists like to think they're doing something for the world, and I don't have a very anthropocentric perspective. We may be the most important animal that has evolved, because we are so much in control and we can make things wonderful or totally destroy them, but that doesn't make me think we're the only ones that count.

People have different values and priorities even within the Forest Service, but I don't have to justify putting time and money into wildlife protection, because we have the Endangered Species Act backing us up. I like that. In addition, Forest Service policy on sensitive species is to treat them as though they were endangered.

But then some people say, "Well, humans come first," or words to that effect, and I'll agree—*if* you're talking about life or death. In considering whether a grizzly bear is going to die or some human being is going to live, I'll go for the human every time. But that's not usually what we're talking about. We're talking about whether every human has the right to his own large house—heated inefficiently—to use up energy and all sorts of water to make the lawn green and the dishes clean, or to over-irrigate commercial farmland. Does that justify sacrificing other species?

If we had to force ourselves to live within our means, we could probably do it, because we're so rich in natural resources and comparatively low in population density. But in the wasting of natural resources, Americans are the hogs of the world. If people all over the world adopted our standards, every other living thing would have to be sacrificed. Think of the population of India—three times as great as the United States. I once read that in consumption of natural resources, one American equals five Indians. I'm not arguing that India remain mired in poverty, but if they ever reach our level of consumption . . .

I think individuals should try to achieve a measure of self-sufficiency, and you can work toward that partly by controlling waste. I get violent about people wasting water, because I know what it does to wildlife populations. We drastically reduced salmon and steelhead populations in the northwestern rivers because we thought we needed to dam them all up, so that we could use water however we pleased. But regional economic self-sufficiency? No; the country is too connected, and it's good that it is. I like to be able to buy bananas, and Idaho is never going to grow bananas. We can't be independent. Learning to live within our means is a national problem.

The biggest long-term threat is population. I always give money to Planned Parenthood. I think it's the only long-term answer. The more people there are, and the more affluent they are, the harder it is to be conservative. If you're affluent, you can afford waste, so the number one thing is not letting the world population get too big.

I really don't see any hope of people changing. Some people will, but we're getting too separated from natural things. I remember a time in a wilderness area in the Laguna Mountains, in Cleveland National Forest, and coming across two women who were just furious because they had just seen a rattlesnake. They were furious at the Forest Service for failing to do something about rattlesnakes. *That's* anthropocentric. We'll always have an anthropocentric view of the world.

Changing the attitudes of people who have become basically urban is very difficult. They are confused about who they are, and who their friends and foes are. The wildlife field is divided. You have the hunting-and-fishing crowd and you have the anmal-protection crowd. The animal-protection people are called the environmentalists, which drives me crazy, because I'm not an animal-protectionist but I consider myself an environmentalist.

To have these two groups arguing is pointless, when there are so many other people in this world who don't care at all what happens to the caribou or the bald eagle or the grizzly or the elk or any animal species. Both of these groups care about wildlife. One wants to shoot it, the other doesn't, but they have the same objective. In order to have that animal in sight —whether it is in sight of a gun or a camera—you have to plan. Both of these groups are basically interested in giving that animal a place to live, and there are so many more people out there who couldn't care less.

It isn't all black and white. Some people who think of themselves as animal-protectionists really have very little appreciation of animals—not much more than the zoo visitor who says: "Mom, look at the buffalo; what does it do?"

A study was once done in which different kinds of people were asked questions about the environment and animals. Among those asked were hunters, recreationists, snowmobilers, baseball fans, and birders. Hunters were down at the bottom with baseball fans. On the average, they knew nothing. The people who ranked highest were birders and trappers. Trappers weren't in the original study, but there was another study that compared trappers to the others, and they scored way up there.

That's not surprising, because anybody who traps has to know hard-core stuff about the habits of animals—what kind of habitat the animal likes, where it goes during the day, its behavior patterns, and how it fits in with other critters. Birders have to know the same things. I'm not the world's greatest birder, but when you get hard-core birders, they'll differentiate the Empidonax Flycatchers by habitat. Jiminy Cricket, they look identical except by where they are located.

Both these groups are really into watching and appreciating animals. Birders are non-consumptive, and trappers are consumptive, but both are into hard-core appreciation. Some hunters appreciate, and some haven't a clue.

If the hunters and the anti-hunters could find a way to accommodate each other, they might—combined with all the television shows on wildlife—slow the encroachment a bit. You can almost measure that encroachment in five-acre increments. That's the size of a typical country housing plot, all around the city, any city, every city; and when you surround a city with five-acre tracts, that's a vast amount of land.

The old idea of a city was that you had smaller lots, or people living in apartment houses, with green areas that were common property. Parks were within the city, and the woods beyond. It was much more efficient from the land-use standpoint. Now everyone wants to own his own privacy, and wildlife takes it in the shorts.

That's why setting land aside is so important, and why setting more federal land aside is *really* important for the long-term maintenance of wildlife populations. On private land, immediate short-term economic gain will always be the highest priority. The Midwest is a classic example, and areas throughout the West where they've gone to irrigation farming.

Farmers used to have windbreaks—weeds and bushes and trees at the edge of the field—but farming has become so expensive that from an efficiency standpoint, you plow everything right out to the road, and you forget how incredibly important those windbreaks are. Some people remember how Roosevelt's shelterbelts were planted to fight soil erosion in the thirties, but they forget how windbreaks also served to shelter birds. They were always full of birds, and the weeds along the side of the field were pheasant habitat.

You can't maximize more than one resource at the same time; it comes down to that. You have to decide what's the most important thing. With endangered species, the decision is legislated, and that makes it easier for you. But what about wildlife that doesn't have that kind of legislative protection? Around here, there is a special concern for the elk. Elk can exist with timber-cutting development; in fact, if you do it right you can improve the habitat for them. But you have to deal with it correctly. It doesn't matter how well you do something— if you do too much of it you can't do it well. If we were to decide to absolutely maximize timber production in Region 1 [Northern Rockies] we could say we're going to mitigate for elk as much as we can, but we would come nowhere near the potential for producing elk that would be possible otherwise.

The thing is, if population keeps on increasing, no matter what we say or do, when push comes to shove it will always be: "We *need* this wood, we *need* this oil, we *need* this gas, we *need* these jobs," and we'll accept the trade-off. It all comes down to the population factor.

Planning for diversity is a particular concern of mine, from my perspecetive on the Panhandle. One of the things I'm most involved with is old-growth management. The Idaho Panhandle National Forest is 2.5 million acres—a large forest in which to try to maintain diversity, and a challenge in terms of old-growth management.

To maximize timber production you would essentially truncate succession at the mature stage. This means that trees grow from their round seed to a sapling to a pole to an immature saw timber, as we call it, to a mature tree—at which point, in the context of optimum timber production, you harvest it. Maturity around here is about 100-120 years. You harvest it then. "Succession" simply means the sequence of growth of the plant communities. There's a sequence of plants that habitate an area over time. Succession on its own—without interference and without humans cutting this tree down—will continue, and that tree would eventually get old.

Succession is interrupted naturally by such things as fire, floods, and volcanoes. They create bare ground and the process starts all over again. But humans do it faster than anything else and on a larger scale. If you manage a forest to optimize timber, you proceed through the first parts of succession and then you cut it at maturity and start over. If you do that, you eliminate the old-growth stage—and a lot of life depends on old growth.

If you don't consider that, you just keep thinking, "We need this tree," without asking why, or whether there might be better uses for it. When you begin asking those questions, you begin thinking, for the first time, about the long-term. That's where we are.

I think the forest-planning process that we have been involved in is wonderful, but I'm sick to death of participating in it. It's meant working in an office for two and a half years, in an inter-disciplinary atmosphere, with a bunch of specialists who sit there and argue and crunch numbers, trying to duplicate a natural system in the computer. It's so rough and crude and so frustrating, because you want it to be good.

Until now, environmental assessments have been coming in on isolated species. "The elk habitat quality has declined such-and-such." It means nothing because it is in relation to nothing. How is one small area going to relate to a general picture of what we want? We don't know. The forest plan is the first attempt of the Forest Service to try to put it all together.

We've always had timber management plans. Now we're saying, "Let's have a plan that takes all the resources into consideration and shows the trade-offs." With the forest plan we can have a timber plan that has wildlife in it, minerals, recreation, and watershed concerns. And if you select any variable— "We want this much timber"—you can see the trade-offs with the other resources. This is the first time we've ever attempted something so complex on this scale. It's going to be crude, but each time we do it we're going to get it closer to the real world.

The difficulties are vast. Eventually, I think we have to attempt regional planning, but that will be even more difficult. With the forest plan, we are dealing with Forest Service land, and we have some sort of control over it. But doing regional planning will require dealing with private lands, mixed in with federal lands, mixed in with state lands. We have a computer program that tries to model a forest. It's mind-boggling to do that, but trying it on a regional scale is very, very difficult; however, I think it's critical, because it makes people stop and think about the alternatives open to us.

It is important to have federal lands. The alternative is to have everything piecemealed off into twenty-acre subdivisions, which would be disastrous from a variety of perspectives, including wildlife. Federal land forces non-development in some areas.

Southern California illustrates the point. If you go from Santa Barbara, north of Los Angeles, down to San Diego, it's almost continuous human development—the major exception being Camp Pendleton, the Marine base, about thirty miles north of San Diego. It's a very large tract of land in a prime location on the California coast and must be worth millions and millions of dollars now. It's federal land; it's undeveloped; it has some least tern nests and some endangered plants. If you want to know what the whole southern California coast was like once, Camp Pendleton is about the only place left to see it in its undisturbed state.

Federal lands don't have to be preserves. I'm not for turning federal lands into national parks. I work for the Forest Service and I think a huge diversity of uses is wonderful. We can continue producing timber in the national forests, and I think it's only fair that we should. We can still maintain viable wildlife populations, but if we were to carve these lands into twenty-acre subdivisions, we couldn't do either one. We wouldn't have the timber and we wouldn't be able to maintain viable populations of wildlife in smaller chunks of land, because the bigger animals that require more territory would be eliminated. They couldn't maintain them back East and we can't out here.

In the West, I want the federal lands to stay federal, or public. Even if I didn't work for the Forest Service, I'd feel that way. I like the wide open spaces, and the wide open spaces here are public.

Federal agencies are criticized for their bureaucracy, and a lot of the criticisms are true. Last year I saw a study done by the University of Pennsylvania that attempted to rank the ten most efficient public or private organizations, regardless of size. They had a bunch of criteria, but what amazed me was that the Forest Service made the list. Well, people do interact more in federal agencies than they do in most private organizations of the same size. I don't know that the Forest Service is a model of efficiency, but I don't think efficiency is a function of being federal or non-federal.

Private organizations can have a role in land management, certainly, but generally when private organizations manage land, it isn't open to everybody. My folks have 1500 acres in the Adirondacks. They lease hunting rights to two clubs, and each club has thirty or forty members, and they pay for hunting rights, which gives them access. I love visiting that land, but I couldn't afford to do it that way.

People criticize wilderness areas and claim they're only for the strong and healthy and the backpackers, but they're taking an anthropocentric view of things. As far as I'm concerned, wilderness areas are prime places to maintain certain kinds of wildlife habitat. I'm for maintaining wildlife for wildlife's sake, but if you want to look at it from a detached scientific perspective, we have a very incomplete understanding of the world around us—not how we run the world, but how the world runs by itself.

When we plan, we have to have something to measure results against—a base line or a point of comparison. You need a base line for data on any topic you want to study, and the only way to know how the world runs by itself is to leave some undisturbed areas of large acreages. Some people believe that we need just a few places for that, but that's not true, because our country is divided into so many types of natural ecosystems that to have base lines you really need to have an appropriate ecosystem and you have to be able to make comparisons between them. Without base lines, you have no frame of reference.

We need indicators of what we're doing to ourselves. Thomas Jefferson didn't think grazing would ever be important in the United States and didn't think ranching or dairy farming would be viable occupations—because of timber wolves. Well, you don't find timber wolves in Virginia today. You find only a few of them anywhere. A whole frame of reference changes. How much more can it change? And what do we compare it to?

Predators are at the top of the food chain, so they're one of the quickest indicators of change in the habitat. Wolves, as it happens, are one of the best barometers we have on deviation from the natural. When you eliminate wolves, which were plentiful in their natural habitat, you've done something drastic. Then it's up to you to figure out what you've done.

In that context—the context of providing a base line, and some guidance about where we may or may not want to go—this region is unusual and valuable to the country. It has forms of wildlife that have been eliminated everywhere else except Alaska. In the lower forty-eight states, this is the only region that still has representative populations of the big animals, such as: moose, grizzly, elk, wolverines. These animals require large territories. People have a hard time dealing with the realization that a single caribou may require thousands of acres. We have 175,000 acres in the Panhandle that we decided to dedicate to caribou, and the fifteen to twenty caribou we have require the entire acreage. That many acres should support a lot of caribou, and we want to increase the numbers, but they're eating only lichens all winter long, and lichens can't take much abuse.

The Endangered Species Act is a real concern of mine. There's a constant danger that the law will be watered down. To protect against that, and to provide for long-term maintenance of wildlife populations, there has to be a recognition of their economic value. I personally would prefer to value wildlife for other reasons, but I'm enough of a realist to realize when push comes to shove, wildlife will always be shoved. Probably the best way to prevent that is to come up with an economic base that is strongly dependent on wildlife.

When this country was being settled, fishing was the first industry; then trappers opened the West. Trapping may not provide an economic base today, but fishing can, and I'm all for trying to maintain it as an important part of the regional economy.

The recreational base is significant for hunting and, as in Africa, the game farm may be the only way to save some wildlife populations. If we can ever get back to something like that for the buffalo, I'd be all for it. I think it's fine that people are raising buffalo now for meat, and that they can butcher them and sell the meat commercially at a profit. I'd rather raise buffalo just for the sake of raising buffalo, but I'll settle for doing it in the context of creating an economic base dependent on wildlife. It's better to be slaughtered in a slaughterhouse than not to survive as a species.

Burtt Trueblood

Burtt Trueblood runs a seed farm operation on the fertile Snake River Plain west of Boise. Burtt and his wife Mary were early pioneers in Idaho's efforts to conserve wildlife. Their model Homedale farm draws visitors from throughout the nation who are interested in observing an approach to farming that integrates wildlife management with progressive farming methods.

HOW DID I GET TO IDAHO? IT WAS REALLY EASY. I was born right here. My family came in 1912. My great-aunt Ada really led the family—Ada County is named after her. She settled down in the area by Star and Eagle and she attracted my grandmother and then she communicated with my parents who were working for the railroad in Laramie, Wyoming. My aunt told them about this land, so they decided to quit and move here. My wife Mary's family had been here for a while before that.

My father worked as an engineer on the Boise Project which was the first big irrigation development around here. Up and down the Boise River are the old settlers' canals and the riverside canal, irrigation that was put in in the 1860s and 1870s. Some were built for mining gold. Those ditches became an irrigation system for farming after the mining closed down.

The Boise Project was one of the first Bureau of Reclamation projects and it was a cheap and practical one. It's made up of five different irrigation districts, Wilder being ours here. My folks homesteaded and Dad worked at the Bureau until 1919; then he farmed full-time until 1933. I took over during my high school period and farmed some prior to World War II. I farmed all during the war, and didn't go to service.

Mary and I went to Alaska in 1950, for two or three reasons. My folks had retired at that time, and my dad had independent income, but my parents felt the income off the

174

farm should be divided equally between himself and me. They wanted to spend a little more than the land was capable of producing and there was just no way Mary and I felt that we could raise a family and give the children the kind of education that we wanted them to have and support two families on this eighty acres. When I suggested that my father think about either enlarging our acreage or going into a more intensive type of cropping system, he was not the least bit cooperative.

In Alaska, we lived out in the boondocks at a place called Shaw Creek, seventy-seven miles from Fairbanks. I worked in construction; helped to build a piece of every road in Alaska. It was a slack time—before the pipeline and after the Korean crisis. I also worked for RCA on communications for intercontinental ballistic missiles.

We came back from Alaska in 1964. My father had passed away two years after we left for Alaska, and when we came back my mother had mortgaged the place to where all the credit was used up and there was no other source, and she was about to lose it. We were not really ready to come back at that time, as the kids were through high school and we wanted to play for a year or two. That phase of our lives had been quite a struggle. You have to generate wealth to send kids to MIT; it costs nothing but loot. We had to hustle around to get a couple of bucks to get them ready and enough to also come back and farm here.

If I have heard it once, I have heard it a thousand times: "Let's make all we can this year." Take a heritage that will feed the family and its sons and daughters forever if proper care is taken. Trade it off in one year for a trip back East or to Europe. It's shortsightedness. This happened on this land and we had a horrible period restoring the fertility of this soil and getting it up to where we could get a decent crop.

It was a heartbreak. We had excellent crops that last year I farmed here, which was 1950. I came back in 1964, and you didn't have to look at the ground; all you had to do was walk across it and you could feel the difference with your feet. The Navajo say, "Don't walk on Mother Earth in the Spring of the year because she is pregnant." You could feel that thing. I never had it put to me so forcefully as here. I had a recollection of what it was like when I was farming here. You could walk across the field and it felt cushiony—like a rug—and all of a sudden, it was hard like the pavement. Anytime a country boy goes to the city and walks on the sidewalk, his feet hurt; his legs hurt. He gets so tired he cannot stand it in just two or three hours because he is not used to that. A city person becomes acclimated to that, but a country boy hurts when he goes to the city. That's exactly what we had here. The land had what I prefer to call "widow woman blight."

Why that name? Sixty-five percent of Canyon County is absentee owned. Usually farm women outlive their husbands by about ten years. The woman says, "We want to make all we can this year," and so the renter is forced to withdraw and withdraw until he creates a semi-sterile condition. There is a 40 acre section down the road that was like that when we took it over—nine sacks of beans to the acre. Right across the ditch, we had thirty sacks. That acreage was almost destroyed. I got the drain water off it, and I built ponds and dikes and gained two acres in a field. We had gullies four to six feet deep when I took that place. I diked all those up and caught all the silt, and then I would haul it up in the field to low spots and keep filling them in. When I took that place, that field was 6.2 acres and now it is 8 acres. I have gained almost 2 acres off that one 40 acre plot.

This sort of thing happens all the time. The old concrete

irrigation structures that my dad put in around 1924 were four feet deep when he laid them in. When I came back from Alaska, I plowed into one of them and broke it open with the plow. They were buried less than a foot. I figured a foot and a half of topsoil disappeared during the twelve years that we were in Alaska. If you move off a foot and a half of topsoil in a land where you have no "A" horizon (rich organic topsoil) you have nothing. You have a sterile condition, as well as the addition of chemicals in certain fields that I wouldn't think of using myself. I use lots of chemicals, but the ones I use are biodegradable—and quickly biodegradable. These were not. So this is what I came back to, and it was a heartbreak.

The fields were as much as thirty to thirty-five percent noxious weeds. In addition to the fertility loss of the topsoil, the weeds had taken over because there was no organic content. A well-balanced soil has much fewer problems with weeds.

The first year, I plowed up a field and planted corn. After it came up, I gave it the first irrigation. I ran water five days and the corn still wilted. The soil could not take or hold water. That fall we had about fifteen tons per acre. I sold it for ensilage, because the ears were so small. Corn is probably one of the most soil-depleting crops we raise, next to alfalfa hay. I had some clover seed that a previous renter had planted and I put thirty acres of clover chaff on this field. The next year I had thirty-two tons of corn ensilage. We doubled the yield in one year and kept on.

It cost a fortune. It would have been a lot better to go buy a good eighty acres in production—some that had been taken care of—than to restore the family farm for sentimental reasons. But I don't have any regrets. This is what I wanted to do. I have this delightful habitat for wildlife and it has a great deal of sentimental value. After all, I have lived here all my life,

with the exception of the period we were in Alaska. I know the neighbors from way back. The boy who's renting land from us is the great-grandson of a nice old gentleman I knew as a kid.

These soils weren't half as productive when my dad home-steaded as they are now under my management. No way would they produce then like they will now. It's a matter of steward-ship. The word "stewardship" comes from Old English. The steward was the guy smart enough to manage the pigs. He was the livestock manager in the family group, and the most tal-ented, because livestock was the most valuable product.

A soil is not infinite. There is only so much phosphorous, potash, and other plant food in that soil. Some time, some way, it has to be replaced. When you haul tons and tons of corn off an Iowa field year after year and ship it overseas, you are extracting the wealth from it. Maybe in twenty years, we won't be able to feed our own population, much less the world's.

The scientific studies I've read show that about fifty percent of Idaho's soil is now gone—or Illinois's, or Indiana's. You can name any state. The soil here had about one-percent organic matter when it was first homesteaded—even after all the abuse with the great cattle herds that were brought through here. There was enough organic matter that my uncle said that the winds "blew black." Organic matter in the end is humus; in this form, it has the dead bodies of little microorganisms that break down other organic matter; and it is blowable and leachable.

In the early days, these guys tore up the sagebrush and started leveling the fields. The winds blew black for a few years. It was their humus blowing away. That's what happened to the other place down the road here before we took it on. It had been rented out to a neighbor who is a notorious exploiter as far as soil is concerned. The owner asked me to take it on.

176

We decided to put it into corn. Corn is a grass and it will give you more pounds of plow-down than any other crop we raise in this area. You need the plow-down (plowing under the stalks to return organic matter to the soil) to build up the soil.

If you plant 18,000 corn seeds to the acre—which they generally do in the Midwest—you will have a twelve-inch, twelve-ounce ear of corn. If you plant 28,000 plants, you will have an eight-inch, eight-ounce ear. If you plant 38,000 plants, you will probably have a four- to five-inch ear weighing four to five ounces. So we planted 36,000 plants to the acre and double-fertilized with the plan of getting maximum plow-down of organic matter.

At the end of three years, we were $3,300 in the hole. We were spending a fortune on fertilizer to accomplish what we needed to do. We had corn to sell, and it made from 130 to 150 bushels per acre, but even so I had not been able to draw anything for my own labor and management.

The fourth year, we seeded with alfalfa, and we had a $6,000 net profit. It was ready to produce, you see, and this was despite the fact that in the second year we had a two-acre plot of alfalfa as a test that wouldn't seed. The bees would land on the blossom and fly away. The nutrient level was so poor in this second-year alfalfa that they couldn't live on it.

So the fourth year, we netted $6,000. The fifth year, we had a nice crop. It got damaged some by a rainstorm, but we still netted $9,000. At the end of five years, I was $3,200-$3,300 ahead for my labor and management. The sixth year, we had a $31,000 gross and a $19,000 net. This is what you can do: you can take a soil that won't even break even and turn it around. That land has been highly profitable ever since. You have to be willing to invest that first $10,000 in order to get a long-term return.

This is a hard thing. Here we have a soil where we have to replace everything we take out as we go along. This country has always needed fertilizing, but the potbellied fertilizer man comes along and says, "What are you doing wasting your time hauling manure when I can do the same for you with commercial fertilizer?" So the guy down the road, a really good friend of mine, takes the potbellied fertilizer salesman's word and quits hauling manure. For three years he has the best crops he's ever had, but by the sixth year, he has his farm up for sale.

He had all that nice land, and kept one forty acre piece, but now he is running a machine shop. He forgot that it takes a balanced program. It doesn't matter whether you use it first by letting the cow extract all the nutriments and then putting the manure as fertilizer back on the soil. Or you can take it from the crop directly by plowing down and back into the soil. Some has to go back.

Conservation is the wise use of our natural resources for the greatest benefit of all life. People are only one of the things that we are thinking of conserving. Gifford Pinchot said, "Conservation is the wise use of resources for the good of man." He was wrong. It isn't just for the use of man! If I can't have angleworms out in this field, I can't feed man. And it takes ten years to build a culture of angleworms! I don't think I am one bit better than an angleworm. His place in the overall picture, the total circle, is just as important as my place.

I see conservation as benefiting all life, and then I include people as one of the animals that we are interested in preserving. I feel that these Labrador dogs own a share of this property. How can you say they are not something special? This is as stupid as ERA. There never should have been a need for ERA because nobody should have ever thought a man was better than a woman. I know a lot of people who would jump all over me for that, but in all my life I have always looked at an individual—white or colored or Indian—pure and simple. I don't think you can live with wildlife and think that you are better than anything else.

My dad was a conservationist and I think that is probably where Ted and I got our initial conservation training. We used to go over across the river fifteen miles to what we called the "Leaf Mines" where there were great areas of fossilized leaves in shale. They are all gone now. People have gathered them up. Or we would have a picnic at what we called the "Petrified Forest" where there must have been an area a quarter of a mile across with logs as much as three feet high, lying there petrified, with some of them opalized. It was beautiful! Dad said, "You can bring home two or three extra nice pieces, but leave the rest for the other people. If there is something there that you think is good enough to send to the Smithsonian, we will take it. But leave the remainder for other people to see." That was his approach. He gave each of us a rifle when we were six. We traveled the hills back of here and shot jackrabbits. It was all right to go alone or the two of us together, but never with another boy. He said three boys always made trouble. He would rather that we go by ourselves, which we did most of the time. If there wasn't work to do, both Ted and I were going down to the river fishing or hunting in the fall.

I got into trapping in high school when Ted was trying to go to the College of Idaho. Ted never did trap. I remember one time in 1933 I had twenty dollar bills saved up and I loaned them to Ted so he could finish a semester of school. I made that money trapping because that was a period when money was awfully precious. My mother always said that only ne'er-do-wells trapped. Everybody that trapped was a cinch to have a red nose and be a drunkard and living in sin. My parents, you

see, were violently opposed to some things—neither of them smoked or drank. Trappers were always drunkards. They always stopped in the beer parlor on the way home and they were just bad, she would say. But I made that money for Ted—by trapping.

As I got older, I got very interested in Future Farmers of America. I had all sorts of projects going. I had a bunch of calves in 1932 when times were so bad that if you got a dollar per hundred pounds for a beef that was all you could expect.

I had a real interesting experience one time. On the far northwest corner of our property, there was a house that was single-wall construction. There was no inside finish at all and it must have been cold. In those days, people took flour and pasted newspapers between the studs to stop the wind. There was a nice man living there. It was in the fall of 1932, and he had been going around, trying to find a day's work at a time. The farmers would also let him go out in the fields and pick up potatoes. He had a cellar dug and a year's supply of potatoes, onions and produce.

One afternoon, when I was a freshman in high school, I came home and was leaning over the fence watching all my critters. I would go around to the neighbors and they would give me a bull dairy-calf, or anything else to raise in hopes of getting something for it. He came up to me and spoke. Here I was a thirteen-year-old in high school and he was a mature man. I remember that he talked to me completely as an equal. He said, "You know, my family hasn't had any meat for a very long time and they need some meat."

I said, "Well, I can sure understand that," or some dumb answer to that effect. He said, "What will you take for that calf out there?" I said, "Well, I figure that calf at $5." It weighed about 500 pounds. I said, "I am trying to get $1 a hundred pounds." He said, "That's a good price, but I don't have $5." What do you want for that one? And I answered, "Three." "Well," he said, "It may weigh over 300, that's a good buy, but I don't have $3."

There was a little, scrawny-looking one that weighed maybe 175–200 pounds, and he said, "What do you want for it?" And I said, "It's worth $2.00." He said, "Well, I just can't do it."

A neighbor had given me a pair of twin billy goats and I fed them on skim milk. One was named Edward, and just then he made the biggest mistake of his life. He came walking along and this guy said, "What do you want for that goat?" Edward probably would have weighed 125 or 135 pounds. Pheasant season was going to open on about the fifteenth, and this was the seventh or eighth of October. I didn't have shell one, and I was really desperate trying to figure out how to get a box of shotgun shells. I thought, "Oh, oh, if I can get a dollar out of that goat, I can get me a box of shotgun shells. . . ."

I said, "I will take a dollar for that goat." This fella looked at me and he said, "Well, I have a dollar." He had a silver dollar and he handed it to me. I said, "I will get a string. You just bought yourself a goat." So, he had some meat for his family and I had some shotgun shells. Times were hard.

In 1946, I did a study for the state Fish and Game people, looking at what wildlife was here before my folks homesteaded. It may have been one of the first such studies done anywhere in the West. My conclusion was that there was about three percent as much wildlife here before irrigation as afterwards. This was after the great cattle drives. The grass was gone; sagebrush had taken over. There were no ducks or geese here then except during migration. Now in the evening, you can

go out and see several thousand wild geese and ducks around here because they stay all year. I contributed to that. People along the river used to keep live geese with the wings clipped as decoys. When the Migratory Bird Treaty Act made it illegal, we went out and gathered the clipped geese and took them over to the Deerflat National Wildlife Refuge, which is our irrigation lake. They made it through the winter. Next summer the little guys grew. They could fly, but their folks couldn't—so they all stayed around. Before long, we had a non-migratory flock of geese. It now numbers 3,500 or so. All of this is man-made.

Right now we have 174 pheasants on this block of 160 acres. You can walk out any day and see them. We leave every fifth row of our seed corn—the "boll row" or pollenizer row—for the wildlife, and it's very attractive for the ducks and geese as well. It's remarkable that we are able to manage and hold such a population of wildlife, given all of the people pressures. Of course, we limit hunting and we know the bird population —what our take is and what the available take can be. It's no different from our corn. I am a management-use conservationist. I am not a preservationist. I want to keep wildlife in such a way that it is at maximum productivity.

The man who is raising beef cattle doesn't keep the steers until they get as big as the English animals became in the sixteenth cenutry—the great oxen. They harvest their beef when it is ready, and you harvest your crop when it is ready. Wildlife is part of the production of the land and part of the value of your land. Other people are learning this, too. Management of wildlife habitat is now one of the two top priorities in Canyon Country, under the Agricultural Soil Conservation Service.

I believe the advocates of the Sagebrush Rebellion are a bunch of damn thieves. They are trying to steal something that belongs to all of us.

The succession of plants in this region is almost to its climax —when one type of vegetation changes to another because of improvements or fluctuations in the soil or climate. The sagebrush is dying out rapidly in Owyhee County, and is being replaced by a grass culture, except where the juniper have taken over. The range is improving and has improved much since 1920 when I first started going out there to watch those hillsides ooze when the snow melted. There was nothing left but pea gravel—no topsoil left at all. Clumps of grass were here and there, maybe three or four inches in diameter—little islands all by themselves, resembling biscuits. Now all this is changing. Grass is coming back. Grass is the soil-builder. All of our great soils have been made by grass, and nothing else. How deep is the soil in the forest? You dig down two or three inches and you are into minerals. You go out into the tall grass prairie and you dig half a day to get to the bottom of the "A" Horizon. This is beginning to occur in the area that I am familiar with that extends from here to Burley to Idaho Falls; and from Nevada to Oregon.

Some of these Sagebrush guys can see this change coming. They saw what the BLM did out here on the controlled burn areas—those 15,000 acre blocks of grass, knee to waist high with fat, lazy deer running around during the winter in perfect condition, having healthy fawns in the spring. This is what the Sagebrush guys see coming. They are going to have an opportunity to run twice as many, and maybe three or four times as many cattle on these public lands in just ten or fifteen years. Public awareness is the only way to stop this.

My family and I have been involved in the conservation effort close to fifty years. It goes back to the time in 1936–1938, when Ted worked for $15 a week to promote the initiative that brought the Idaho Fish and Game Commission into effect.

Also at that time, we demonstrated that you could catch salmon on a lure. People in those days would drive saddle horses up and down the streams during spawning runs spearing salmon. The eggs were lying there, freshly fertilized, and guys would take spears and ride saddle horses and chase the salmon up and down Bear Valley Creek and Sulphur Creek and all the streams up there on the headwaters of the Salmon River. This was during the 1920s and 1930s. It then became illegal for a period of time to ride a saddle horse up and down a stream. We got busy in the late 1930s, and Ted learned how to get king salmon on a lure. He and I walked the Middle Fork of the Salmon River in 1937, and he went back in 1939 and spent the whole summer fishing for salmon and learning how to use lures. Shortly thereafter, we made a movie. Mary and I did the fishing and Ted took the film. The Fish and Game Commission bought the camera and film, and that thing was copied and shown and run until it was just about worn out. In a few years we had a law that stopped salmon spearing.

Salmon are almost gone now; they are almost extinct, but we were able to save some of the run. There are only about 300 left. But here we are this year with the best steelhead trout run in ten or fifteen years. It makes me feel good. We've had a good take, but there's plenty left for spawning. That was a long, hard battle and the younger people in Idaho don't even know how we fought to stop salmon spearing. This was long before the big fuss about dams and all that stuff about how to save the salmon. We were years ahead!

I am deeply concerned in one area, and that is the population problem. That isn't my area of expertise and I don't know the answers to it. I can only stand back and shiver. The pressure on our land is getting great. I am terribly frightened about the lack of birth control. There are too many births in the world. There are too many people. I am afraid the pressure is going to be so massive that I won't be able to hold onto this 200 acres to produce food. People want to live on the land. Look what happened in Egypt; look what happened in Central America, where the father leaves the farm to the family and they divide it into little pieces, and finally there is only room enough for a house. Then they no longer are self-sufficient in their food supply. We are under intense pressure to sell this land for housing. Constantly, people want to buy our land. Perhaps they will make an amazing discovery. When they get to living on this beautiful farmland they will discover it isn't what they thought. We have been Californized something terrible by the people who come up here and get a piece of land all their own. They are just like a bunch of pigs in a pen: they ruin what they are after.

Farmers *can* go ahead and produce food, but economics and political pressures are the bases of all problems right now. Always remember that there never has been a state since Rome where government policy hasn't been "cheap food and the hell with the land," except in modern Israel. Right now we are trading our wealth out of our soils for oil. If it were not for the foreign exchange from agriculture, where would we be as far as being able to buy oil so people can drive up and down the highways and do all the things they do in wasting gasoline?

But are we ready for the kind of government that will tell a man he can't do that, or tell a farmer that he must not sell or subdivide if he wants to? Do you want blood on the streets? If anybody came here and told me, independent as I am, "You will do something to this land," he would never leave the place alive. That's a fact. I don't think you can tell a man, "You *will* do such and such with your fields." It's the ethic of the American farmer that he is in the best class of citizens. He is not about to sell out if he can help it. But if he is forced to, he will.

Arnold Silverman

I REMEMBER THE FIRST TIME I DROVE OVER THE CONTINENTAL DIVIDE and dropped into the Butte Valley. It was twilight on a June afternoon in 1954, and I remember it as though it were yesterday! There it was: my first view of Butte, Montana, which I had been reading about and learning about through geology texts—and there *I* was, driving in to Butte from New York City!

I was doing my dissertation work then, and I had the same sense of the West that I suppose most easterners have especially geologists—that this was the great frontier, on which the industrial wealth, the mineral wealth, and, in a sense, the social wealth of this country evolved. The wars of the copper kings. The Anaconda Company. And the grandeur of the physical, geological processes that could produce a Butte in this world.

Butte is one of the truly great, world-class mineral deposits —an inspiration to any young geologist with intellectual aspirations. To come here, to walk around the hills, to drive up to the silver and manganese mines of Philipsburg and then on into northern Idaho and the great Coeur d'Alene mining district were some of the great thrills of my early professional life. And

then to have the opportunity to come back, four years later, to teach at Missoula was like coming to Mecca.

In my eastern mind I connected Montana with the remoteness of Alaska and western Canada. Not only did it play a vital role in the intellectual development of my field, it also played a vital role in my personal imagery of space and time. Geographically, it seemed much farther away than California. I came here with a sense of awe, as to a new land, and that sense heightened my almost reckless expectations; anything was possible.

Culturally, I had a certain awareness of connections that balanced, in a way, the physical remoteness of Montana. There was a very strong, progressive labor tradition in the West, created largely by the Mine, Mill and Smelter Workers' Union and the Farmers' Union. They were important political and social forces in Montana, and their members were the people I immediately associated with and felt comfortable with; they made me feel welcome. I met people who were both exciting and, if you will, settling. Knowing them made it possible for me to come from the East and settle, without feeling like an outlander. Wherever the Mine-Mill had a presence, there was a sense of connection for anyone who had grown up in the East and understood the role that the union movement had played in bettering the lives of working people. Butte and Anaconda were *the* Mine-Mill towns of the West, of course. The traditions there helped make Montana accessible to me.

That was about thirty years ago. My sense of the physical Montana is that it has changed very little since. Except for a modest increase in population, which is particularly noticeable in a few communities—Great Falls, Billings, Missoula—the place has not changed much at all. I have the same sense of the relationship of the landscapes, the valleys and the mountains and the plains and prairies and plateau regions, that I had when I first came here. I see them in the same physical light, their reflections not having been disturbed in any dramatic way.

Of course, there are places in eastern Montana where coal mining has developed and expanded relentlessly, but, on the other hand, Anaconda and Butte have changed very little physically. The northwestern part of the state has not changed much, except for the construction of the Libby Dam and the opening up of a rich copper-silver mine near Bull Lake, south of Troy. People are still generally pursuing the same activities for their livelihood—with the exception of the significant reduction in hardrock mining—as they did thirty years ago.

There was an interest in oil exploration when I first came out here, and there still is today. There are a few more oil wells in the state now, but the level of activity is not much greater than it was then. Maybe there's a little more excitement because of the Overthrust Belt development and new discoveries deep in the Williston Basin. We've built some reservoirs (Yellowtail), impounded some water, generated some hydroelectric production; but, by and large, it's still the same Montana, both physically and mentally.

People characterize this as a very fragile part of the country. The word is inaccurate, because it seems to suggest that Montana shouldn't be disturbed by any activity of man because the entire ecological system will be disrupted by that disturbance beyond recovery. I don't think that's a correct view of fragility. What the term means to me is that there are limits to the extent and intensity of man-made changes that can be accommodated without seeing long-term effects or irreversible changes. So one can argue that the basic physical character of the state would not change dramatically if the rate of growth and the extent

and kind of individual projects were contained within some reasonable limits, within the carrying capacity of the land.

To argue that you can't mine in Montana without losing the essence of Montana as we have known it throughout modern history is absurd to me; to argue that you can't cut timber without ruining the forests is absurd; to argue that you can't ranch or grow crops without ruining the land is absurd. If you're sensitive to questions of size and scale and scope and sequential development, you can preserve the physical character of Montana, and its environmenal integrity.

But what I *will* argue is that if you are not sufficiently concerned about where and how you do it, at what rate expansion takes place, how you reclaim and reseed and what technology is compatible with the environment—then you can ruin this state. And the state is threatened by the undisciplined, unrealistic, unthinking assumption that Montana should be nothing more than energy resource center for the entire country, for a long time into the future.

That assumption could destroy a very large portion of what we value—wilderness, clean air, good water—and it can destroy a large amount of land that is productive now in a variety of ways and could be productive forever. It could destroy, too, a sense of economic and social community that is terribly important to the way Montanans live, and it could destroy Montana's political character, which is, in some ways, unique—because of the way people can still reach out to the system and influence it in ways that are unheard of in places like California and New York.

I think we can control what happens to our community, the Northern Rockies, if we're sensible and committed. To begin with, we don't have to accept the forecasts of some futurists who argue that America can survive only by devouring

Montana. Looking ahead twenty or thirty years, there will be a very modest increase in total demand for energy, meaning a relatively small increase in the demand to exploit the physical resources of Montana—much less than some analysts, particularly in the government, have been claiming the past ten years.

I would argue that "relatively modest" means perhaps twice the size of current mining activity, as opposed to projections of ten times the current size, or twenty times the size. And it's certainly possible to project a future in which less exploitation of energy resources takes place. To some extent, projections of physical change are going to be governed by changes that take place culturally and politically.

In that respect, I think Montana has become dramatically more open and sensitive to public concerns and public-interest movements; dramatically more open and accessible to a wide variety of people who can occupy community positions with great power to influence the court of our political evolution. In terms of the distribution of power, and in terms of democratic influence on the decisions of state government, I think there has been a quantum leap in the past twenty years toward open politics.

I have a sense of an evolving, developing, participatory democracy in Montana that, in my earlier years, I never really believed could be possible, because it wasn't possible in the urbanized, centralized, overpopulated communities where I spent most of my early life. There was a sense in those places of being a victim—of being dragged along rather than doing the pushing. I'm encouraged by the contrast between that kind of political life and the evolution I've seen in Montana in the past two decades.

I think a very dynamic politics is alive and well in Montana. I see it in a "new guard" evolving in the legislature. They are

Arnold Silverman is the chairman of the geology department at the University of Montana. A nationally recognized expert on strategic minerals and energy development in the West, he is a member of the board of the Northern Lights Institute. He lives in Missoula, Montana.

the cadre now and not the leaders, but they are going to shape this state ten years from now. We saw this group emerging in the most recent legislative session, and to some extent in the previous session.

If we were to build political strength on the local level on the same basis—that is, young people interested in a commitment to a community, and interested in community politics and community organization—we would see a political future in Montana very much sensitized to what people want—a future of not being pushed and hauled by old-guard reactions, either to the way politics was practiced in the old days or to the politics of tough muscle from outside forces.

Politics will always be subject to corporate muscle in the Rockies, and the only way we'll survive that is if bright, committed people have a sense that they can deal with it, are not intimidated by it, and can still sort out for themselves what the critical life issues are.

That can happen, and there are a lot of people around who can make it happen. Just suppose we didn't have to deal with the El Salvador, Afghan, African, and Vietnam kinds of issues that consume so much energy and intellect. My God, what an enormous amount of vitality and commitment could be devoted to dealing with the future survival of an integrated bio-social system for the Northern Rockies!

I don't know that we'll ever have that luxury, but there are enough sensitive people out there, willing to contribute, that I'm sure we will get a hearing about the future of the region. And if we're diligent and intelligent and committed, we can have a good part of that future our way.

I'm not arguing that we've consistently made progressive, democratic political decisions in Montana; I'm not arguing that we've always known what we wanted to do; I'm not claiming that the best of our people have always had a chance to become the representatives of our society; but what I am saying is that the *availability* is there—so much more so than twenty years ago.

Most of the industrialized urban centers along the Great Lakes and in the East still are so totally the captives of the indigenous primary industries that what passes for political freedom is a sham. That happened to Montana, too, in the early days of development, and perhaps to an even greater degree than elsewhere, but it is not the case now. Montana is

ahead of every other state in the Rocky Mountains in articulating a community of shared, basic public concerns. In that respect Montana is far ahead of Wyoming and Idaho. That may be unfair, but let me tell you why I feel that way. There are three reasons.

First, I think I can go to any community in Montana— I mean every single one—and find at least one kindred soul. I don't think I could do that in Wyoming and Idaho, but I can do it here, because communication is immediate and sympathetic and vital. You're not alone. You can find a sense of understanding, a spirit that is shared by somebody everywhere, and that's important to the way I view change taking place.

Second, I'm impressed with the fact that we can be very stupid about choosing our leaders in Montana, but very shrewd about how we later evaluate them. And I think that's also important to the democratic process, because there may come a time—and it may come soon—when we will do away with that dichotomy, when we'll get a coincidence of how we feel and vote and what we expect from the people we voted for. The potential for that seems much better in Montana than in Idaho and Wyoming.

The third reason has to do with my point of view as an educator. My perspective of the University of Montana, on Montana State University, and on the whole educational system in the state, gives me the sense that our kids get an opportunity to understand more of what's relevant in living their lives than they would in other places. I think the University of Montana, for instance, contributes more to the education of a student than any legislator expects or suspects.

It has always been very important that a small but good liberal-arts school, such as the University of Montana, has been able to produce people who have stayed in the state and who have had a reasonable understanding of themselves and their world.

I have admired people that I've met at the University of Idaho, but the institution has not had credibility for me. I would never want to work there, and I've been appalled by the University of Wyoming. They have money, facilities, equipment, laboratories, and some very competent people, but, as a community, what has gone on there—at least until the very recent past—has been a great disappointment. These two institutions have not been a focus for community understanding and service; they have not led the people in their state in the search for understanding and truth about the great issues of life in the Northern Rockies: energy, nuclear weapons, and the responsibility of citizenship.

At Wyoming, presidents would tell faculty members they didn't like the conclusions of their studies: "You better change that, if you want to have a future here." They always made it stick. The dynamic of the University of Wyoming was to follow the political lead rather than lead the political life: "Treat me well and you can count on me to be the handmaiden of your political and social views for life. You won't get criticism from me."

That's the sense I have, and the sense a lot of people have who have worked at the University of Wyoming. It may have changed; I can't speak for it today, but I *can* say that in the mid–seventies it was like that.

That is not to say that people in Idaho and Wyoming aren't moving on important issues, but people in Montana began to move on some of those issues in the late fifties and early sixties—air pollution, water resources, and mined-land reclamation, for instance. The important state constitutional convention of 1972 was an outgrowth of the sixties, when people began to tie together in their social and political consciousness, the strings between environmental concerns and economic independence.

Once we in Montana were dominated by one railroad, one power company, one mining company and, to some extent, by the logging industry, but the economic base diversified so rapidly that a very different perception of economic life entered our thinking and our vocabulary. Aside from little boomlets and bustlets related to resources such as uranium, oil and gas, which brought a few people in and then out again, the job growth in this state occurred primarily in the public sector—in state and local government. It brought into this sector an active, intelligent, educated group of people who shared a concern about the way their fellow citizens lived and worked. This has contributed to a broader sharing of political power that has worked remarkably well in recent years, and it has been exciting for me to have been involved in it and to have had some small impact on it.

I have had a fear—although it's less of a fear today than it was a year or two ago—that Montana would fall into the national malaise of believing that state and local political organizations can deal with every important issue, and that we would withdraw from our belief in federalism and its place in American life. That would set us back in every area from education to health and literacy, from political structure to political enfranchisement and civil rights. We would wind up embracing the idea that prevailed in Washington during the first year or two of Reagan and Stockman—the idea that there's really not much for the government to do, except perhaps build MX missiles.

If that happened, we would eventually find ourselves overwhelmed by problems that could only be solved by addressing them, on the national, federal level. Without that approach, it's every man for himself, and every community, and I think that would be devastating for Montana.

I don't necessarily feel we need to accept every kind of federal decision that affects us, but I do feel we have to engage in shaping those decisions. To argue for political isolationism domestically is as destructive as arguing for it internationally. If we're engaged in the national dialogue, there's a better chance for a reasonable outcome.

I'm not as worried now as I was a year or so ago, because I perceive the coming failure of the anti-federalism view in this country. I think that by the end of the eighties we'll be in another very exciting period of creative federalism, carrying on, I hope, into the next century. It could still go the other way, but I doubt that it will, because we're beginning to understand the implications of removing the federal government from the kind of creative role it ought to fill in our society.

I was also afraid we'd see a collapse of the economy and, with that collapse, a growing fear about economic survival that would override every other concern. That fear could be so profound as to destroy, irrationally and completely, what had been built up over the past twenty years. If we had a basic nationwide political retrenchment followed by economic collapse, I'm not sure how Montana would survive.

We need a viable economy to support and maintain political dynamism. We have the resources to do well. We can be creative and productive resource extractionists; we can be creative and productive venturists; and we have to be, in order to sustain an economic system that gives us the freedom to be politically progressive. If we have to fight an economic recession, or depression, so profound that we lose sight of our other goals, then we'll destroy the Montana community—a community built in this region across a span of generations.

We have to nurture that sense of community, guide it, reflect on it, alter it as need be, so that we can succeed at living together at some level of economic and social well-being. If we turn on ourselves because of economic depression, there are people waiting to exploit us. Wherever there's a soft underbelly to the economy and community strength, the exploiters will be there, trying to hustle an extra percent of profit at our expense. That could propel us back into economic colonialism at a moment in history when we've nearly put it behind.

We have the capacity now to make good, solid, reasonable political decisions about our development without swinging to hysterical extremes. Energy development, for instance, involves long lead times, which provide an opportunity to try to understand real needs and to figure out what a workable energy system might look like twenty or forty years from today. We don't have to take the position that everything is up for grabs because we're in a recession, or that nothing is up for grabs because we're in danger of self-destruction. Neither extreme makes any sense.

To make the state of Montana into a national park, in effect, is beyond the realm of possibility, and even if you could do it, why do it? It would mean displacing 800,000 people economically and psychologically. On the other hand, to make Montana a goddam boiler room for national demands that we cannot understand or control—well, that would be the other extreme absurdity.

I do not believe that we're going to see, in the next quarter-century, the kind of explosive, wild, unplanned, uncontrolled growth that was being predicted a few years ago. The development of resources will be more affected by the long struggle back to some sort of economic plateau—the struggle that will follow this horrendous recession. The region will have a positive but slow economic evolution; we won't have to confront the extreme changes that were being predicted.

The Montana I see today is essentially the Montana that I saw for the first time in 1954, and I think it will be recognizable in 1994 and recognizable for a long time beyond that, *if* we have a continuing, collective understanding of what's important to us and if we are cautious and constrained about social and economic transformations that would place heavy additional burdens on the natural systems that support us. Without arguing for the elimination of anything—mining, growing crops, grazing cows, cutting wood—we have to be future-cautious and identify the incremental changes that put us closer to the carrying capacity of the land. We have to understand that we're close to the limits of carrying capacity now—that understanding has to influence every decision we make. We have to remember that what we do today still matters for the future. In historical terms, we've only recently grasped that point; we can't let go.

Whatever we want to do in the future, our water resource is going to be the key ingredient in allowing anything to happen. We have to husband that resource, protect it, nurse it, and use it wisely. On the other hand, there's an argument to be made that the resource may be sufficient for most needs, if some problems that seem important at the moment diminish in importance in the future. How much more land are you going to be able to irrigate in Wyoming and Montana? I think it's much less than people tend to assume; consequently, when you're conserving water for irrigation you may be saving it for a purpose that will never materialize and for which that water will never be needed.

It may also be fallacious to think that every community in Montana will grow to a population of 100,000 or more. When one talks about Billings and Great Falls, one isn't talking about Bozeman and Helena, so to argue that there will be a dramatic drain on water resources from population increases might also misrepresent the real situation.

There is, in my judgment, one critical issue related to water. Right now we don't know—although we're getting close to knowing—what we need to maintain fluvial ecosystems in their current state, and I think that's *the* water issue in Montana. If we knew, we might well be able to decide to reserve a small amount of water to develop energy sources that are important to us in the region. I think it's foolish to argue that we know how much water we can afford to give away, but it's certainly just as foolish to argue that we're not ever going to be in a position to make some reasonable judgments about the future.

The situation is somewhat different with soil resources. In the Northern Rockies and the Northern Great Plains, we're talking about soil horizons that have taken thousands of years to evolve. If you lose that soil, you've lost a resource that is not quickly replaceable, in any historical sense that we can understand and deal with. So when we talk about what to do with soil, we have to talk about maintaining a soil base in the context of a time frame we can't even imagine: 10,000 to 15,000 years to evolve.

Water is truly renewable in the sense that we're not talking about 10,000-year cycles. We do have cycles of drought and abundance, but within time frames of four to seven years, so we're talking about a resource base of water that is sustainable and renewable for ecosystem maintenance. There's plenty of water for that. In addition, we do not expect any severe climatic variation that would lead us into a long-term drought cycle in the Northern Rockies that would mean constraining current activities. It's also clear that agricultural economics is not going

to provide us with a very large expansion of new irrigable land.

So we can ask: water for what? Well, once we fully understand hydrologic systems, once we fully understand water in an integrated cycle in a specific basin, I think we'll be able to say a lot about how we can most effectively use water for the benefit of the natural ecosystem and the people who live in the basin, and it may surprise us to learn that we can use some of that water for what some derisively call "development."

With reason, we're all afraid of the "rape and run" mentality. The Anacondas and the Arcos come in and take all there is to take and give little, and when they're finished, they run. But perhaps we can develop an economic base in which the developers understand the need for a different commitment if they want to be here in our community.

It could be that we will come to understand that the sustaining of the Northern Rockies as an integrated social, political, economic and environmental whole demands that we use resources wisely—yes, that we *use* them. I'd be disturbed if we were to create a social and political slum in the Northern Rockies because we were both indifferent and unresponsive to our ability to use them.

We can work toward a better future in the region, but the future of mining towns like Butte and Anaconda is most likely to be very different from the past. That's a sadness that really speaks to the uncertainties of human endeavor. I wish Butte could go on forever, because I think Butte is a national treasure —not only for the gold and silver in its veins, but as a place where people try to structure a life around a kind of work that makes them a special kind of community. I'm sorry to see Butte go, but I think Butte has gone, because in American life today

there is an economic payback that requires some arbitrary minimum return, and when it's not reached, then the structure is not worth maintaining.

To save the old Butte, you would have to prevail in arguing that if it's valuable to us as a community of people and skills, in the national interest, then Butte, and the American steel industry, and perhaps other segments as well, will have to be maintained by the nation. I think there's good reason to do that, to have a national mining community with skill and dedication. It would be in the national interest to help Butte survive a down-cycle in world mineral activity, because Butte might be able to sustain itself very comfortably from the year 1990 to the year 2050. One can make that argument for the Buttes of this world—that they're a resource, a valuable resource, which with a very small amount of social concern and government help could live through their economic downturn and survive for the future.

Labor has always had a hard time in Montana. It is not what you would call a classic labor union state. It's more a farmer/rancher state, with a philosophy of not necessarily needing daily solidarity to survive. You could live on a ranch twenty miles from the nearest neighbor and make it through three generations and never get any closer, but in a mine you can't wander more than a few feet from your partner without raising the risk to your life. It is a drastically different kind of environment, which produces a different understanding of the way people live and communicate and survive.

When you extend that to the community, and take the Butte miner and put him on the Butte City Council, the community reflects the life of the underground; but build an agriculture-based town such as Billings—well, the unions have always found it very hard going. There's a strong, conservative, long-standing, historical bias against organized labor because of the perception that labor is socialist, labor is collectivist, labor is liberal, and labor is the people. That may be a very important element in anti-union feeling here: labor as representing the working masses, versus the uncrowded, unpeopled ranches, the vast empty land, the open sky, even the big sky.

The single most important issue for the West and Montana is not the future of the Yellowstone River or the future of the Bob Marshall Wilderness, or anything else specific to the region; it's the issue of nuclear war. There's nothing more important than that. That was clear certainly by the early sixties.

In the fifties we learned that nuclear technology could be so widely distributed and so readily available and so immediately usable and so indefensible that it had to be perceived as a plague, an epidemic, against which there was no easy vaccination or antidote. It's like the threat of cancer: you understand its potential, its universality, and you look for an antidote; such as worldwide nuclear disarmament. We are still looking for a way to live with nuclear knowledge and yet not feel threatened by it. That seems to me to be *the* challenge for the genius of mankind—to live with the knowledge of the nuclear phenomenon, and to extend it through man's intellectual capacity, and yet be able to do that with the tranquility and calmness and optimism to know that it need not be a life-threatening, evolution-threatening situation.

That challenge became obvious the moment we knew that nuclear weapons could be made and delivered rather easily. To wipe us all out, what does a Reagan or a Gorbachev need to do? Very little.

The early sixties generated a different psychology. It was the psychology of "You can survive." It was more appealing to many people than coming to grips with how casually we might all be annihilated, and it still is. All the talk about fallout shelters was the early application of that psychology. The discussions are more sophisticated now, but they still turn on the question of whether people can be persuaded that a nuclear war can somehow be "won," which would make it much more likely to occur.

There were many of us who used to go around saying, "When you understand that nuclear war's the issue, if you're not right politically on that issue, you're not good on any issue." That was sort of naive—not recognizing where people are, and how they need to come to their own understanding of what's possible and acceptable. But personally I don't think it was hard to come to an anti-nuclear weapons position very early. You didn't really need some scientifiic insight into the physics and chemistry of nuclear weapons. You needed some dynamic understanding of potential and consequences, and the moment you had that, you would know, instinctively, that it was the one overriding issue for our lives. It would be instinctive, and you would know.

A Guide to the Northern Rockies

THE THREE STATES OF THE NORTHERN ROCKIES — IDAHO, MONTANA AND WYOMING — HAVE A LAND AREA OF 328,609 SQUARE MILES. Montana is the largest of the three with 147,138 and the fourth largest state in the Union after Alaska, Texas and California. Wyoming is ninth largest, with 97,914 square miles, and Idaho has 83,557 square miles and is the fourteenth largest. Together, the states are larger than Texas but smaller than Alaska. They are only slightly smaller than the combined land area of France, Luxembourg, Belgium, the Netherlands, Switzerland and West Germany. On the other hand, they are smaller than the Canadian province of British Columbia, immediately to the north.

Perhaps the best place to feel the power of this space is not in the great mountain ranges, but over in the Powder River country of Montana and Wyoming. Among the rolling, sagebrush-covered hills, there is often an unbroken line of sight in all directions. The brittle, grey-green sage (*artemisia tridentata*) provides a smooth coating on the baked hills, and it recalls a calm day on the ocean. There is a profound sense of freedom, of possibilities as limitless as the horizon.

A lot of people don't like that country. They think it is forbidding, desolate, bleak, and frightening, even. A government type from Washington, D.C., out visiting on a coal mine tour, said she thought it was a "wasteland." She added, not coincidentally, that it seemed to her that the best use for it would be coal mining.

Well, there is a lot of coal there to mine. About 1.5 trillion tons of coal exist in the Powder River and Williston Basins of Montana, North Dakota and Wyoming. In the 1970s, coal was the hot issue in the area, but by the 1980s, massive coal strip mining was a fact of life and hardly controversial at all.

Coal is only one of a number of valuable minerals that pace economic growth in the West. The Northern Rockies area is heavily reliant upon extractable minerals for attracting employers, jobs and investment. Dr. Dwayne Ward of Helena, Montana, has calculated "location quotients" for the Northern Rockies which measure how important an industry is to a state relative to its importance to the rest of the country. The agriculture, forestry, fisheries, and mining sectors are three times more important to Idaho and Montana and five times more important to Wyoming than to the country as a whole. Manufacturing, on the other hand, is about one-quarter as important to the states as it is to the nation.

From the gold rush of the 1800s to the coal rush of the 1970s, prospectors and resource exploiters joined the ranchers and farmers in settlement. This reliance on minerals has been a mixed blessing. The boom-and-bust phenomenon of the volatile mineral economy has plagued economic health and growth.

The mineral wealth of the West is impressive indeed. Idaho is the nation's largest producer of antimony, silver and garnets. It was the number two producer of lead and phosphate and third in zinc and vanadium. Wyoming is the nation's largest producer of trona and bentonite and is second in uranium, third in coal and sixth in oil and gas. Montana has the largest demonstrated reserve of coal in the country and has long been a major copper producer. Butte is the home of the fabled "Richest Hill on Earth."

The sense of grandeur and of a remaining frontier that the area's geology and mineral wealth create has drawn people west in large numbers over the past fifteen years. Wyoming, spurred by a boom in coal and uranium, was the fourth fastest growing state in the Union over the decade of the 1970s. The total population increased 41.3 percent to a total of 468,557 by 1980. Only Arizona, Florida and Nevada grew faster. Idaho grew 32.4 percent from 713,015 in 1970 to 943,925 in 1980. In December of 1984, the state etimated that its population had topped one million. Montana ran a sedate and unhurried third among the three Northern Rockies states in this population race, up 13.3 percent for the decade. Montana's total population in 1980 was 786,690. By way of comparison, the United States as a whole grew 11.4 percent over the decade.

Taken together, the three Northern Rockies states had a population in 1980 of 2,200,182 or about the same total population as Brooklyn (which was losing population). Among the fifty states, Idaho is 41st in population, Montana 44th and Wyoming 49th.

In 1880, there were 92,558 people in all three states. So, over the course of the last 100 or so years, the Northern Rockies states have grown by 2,377.08 percent. At this rate, by the year 2080, there will be 52.3 million people in the Northern Rockies, roughly the same population as France, Turkey, or Vietnam—but only if Malthus was right.

When you combine all today's people and all that space, you find that, on the average, there are still great distances between neighbors. Idaho has 11.5 people per square mile, Montana 5.4 and Wyoming 4.8. New York City has 64,922 people per square mile. The average square mile in the United States has 62.6 people in it.

In the West, it is considerably easier to find some land that has few people on it. In fact, the Northern Rockies area is a national repository of wilderness lands where the hand of humankind is substantially invisible. As of early 1984, the three states had 39.3 percent of the federally designated wilderness acreage outside of Alaska. Idaho had 3.7 million acres, including the largest single wilderness, the River of No Return. Montana had 3.1 million acres of wilderness and Wyoming 2.2 million. Legislation passed in late 1984 for both Idaho and Wyoming, and pending in Montana, will add considerably more land to the national wilderness system in the three states.

Wyoming is the home of Yellowstone, crown jewel of the national park system, and also its spectacular sister park, Grand Teton; Montana has Glacier National Park. It has been unofficially confirmed, by the way, that the mountain, Grand Teton, for which the park is named, is the most photographed peak in the lower 48. Kodak has made a fortune from it.

This large land has created a large mythology about cowboys, cattle barons, outlaws, and missionaries. Mari Sandoz in her book *The Cattlemen* calls Wyoming "the purest cow country" and dates the beginning of the cattle era there as 1868, when John W. Iliff bought $40,000 worth of cattle from Colorado pioneer Charles Goodnight to be delivered near Cheyenne. In his *History of Wyoming*, T. A. Larson says that Nelson Story drove a herd of Texas cattle through eastern Wyoming to Montana in 1866. Ever since, the cowboy and cattle baron have been the fundamental figures in western—and American—mythology.

Real cattle have been less important. While the ranching industry is important to the states themselves, the Northern Rockies states are not really big cattle producers relative to the rest of the country. Montana ranks 12th in the production of cattle and calves, Idaho 25th and Wyoming 30th. In 1981, there were 1.4 million cows and calves in Wyoming, 1.9 million in Idaho and 2.9 million in Montana. Combined, the states raise about 6.2 million head of cattle, less than half of Texas's output of 13.7 million. Georgia, Pennsylvania and Virginia all produce more cows (including dairy cows) than Wyoming, "the purest cow country."

Curiously, one of the enduring images of the cattle baron mythology is the helpless sheepman being brutally used by a virtually inexhaustible supply of hired thugs. The sheepmen usually hired Alan Ladd to fight against these insurmountable odds. But while the cattlemen may have won the battle, the sheepmen won the war. Wyoming is ranked third nationally in the production of sheep and lambs, a statistic that will surprise anyone who has ever tried to buy lamb chops in that state's supermarkets. Montana is sixth in the nation and Idaho ninth. The first year in history that cattle outnumbered sheep in Wyoming was 1976.

The second part of the mythology of the West, of course, is the Indian. Early white settlers viewed the tribes as the embodiment of backwardness and savagery. Modern whites see a more complex society, but one that nearly equally disturbs them. The forces in conflict on the reservations, in the tribal histories, and with the whites are very intricate, and most writing by whites about the Indian is filtered through white ideals, mores and ambitions.

There are 32,478 Indians on reservations in Idaho, Montana and Wyoming. They represent many different tribes on 12 separate reservations. The tribes include the Sioux, Assiniboine, Blackfeet, Chippewa-Cree, Northern Cheyenne, Crow, Gros Ventre, and confederated Salish and Kootenai in Montana; the Shoshone and Arapaho in Wyoming; and the Shoshone-Bannock, Nez Perce, Coeur d'Alene, Kootenai and Shoshone-Paiute in Idaho.

The Northern Rockies states are mostly conservative and mostly Republican. In Idaho and Wyoming, the legislatures are dominated by the Republican party, as are the congressional delegations. In Montana, the reverse has been true, with Democrats dominating the state legislature for thirty years until 1981. The Republicans took control of both houses that year, and the two parties have each had their innings since then.

But none of the states is exclusively Republican or Democratic—all three had Democratic governors in 1985, for instance, and all but one of Montana's federal legislators is a Democrat. Party labels are not really meaningful gauges of political posture. More importantly, being "conservative" in the West doesn't mean the same thing as it means in North Carolina. For the most part, it simply indicates a healthy respect for the individual and his rights.

There is a saying that "All politics are local politics." In the Northern Rockies, this its true in spades. The states are small enough that people know the politicians who represent them. This personal form of government keeps some of the old-fashioned virtues current as well. For instance, citizens take their rights and responsibilities seriously. Idaho consistently ranks number one or two in the country in the percent of its population voting for president. Montana is always in the top ten.

The attitude toward government leads to some results that may surprise folks from more "progressive" parts of the country. For instance, the number of women holding state and local public offices more than doubled in the three states between 1975 and 1980. Wyoming and Montana have tough environmental control and plant siting laws because of conservationist respect for the land. Wyoming's air quality standards are tougher than those laid down by the federal government. The government is still such that it can respond to the people. Of course, it doesn't always.

Politics and land intermingle considerably in the Northern Rockies. Much of the land is owned by the federal government, a fact about which local politicians remind the voters from time to time. There are 52.7 million acres of land in Idaho, 33.3 million of which—or 63.1 percent—are owned by the federal government. Montana has 93.1 million acres, 27.1 million federal (29.1 percent), Wyoming has 62.1 million total acres, 29.5 million federal (47.5 percent). In the nation at large, the federal government owns 33 percent of the U.S. land mass. In this scheme of things, the Northern Rockies states are better off (or worse depending on your point of view) than Nevada, which is 86 percent federal property, and worse than Connecticut, which is 0.3 percent federal. Washington, D.C., is 32.9 percent.

This federal land has led to problems in one of the largest and most confusing areas of western life and politics—water. The federal government has reserved some rights to itself. Indian tribes—separate nations within the U.S.—have been allocated rights, and there are the complex questions of private water rights.

In 1878, Major John Wesley Powell issued from the presses of the usually bland and unremarkable Government Printing Office perhaps the most radical document ever printed by that office, *Lands of the Arid Region of the United States.* Had Powell's recommendations about water and land use been adopted, the West today would be very different. Powell recommended that the size of irrigated farms be reduced to 80 acres from the 160 acres allotted under the 1862 Homestead Act. He proposed that unirrigated grazing tracts be increased from 160 acres to 2,560 acres. And he suggested that all homesteads or pasturage units offered for settlement should be given equal access to water. This could be accomplished by scrapping the normal system of rectangular tracts and fashioning irregular streamside tracts as necessary to provide access to water.

Powell's proposals may have saved a lot of hardship at the time. The Homestead Act, which allowed everyone over twenty-one to claim 160 acres of land, worked fairly well in the semi-humid lands of the East. In the West it was little short of disaster. Idaho's Senator William E. Borah said at the time: "The government bets 160 acres against the entry fee . . . that the settler can't live on the land for five years without starving to death." While the homestead rush has lived on in western myth as a great attraction, it was by most standards a failure. According to T. H. Watkins' introduction to a 1979 reissue of Major Powell's historic report, of the 552,112 claims entered between 1862 and 1882, only 194,488 were held to full title.

Water, then and now, is subject to much misunderstanding and just plain wishful thinking. Wyoming historian T. A. Larson offers a dose of realism: "In the next few years, I think we're going to have some real knockdown, drag-out fights over the water issue. Water development is terribly expensive. It's not wise politically to proclaim this from the housetops, but there is no question in my mind that this water can be put to better use downstream, and is being put to better use in Arizona, California, Mississippi, the Dakotas—places where you have better soil, faster growing seasons, and a lot more people to take care of. So that's probably where the water ought to go—where it's going right now."

Larson's approach to this problem is little short of radical in the water-short western states. The sentiment is often expressed that "water is the future of the West," and the parallel sentiment has been "use it or lose it." Traditionally, this "future" has meant the construction of large water projects to store the precious flow of rivers and streams. The stored water has usually been used for irrigation.

Now, however, the era of the large water project is over. The obvious, cost-effective ones have all been built. New water development will be too expensive for irrigation, so it will probably be built for industry. The question then becomes, what kind of industry? In the past, that question has been answered by the largest, most polluting industries—coal gasification, oil shale extraction, natural gas sweetening plants, phosphate mines, copper smelters.

The lands west of the 100th meridian—which slices through Nebraska at approximately the location of the town of North Platte and through North Dakota near Rugby, "the geographical center of North America"—are semi-arid. That is to say, they receive an annual average of less than 20 inches of rainfall. Yet, the three Northern Rockies states are far and away the largest per capita water users in the United States. Idaho withdraws 19,007 gallons of water per day per person, Montana 13,959 and Wyoming 11,368 per capita per day. California uses 2,272 gallons per capita per day and New York, 967.

The three states are also prodigious consumers of energy. In 1980 the average per capita consumption of energy in the United States was 334 million BTU. Wyoming consumed 842 million BTU per person, better than two-and-a-half times the national average. Montana used 465 million BTU and Idaho 376 million.

Distance is a characteristic of the Northern Rockies that is associated with all that space. The two are related, of course, but are not exactly the same. Space is an area you exist in; distance is ground you have to cover. Most of the distance in the West is covered by automobile, and the Rocky Mountain measure of distance in auto travel is the six-pack.

As a group, folks in the Northern Rockies are relatively healthier than the nation at large—until they get behind the wheel. A combination of distance, speed, alcohol and lousy drivers has put the Northern Rockies among the top ten states in traffic death statistics. In 1979 Wyoming, Montana and Idaho were fourth, sixth, and eighth highest, respectively, in the United States in deaths per hundred million vehicle miles.

Statistics only tell part of the story of a place and of the ways in which people live in it. The many varied voices of those who call the Rockies home offer a richer understanding. They are the folk that struggle with the issues to which Wallace Stegner referred when he wrote in *The Sound of Mountain Water:* "Angry as one may be at what heedless men have done and still do to a noble habitat, one cannot be pessimistic about the West. This is the native home of hope. When it fully learns that cooperation, not rugged individualism, is the quality that most characterizes and preserves it, then it will have achieved itself and outlived its origins. Then it has a chance to create a society to match its scenery."

DAN WHIPPLE
NORTHERN LIGHTS INSTITUTE